Labor and the American Revolution

LABOR and the AMERICAN REVOLUTION

_____*by Philip S. Foner*

(G
P)
GREENWOOD PRESS
WESTPORT, CONNECTICUT • LONDON, ENGLAND

Library of Congress Cataloging in Publication Data

Foner, Philip Sheldon, 1910-
    Labor and the American Revolution.

    Bibliography: p.
    Includes index.
    1.   United States—History—Revolution, 1775-1783.
2.   Labor and laboring classes—United States—Political activity—History.
I.   Title.
E209.F67   973.3'15'0623   76-18034
ISBN   0-8371-9003-7

Library of Congress Catalog Card Number: 76-18034
ISBN: 0-8371-9003-7

First published in 1976

Greenwood Press, a division of Williamhouse-Regency Inc.
51 Riverside Avenue, Westport, Connecticut 06880

Printed in the United States of America

"Our ancestors, the Mechanics and Working Men of
1776, who laid the foundation stone of our nation; may
the workers of today and the future complete the super-
structure, and may it stand as firm as the foundation
stone it rests on."

Toast at Mechanics' and Working Men's
Celebration, Fourth of July, 1831

New York Daily Sentinel, July 8, 1831

Contents

Preface

In an address delivered on July 4, 1835, before the Mechanic Apprentices' Library Association of Boston, Henry Seaver said:

> To us this great struggle, the American revolution, is rife with pleasing thoughts—not only on account of the great political changes resulting from it, but from the contemplation of the fact that it was the mechanics of our native city that first lighted the fire, which since '76 has covered the whole western sphere in a bright halo of glory, and whose heat extends to the furthermost corner of the earth. It was the mechanics of Boston, that first rocked the bantling in the cradle of liberty, and first set in motion the ball of the revolution. It was the men of the stout hearts and the brawny arms—"men who knew their rights and knowing dared maintain them"—that first stepped forth as the friends and defenders of liberty.[1]

Yet in 1877, in a volume of almost nine hundred pages of orations delivered on the occasion of the Centennial of American Independence, there is only one mention that the colonial workers—the mechanics, artisans, tradesmen, artificers, laborers, journeymen, and seamen—had played a vital role in both the resistance movement against British tyranny and the achievement of American independence. That single reference was by Professor John M. Langston, a black teacher at Howard University, during the course of his Fourth of July oration at Portsmouth, Virginia. Langston urged that, in celebrating the one hundredth anniversary of the Declaration of Independence, Americans should not forget Crispus Attucks, "brave and courageous, who gave up his life . . . on the sacred soil of Massachusetts in order to make the Independence we now celebrate possible."[2] Crispus Attucks was the runaway slave, turned seaman and stevedore, who, with four white workers, was killed by the Red Coats in the Boston Massacre on March 5, 1770.

This neglect of labor's contributions to America's revolution and independence continued well into the twentieth century. In a paper read before the American Historical Association in December 1940, Herbert M. Morais said regretfully:

> Although colonial craftsmen and workingmen rendered distinguished service to the cause of the American Revolution, their work has been largely ignored or insufficiently treated. Historians and poets of our revolutionary saga have for the most part left untold and unsung the contributions made by them. Their story, like the short and simple annals of the poor, has been buried in the scrapheap of History.[3]

Since these words were written, a veritable flood of articles, monographs, and academic dissertations has appeared, resurrecting various aspects of this forgotten story.[4] Most of these studies are confined to a specific locality, and the scholars themselves frequently disagree on crucial issues. Their contributions have had little effect on either the average textbook writer or the scholars of the intellectual aspects of the period—scholars such as Daniel J. Boorstin, Bernard Bailyn, and Robert Brown, who argue that the American Revolution was essentially conservative, aiming not to overthrow or even change the existing social order, but to conserve liberties long possessed. (Indeed, the Revolution, according to Boorstin, was not a real revolution at all, but only an act of separation from the old British Empire.)[5] Nevertheless, the dissertations, articles, and monographs have begun the long-needed analysis of the story of the American Revolution "from the bottom up."

The present work is an attempt to present, in a single volume covering the major urban centers, the story the late Dr. Morais hoped would someday be told. The bicentennial of the American Revolution is a fitting time to make this story available.

In the preparation of this volume, I have had the generous assistance and cooperation of the libraries and personnel of the Library of Congress, the New York Public Library, the New York Historical Society, the American Philosophical Society, the Historical Society of Pennsylvania, the Library Company of Philadelphia, the Boston Public Library, Yale University Library, Columbia University Library, Harvard University Library, Bancroft Library, the University of California, Henry E. Huntington Library, the John Carter Brown Library of Brown University, Rhode Island Historical Society, Connecticut Historical Society, Massachusetts Historical Society, the University of Wisconsin Library, the University of Chicago Library, New Jersey Historical Society, Maryland Historical Society, Charleston Historical Society, the University of South Carolina Library, Public Archives of Nova Scotia, Halifax, Library of the Farmington Division, the University of Maine, Tamiment Library of New York University, and the Langston Hughes Memorial Library of Lincoln University, Pennsylvania. I have also had the opportunity to discuss important issues connected with this subject with Professor Michael Kay of the University of Toledo, Professor Alfred F. Young of Northwestern Illinois University, Professor John A. Alexander of the University of Cincinnati, and Professor Eric Foner of the City College of New York. My brother, Henry Foner, read the entire manuscript and made valuable suggestions. I wish to take this opportunity to thank both the institutions and the individuals mentioned.

Philip S. Foner

Lincoln University, Pennsylvania
July 1976

Labor and the American Revolution

1 ___ The Colonial Worker on the Eve of the Revolution

☐ During the period leading up to the American Revolution, the thirteen colonies were basically agrarian and most of their inhabitants lived in rural areas. Approximately one out of every ten people lived in urban centers. Of these, Philadelphia was the most populous city; on the eve of the Revolution, it had some 40,000 inhabitants. It was followed by New York with 25,000 to 35,000, Boston with 20,000, and Newport with 12,000. Only one city developed in the South during the colonial period — Charleston, South Carolina.

The colonial workers who lived in these cities comprised both the free (artisans, mechanics, journeymen, apprentices, sailors, dockworkers, and unskilled laborers) and the unfree (indentured servants and slaves). By Carl Bridenbaugh's estimate, about one-half of the population of Revolutionary Charleston and two-thirds of the population of Boston, Newport, New York, and Philadelphia belonged to the mechanic class. Benjamin Labaree's figure for Newburyport, Massachusetts, in which over half the adult males in 1773 were artisans and laborers, suggests that mechanics constituted a majority in smaller cities as well.[1]

The growing numbers of artisans and mechanics were made up of immigrants who had paid for their passage to America and indentured servants who had worked out their passage and had already served their time. Many were itinerant craftsmen, who went from town to town to make shoes, construct furniture, shoe horses, manufacture soap and candles, and perform other services. The typical artisan, however, worked in a small workshop in a city or town (often his own home), along with one or two journeymen, apprentices, indentured servants, or even slaves in some cases, or else he was an independent craftsman who owned his own tools but worked for wages.

Some craftsmen produced for the marketplace, in anticipation of demand, and a few were even engaged in the export trade. The majority, especially those in the clothing trade, worked for custom orders, waiting on customers to take their measurements and calling when the work was completed.

Historians have been unable to agree on the correct terminology for describing the city artisan, or mechanic, or even tradesman, as he was then called. Some have restricted the term to self-employed craftsmen, arguing that the Revolutionary mechanic was, for the most part, a small businessman or entrepreneur, and not a dependent laborer—in short, in no way a member of the colonial working class.[2] Some even deny that there were any workers in Colonial America and put the words *workers* and *laborers* in quotation marks. Others use the term to refer not only to skilled workers, but to all groups below the ranks of merchants and lawyers, while still others apply the term to the entire urban working population from master craftsmen down to wage-earning journeymen and laborers, apprentices, and indentured servants. In a recent study of labor in colonial Massachusetts, Mary Roys Baker states: "As defined here, labor includes all Bay Colony master craftsmen." The author points out that these craftsmen never "became capitalists" and that "all Bay Colony 'Masters' were called 'Workmen' or 'received pay for their work.'"[3]

It is clear that the terms *artisan* and *mechanic* may be applied to a diverse grouping. We do know that contemporaries defined a mechanic as anyone who worked primarily with his hands.[4] We also know that master craftsmen and journeymen—men who possessed a skill, owned their own tools, and had served an apprenticeship—were clearly distinguished from both the merchants and professionals above them and the unskilled laborers below. Furthermore, contemporaries were careful to draw distinctions within the working population, as is indicated by such phrases in common usage as "mechanics, laborers and cartmen," or "the substantial mechanics," and "the lowest order of mechanics."[5]

As we have noted, the typical artisan worked in a small workshop along with one or two journeymen, apprentices, and indentured servants. He was also an independent craftsman; for example, a bricklayer owned his own tools but worked for wages. There were master artisans like Paul Revere, who, besides his own skilled and lucrative metal work, owned a business and employed workmen.[6] Less fortunately placed mechanics lacked the tools or wealth to enter trade on their own account, and so hired out as workers.[7]

How many artisans and mechanics were masters and how many were wage earners? Unfortunately, the surveys available of various trades in Colonial America are insufficiently comprehensive to permit a clear answer. Again, it depends on the definition used. One historian describes the Charleston mechanic in the Revolutionary era as an artisan employing a "retinue of apprentices, journeymen, and slaves."[8] Another describes the New York mechanic as "a self-employed artisan, a petty tradesman, or a skilled or unskilled wage-earner." Applying this definition to the city on the eve of the Revolution, he notes that the common laborers and seamen probably accounted for 75 percent of the entire group.[9]

One clue is offered in the Federal Processions in Philadelphia and New York City, which celebrated the ratification of the Constitution adopted in 1787. The official count in Philadelphia listed two trades, with masters counted separately from other workers: 16 master cabinet- and chairmakers marched with 100 "apprentices and journeymen" and 10 master bricklayers marched with 100 "workmen."[10] Judging by the published list of mechanics in the New York parade, perhaps a third of the mechanics were master workmen, another third journeymen, and the remaining third apprentices. Among the cabinetmakers in the procession were 16 master workmen, 120 journeymen, and 30 apprentices; among the coopers, 138 master workmen and journeymen and 55 apprentices.[11]

These statistics show that the majority of those called "artisans" and "mechanics" were laborers, not employers. For the purposes of this study, then, we shall use the modern terminology of "labor" and "workers" in speaking of the artisans and mechanics, regardless of whether these include masters, who owned the shops where they produced or sold commodities, or those who owned their own tools and worked for wages. This procedure will be followed for the preindustrial era because, as will become clear, although the economic classes of workers and employers have changed profoundly since the Industrial Revolution, the basic issues and economic goals of American labor groups have remained constant and fairly consistent for centuries.

Then, too, while the term *artisan* as used here includes both the master craftsman who owned his own shop and the artisan-mechanic and journeyman who worked for wages, we must bear in mind that the line separating them was very fine. Even the master craftsman lived marginally; he borrowed money short-term and, in a period of recession, could easily end up in debtor's prison.[12] Moreover, the years of Revolutionary activity between 1765 and 1776, more than merely years of recession, were actually depression years. It is understandable, then, as Richard B. Morris points out, that the term *mechanics* gained "a more distinctly proletarian character" as the Revolutionary period advanced.[13] In Morris's important work, *Government and Labor in Early America*, the term *labor* covers artisans, mechanics, journeymen, and laborers.

"Even in the larger towns many, probably most, of the manufacturing mechanics were their own employers." wrote Victor S. Clark in 1916.[14] More recent studies, however, reveal the existence of a larger wage-earning class than Clark's generalization would have us believe. To be sure, the prevailing mode of production in colonial towns was the small workshop, and there were no factories or business corporations in Colonial America. Nonetheless, even in the small shop, a master employed one to four journeymen and apprentices.[15] Many enterprises were even larger. Printing, for example, required a substantial capital investment and a fairly large number of employees. The New York City printer Rivington employed sixteen men. Shipyards and ropewalks employed at least five, and sometimes as many as twelve, workers. Breweries, soap and candle manufacturing, leather tanning, and hat manufacturing (despite the restrictions imposed on such enterprises by the British government) were also substantial, large-scale businesses.[16]

Regardless of size, the preindustrial small shop found in nearly all trades demanded skilled labor and required that each worker be competent in all or most aspects of his craft. Not all such
workers were free labor. At the eve of the American Revolution,
black slaves and white indentured servants comprised an important section of the colonial working class. An estimated 80
percent of all immigrants who came to the colonies, whether vol-
untarily or in chains, were either white indentured servants or
black slaves.

To escape conditions of unemployment, religious wars, and extreme poverty in England and on the continent, large numbers of
poor people signed contracts to do "any work in which the employer shall employ them" for five to seven years in return for
passage to the New World and the promise of freedom and a plot
of land after their term of bondage was over. Not less than 50
percent, and probably closer to 65 percent, of all white immigrants in America before 1776 were indentured servants.

Some 50,000 white convicts were brought to the New World
during the colonial period. They were sold into bondage for a
term of seven years or, in the case of hardened criminals, fourteen years. Many of the convicts had been imprisoned for failure
to pay small debts. England found it economically and morally
advantageous to use her colonies as a dumping ground for un-
desirables in her overcrowded jails.

Another method of supplying involuntary labor for colonial
employers was through kidnapping. Thousands of children and
adults alike were "shanghaied" aboard ships that were destined
for America. There, they were sold into semi-slavery either for
seven years or until they reached maturity. [17]

Most of the indentured servants were unskilled, but a significant minority had followed skilled trades in Europe. Hence, some
came to this country with a variety of special skills: they were
carpenters, tailors, stone masons, blacksmiths, millers, barrel
makers, weavers, silversmiths, and butchers. They were frequently purchased by colonial artisans as workers in their
shops. [18] An advertisement in the April 29, 1775, issue of the
Pennsylvania Evening Post (published in Philadelphia) read:

Just arrived in the Ship Ann, Capt. Fortin, from Bristol,

A number of healthy men and women servants, whose times are to be disposed of by William Fisher, Esq. and Son, or said Captain on board, at Arch Street wharf.

The men servants are chiefly tradesmen, such as woolcomber, saddletree-plater, weaver, brassfounder, stockingmaker, joiner, tin-plate-worker, upholsterer, collar-maker, barber, coach springmaker, ivory turner, plasterer, shoemaker, blacksmith, broad weaver, brightsmith, etc. Also farmers, coachmen, sawyers, footmen, labourers, and hostlers.

In some colonies, indentured servitude was an important source of labor, but because of its limited term of bondage, it could not meet the growing demand for labor. Hence, the colonists increasingly turned to slavery. Negroes could be forced into lifetime bondage more easily than whites, and once enslaved, they could not easily run away and mingle in strange surroundings. More important, the slavery of blacks could be justified by the ideology of racism. A black skin connoted both evil and inferiority; Negroes were said to be destined to be slaves by the "Curse of Ham." They were pictured as savages and infidels from a barbaric, dark continent without a civilization, and enslavement was considered an improvement in their way of life.

The number of black slaves in the colonies grew slowly at first, but with the expansion of rice, tobacco, and indigo plantations, the growth became more rapid. By 1770, there were about half a million black slaves in the colonies — approximately 20 percent of the colonial population.[19]

Some of the Africans who were brought to America in chains were skilled in woodworking, weaving, construction, and other crafts. In the South, black slaves were not only field hands; many developed a variety of skills that were needed on a nearly self-sufficient plantation. Because skilled labor of whatever color was in great demand, slaves were often hired out to masters who owned shops by the day, month, or year for a stipulated amount. Some were hired out to shipmasters, serving as pilots and managers of ferries. Others were used in the maritime trades as ship-caulkers, longshoremen, and sailmakers. A large number of slaves were employed in Northern cities as house servants, sailors, sailmakers, and carpenters. New York had a higher proportion of skilled slaves than any other colony—coopers, tailors, bakers, tanners, goldsmiths, naval carpenters, tobacconists, caulkers, cabinetmakers, shoemakers, and glaziers. Both in Charleston and in the Northern cities, many artisans utilized slave labor extensively. They found it more profitable to purchase a black slave whom they could keep working in their shops for life than to invest in an indentured servant who would have to be freed in seven years.[20]

The colonial need for skilled workers was also met partly through the apprenticeship system. This system provided a technical education and room, clothing, and board for children who were bound out either by their parents or Overseers of the Poor, officials appointed to supervise those in need. In Boston, the Overseers of the Poor bound out a seven-year-old boy in 1756 as an apprentice to a printer and bookseller until he reached the age of twenty-one. However, the apprenticeship usually lasted only seven years, and by the Revolutionary era, terms of five years or less were more frequent. In signing the indenture of apprenticeship, the master usually obligated himself to feed, clothe, and shelter the apprentice; to teach him to read, write, and cipher; to employ him in his trade; and to teach him its "mysteries." In turn, the apprentice promised to obey his master's lawful command, to keep his secrets, to absent himself only with his master's leave, and to behave as a "good and faithful apprentice" ought to behave. If the master should renege on his agreement, a parent could bring suit and get his son released from his apprenticeship. The apprentices bound out by the Overseers of the Poor, however, were not so fortunate, since the Overseers rarely interfered with masters.

At the end of the apprenticeship, the apprentice received his "freedom dues." In the case of a seaman, the young man was to be presented with a new suit of clothes, shirts, and such mariner's equipment as a quadrant, a forestaff, a compass, and a calendar. Most freedom dues did not include either a cash payment or tools. As Lawrence W. Towner points out, "without freedom dues in cash or tools, a good many years of service as a journeyman probably awaited the poor apprentice when he was freed." Poor young women, who were apprenticed chiefly to serve as household maids and were seldom taught a trade, ended their apprenticeship with the prospect of either continuing as paid household servants or getting married. In the latter case, their choice of husbands was limited insofar as they had no dowries to bring to their marriage. [21]

The indentured servant's labor belonged to his master twenty-four hours a day, seven days a week. Like the black slave, the servant was a chattel. He had no property himself except what his master allowed. Running away and disobedience were severely punished, although not as harshly as in the case of a slave, who might be killed and was often castrated. Stories of inhuman cruelty to white servants were quite common. Still, unlike slaves, white servants had personal rights to life and contract rights to a minimum standard of living. They could bring suit to enforce these rights, and the courts would comply, even to the extent of freeing the servant outright. Only in Massachusetts did a slave have the right to bring suit against his master, but more often than not, this right was little more than academic.

Both servants and slaves ran away from their masters, sometimes even together. It was harder for the slave, because of his color, to escape recapture; therefore, many fugitive slaves headed for ports where they could sign up and ship out as seamen. Slaves had other ways of resisting bondage. Some deliberately damaged tools, disabled work horses and mules, and poisoned wells. Others committed thefts, set fire to barns, and ruined stores crops by other means. There were also slaves who murdered their masters and overseers.

In 1712, rebellious slaves in New York City set fires and killed those whites who rushed to quench the flames. Most of the rebels were themselves killed, and those who survived were executed in a horrible fashion as an example to others who might rebel. In 1739, near the Stono River in South Carolina, a slave led more than a hundred of his brethren in an attempt to fight their way to Florida, where the governor of that Spanish colony had promised freedom to all fugitive slaves. Few made it, but the uprising spread fear among the whites. More than one traveler through the South noted that "every white man was a soldier" and "every town an armed camp." [22]

There were thousands of workers in all colonial cities. Free workers who worked for wages included artisans, mechanics, journeymen, dockworkers, and merchant seamen—the last two constituting the largest single group of wage workers in the colonies. Until the very eve of the War for Independence, however, various forms of unfree labor—slavery, indentured servitude, and apprenticeship—comprised a high percentage of the work force in the cities. Estimates for Philadelphia for example, indicate that in 1775 there were at least as many slaves, apprentices, and indentured servants in that city as there were free wage-earning laborers and journeymen: 800 to 900 indentured servants, 600 to 700 slaves, and 1,500 to 2,000 male apprentices. [23]

* * *

The goal of the free skilled worker was "independence"—the status of a master craftsman. This goal was not difficult to achieve until the 1760s. The scale of artisan business activity was sufficiently small to permit the "new beginner" easy entrance into trade free of competitive disadvantages. It required only a small amount of capital for a skilled worker to set up for himself, and in prosperous times, the number of small-scale enterprises quickly mushroomed. [24]

The primitive state of the American economy made it difficult for most artisans to acquire great wealth. The market for urban manufacturing was extremely limited, since large numbers of rural families produced their own goods and British imports supplied the demands of many other Americans. The shortage of money, high interest rates, and the abundance of cheap land which drew city residents to rural areas, all combined to further hinder the development of manufacturing. In a situation where technology was backward, the market limited, and credit often unavailable, the artisan's opportunity to accumulate wealth was restricted.

Every artisan strove for the security of owning his own shop where he could sell his products, but in 1765 many of the colonies entered into a severe depression which stifled business and threw large numbers of people into unemployment and debt. The depression lasted twenty years; Boston's, which began in 1734, lasted even longer. As a result, many artisans found themselves back in the class of workers for wages from which they believed they had permanently escaped when they had achieved "independence."[25]

Even with the depression, the mechanics of Colonial America were better off then those in Europe. Thomas Paine noted in *The Crisis* (No. 10) that the "income of a common laborer who is industrious is equal to that of the generality of tradesmen in England." Later, Benjamin Franklin observed that American workers in the 1780s "all demand and obtain much higher wages than any other part of the world would afford them." One student of the subject has estimated that the "colonial workman commanded real wages which exceed[ed] by from 30 to 100 per cent the wages of contemporary English workmen."[26]

Despite all of this "evidence," we can but guess at the actual wages of eighteenth-century workers, insofar as we have no reliable statistics on pay scales. We do know as fact, however, that all was not "milk and honey" in the life of a colonial worker. In a letter to the *South Carolina Gazette* of February 2, 1765, a wage-earning Charleston mechanic lamented that it was "past a doubt, that an industrious man who does not earn more than thirty or forty shillings in the day (and few do that) cannot possibly pay house rent, clothe and feed his family, and pay five pounds out of his poor pittance to purchase a cord of firewood." To support a Boston family in 1775 required about £60 sterling a year: £30 for food, £10 for rent, £12 for clothes (if a wife made all but hats, shoes, overcoat, a Sunday suit, and dress), and £5 for schooling, with firewood, taxes, medical expenses, and sundries swallowing up the rest. The artisan just managed. If he hired himself out by the day, and was of only average ability, he earned about £15 to £20 a year, barely adequate if men were healthy and stayed single, but certainly far from enough to support a family.[27]

Unquestionably, some of these workers were able to supplement their income through subsistence farming. Moreover, the work contract frequently included daily or weekly rations of meat, drink, and lodging, which obviously increased a worker's "real" income. Nevertheless, the majority of colonial workers found life exceedingly harsh. Regular working hours were from sunrise to sunset, and even though workers might receive time off for meals, and even for drinking and a nap, they worked a very long day.[28]

High prices and shortages of provisions added to the hardships of workers. A petition to the South Carolina Assembly declared that the laborers found it "very difficult to live due to the scarcity of provisions as well as money." During periods of unemployment, the colonial worker was often unable to keep his children from starving and himself from debtor's prison. In 1737, the lieutenant governor of New York observed that many workers in the colony were "reduced to poverty from want of employ." Even more serious problems faced these workers in the decade and a half preceding the American Revolution. The transition from prosperity to poverty began with the close of the French and Indian War in 1763. The termination of hostilities also brought an end to several war industries, including privateering. Thousands of workers who had received prize money from the captains of hundreds of vessels suddenly saw their jobs and their incomes eliminated. In New Jersey, the number of unemployed workers was so great in 1765 that the Provincial legislature had to appropriate £200 to be used to buy grain for the more distressed families. In Philadelphia, so many artisans were imprisoned for debt during the winter of 1766 that their fellow craftsmen took up collections so that their families might survive and they might have some clothing to wear. [29]

"Poverty among the free labor element," writes Joseph G. Rayback, "was virtually unknown in the seventeenth century and was but a minor incident in the eighteenth." On the contrary, recent studies have shown that a large proportion of the colonial workers was poor. [30] A study of Boston by James A. Henretta estimates that the propertyless poor made up at least 29 percent of the population. Since there were not enough jobs in Boston, resulting in intense competition for work, the number of poor grew greatly during the pre-Revolutionary decade. This trend, Allan Kulikoff demonstrates in his work on equality in Revolutionary Boston, was accelerated when many poor men and women migrated to the city from nearby towns. "The poor of Boston had increased from 14% in 1689 to 29% in 1771," notes Dirk Hoerder. [31]

As John A. Alexander points out, Philadelphia experienced a steady increase in the number and percentage of poor people in the 1760s and 1770s. By the early 1770s, some 410 adult males spent part of the year in such institutions as the almshouse, the workhouse, or the hospital for the sick poor, and another 469 were designated as insolvent or without sufficient property to pay taxes. Uncounted others were aided by various church charities and ethnic societies like the Friendly Sons of St. Patrick and the *Deutsche Gesselschaft*, or various craft organizations. Poverty in Philadelphia especially afflicted day laborers, sailors, waiters, servants, and, of course, many blacks. Even a large number of shoemakers, weavers, and bricklayers are listed among those receiving institutional relief. Gary B. Nash summarizes the situation in Philadelphia as follows:

> By the eve of the Revolution poverty had blighted the lives of a large part of the population. . . . In a city that had 3,673 male taxables, one of every four free men can be classified as having been poor or near poor by the standards of that time. . . . Not including those destitute persons who voluntarily left to seek their fortunes elsewhere, the number of poor in the city, minimally calculated, represented a rate of poverty for the population at large of 71 per 1,000 — eight times the incidence before the Seven Years' War.[32]

Many of the poor found themselves in jail because of the institution of imprisonment for debt. The government made no provision for furnishing debtors with any of the necessities of life — except the prison roof over their heads. Thus, persons jailed because they could not pay their debts, however small, were expected to pay for their own food, clothing, and fuel. Imprisonment for debt often took the sole support from the family, so that the imprisoned debtor's wife and children suffered severely.

The following example cited in a recent article, by Douglas Lamar Jones may not be typical, but it does provide a telling answer to the argument that poverty did not exist in Colonial America. "Peter Frost," writes Jones, ". . . made an extreme choice when he was unable to solve his continuing problems of poverty and personal care. Frost, an Ipswich laborer, bound himself for life in 1700 to William Cogwell, Jr."[33]

In a number of cities, free labor faced ruinous competition from Negro slaves who were employed as mechanics. Throughout the colonial period, free white craftsmen fought a losing battle to exclude blacks from most of the skilled trades. The free mechanics of Philadelphia in 1707 protested the "want of employment and lowness of wages occasioned by the number of *Negroes* . . . hired out to work by the day."[34] Thirty years later, free workers in New York protested the "pernicious practice of breeding slaves to trade," which forced the free worker to leave for other colonies.[35] Some restrictions were in fact imposed on the use of slave artisans, but few were carried into practice. The white workers in colonial Massachusetts were not among those who complained about the competition of black workers. While it is true that the blacks never constituted a large percentage of the Boston population—rarely rising to 2 percent of the colonial Massachusetts population—there were still a number of highly skilled craftsmen among them. Even so, the colonial records, as one student has pointed out, "reveal no conflict whatsoever between black and white workers."[36]

Almost from the beginning, the colonies attempted to deal with the labor shortage by controlling wages, hours, and prices. Authorities instituted regulations adapted from England to keep wages in line and to restrict easy movement between trades that might cause severe labor shortages in key areas. When prices went up, the courts fixed maximum rates and fined workers heavily when they sought or received wages above these rates. A court record in New England reads: "William Dixie paid 3s fine for taking 3s per day; James Smith fined 2s, John Stone and Jno Sibley 3s each for taking excessive wages." This action, employers argued, was necessary "to save the American workingman from himself." One employer remarked in 1769: "It is certain that high wages more frequently make labouring people miserable; they too commonly employ their spare time and cash in debauching their morals and ruining their health."[37] As the argument went, low wages were therefore a blessing in disguise for the workers.

While most wage-control legislation in colonial times was relatively ineffective because of the scarcity of labor and the closeness of the frontier, demands for such laws were made throughout the period and, as we shall see, they were put into effect during the War for Independence.[38]

In later decades, workers would seek to solve the problems of low wages, long hours, and poor working conditions and to attain better living standards by forming trade unions, organizing their own political parties, and achieving a better way of life through legislation. But class lines were still too fluid in early America for trade unionism. Except in depressed times, most of the skilled workers who earned wages had a reasonable opportunity to set themselves up as independent masters after a few years' employment. Unskilled workers could either move to other places or become farmers.

Colonial America teemed with private clubs and societies. Some were craft guilds which sought to follow the practices of the European guilds by regulating their respective industries, fixing prices for their work, and inspecting the workmanship and quality of materials. These were not very successful. The best known was probably the Carpenters' Company of Philadelphia, founded in 1724, with its members limited to masters of six-years' standing. (Norman J. Ware and Herbert Harris claim that from the start the company included not only masters, but also journeymen. Richard B. Morris counters that there is no evidence to support this view.)[39] Benevolent societies also arose among masters for the purpose of "assisting such of their members as should be in need of support or the widows or minor children of the members." They paid sick benefits, provided for indigent members, occasionally loaned money, and provided "strong boxes" for savings. A typical mutual aid society was the Friendly Society of Tradesmen House Carpenters, organized in New York City on March 10, 1767. The society was restricted to house carpenters between twenty-one and forty years of age; fees and dues were regularly collected; a sick benefit of 10s. per week for a maximum of three months was available; and upon a member's death, £4 was paid to his family for funeral expenses.[40]

The employer-interest character of these societies is well illustrated by the names of those formed in the maritime industry. Thus, in 1765, the Sea Captains' Club of Philadelphia was founded as a "Society for the Relief of Poor and Distressed Masters of Ships, their Widows, and Children." In 1770, there was organized "The New York Marine Society, for promoting Maritime Knowledge, and for the Relief of Distressed Masters of Ships, their Widows, and Orphan Children." None of these societies did anything for the common seamen.[41]

The artisan of Colonial America was literate, self-educated, and often interested in science, so the formation of the Library Company is not surprising. Most artisans appear to have owned books, and those who did not could find an evening school or library to satisfy their intellectual curiosities. Craftsmen had a chance to hear lectures on navigation, astronomy, and electricity. The nature of the work, requiring dexterity with tools, mastery of physical materials, and technical knowledge, stimulated interest in science. Indeed, the great scientists of Colonial America—Thomas Godfrey, David Rittenhouse, and Benjamin Franklin, all of Philadelphia—began life as artisans. Godfrey, a glazier, studied Latin in his spare time in order to read Newton's celebrated *Principia Mathematica* and was one of the inventors of the quadrant which proved a great aid in navigation. Rittenhouse, who began his career as a clockmaker, greatly improved the telescope and also made important contributions to astronomy. The work of printer Franklin in electricity won him a worldwide reputation. In 1731, aided by poor tradesmen and mechanics of Philadelphia, Franklin started a subscription library which had a variety of books.

In some cases, mechanics formed their own organizations, such as the Association Library Company of Philadelphia. Moreover, colonial workers did act on occasion to improve their conditions. The Journeymen Caulkers of Boston issued a joint statement in 1741, declaring that they would no longer accept payment for their work in notes to shops for goods, a practice which, they said, had "greatly impoverished themselves and their families." For the future, they continued, they would receive and take "no other pay for their service than good lawful public bills of credit."[42] "This good and commendable example," the *Boston Weekly News-Letter* of February 12, 1741, remarked, "will soon be followed by numbers of other artificers and tradesmen."

The following advertisement in the *New York Weekly Journal* of January 28, 1734, indicates that maidservants were also organizing to improve their working conditions:

Here are many women in this town that these hard times intend to go to service, but as it is proper the world should know our terms, we think it reasonable we should not be beat by our mistresses' husbands, they being too strong, and perhaps may do tender women mischief. If any ladies want servants, and will engage for their husbands, they shall soon be supplied.

In addition to forming self-help organizations, workingmen occasionally resorted to "strike" actions to redress grievances. John R. Commons claims that the Philadelphia printers' strike of 1786 was the first authentic labor strike in American history, but Richard B. Morris cites a strike of New York's journeymen tailors in 1768. [43] The twenty journeymen tailors announced on March 31, 1768, that they would return to work only if they received "three shillings and six pence per day with diet." [44] However, in the *Charleston Gazette* of October 29, 1763, there is an announcement that Negro chimney sweepers "had the insolence by a combination amongst themselves, to raise the usual prices, and to refuse doing their work, unless their exorbitant demands are complied with." This action may not have been a strike of workers against employers, but rather a protest of craftsmen against prices fixed by local authorities. Richard Walsh calls the sweepers "one of America's oldest trade unions," adding that "unfortunately nothing more is known about it than the [Grand] jury's grievances." [45] It may be stretching a point to call its action that of a trade union, but it certainly represents joint activity to solve a common grievance.

Mary Roys Baker insists that American wage earners were performing the "fighting functions of a modern Trade Union" throughout the colonial period "by acting in concert to raise wages, to reduce hours of work, to enforce customary work rules, to increase job security, to obtain specific laws which benefit labor. . . ." She views all of the actions of colonial masters, artisans, and mechanics on the economic front in colonial Massachusetts as the "*preliminary* stages" of trade unionism. Indeed, she sees a "prototype labor movement" existing in the Bay Colony as early as 1677. [46]

Colonial America had a long history of protests of craftsmen against prices fixed by local authorities. In 1684, the truckmen employed by the municipal government of New York refused to move dirt from the streets unless the price per load was increased. The strikers were "suspended and discharged" "for not obeying the command and doing their duties as becomes them in their places." A week later, the carters asked to be returned to their jobs. They were ordered to conform to certain "laws and orders established" and to pay a fine of six shillings each. About a century later, in 1770, the coopers of New York determined "not to sell casks except in accordance with the rates established." The coopers were tried and convicted of a conspiracy to restrain trade, and were ordered to pay fifty shillings "to the church or pious ones." Those who worked for the city were dismissed.[47]

Several years earlier, in 1758, the same city government had been much kinder when the powerful shipping merchants had combined to lower the wage scale for ship carpenters, able seamen, and laborers. In 1764, a colony-wide employers' association was set up in New York City. Each member agreed not to "receive in his service" any workers who could not produce "a recommendation in writing, from the master, or mistress, whom they last served in this Colony."[48] No fines were imposed upon these employers, nor were they prosecuted for conspiracy.

In 1746, a number of Savannah carpenters went on strike. Immediately, the trustees of the colony invoked a parliamentary statute to suppress the strike. The report of their action, dated December 29, 1746, read in part:

> An advertisement being read, signed by several carpenters at Savannah and stuck up at several places in the said town, whereby they have combined and resolved not to work below particular prices specified therein.
>
> Ordered
>
> That the Act of Parliament intitled . . . be sent over to the President and Assistants, with orders for them to apprize the people of the consequences of the said act, and to put the same in force.[49]

It is clear that, while there were no trade unions and few, if any, labor strikes in Colonial America, there were numerous examples of joint action by artisans, mechanics, and journeymen on the economic front to remedy their grievances. This tradition was to be important, as we shall see, when the Revolutionary movement got under way.

There was even a tradition of joint political activity by colonial artisans, mechanics, and laborers, which was to be useful in the Revolutionary movement. It was mainly confined to New York. In 1689, Jacob Leisler led the people of New York City against the mercantile aristocracy, captured the Fort of New York, and overthrew the government. City artisans and laborers, classified by Governor Bellomont as "the scum of the people, tailors and other scandalous persons," formed the majority of Leisler's party. Before the movement was defeated, several important democratic rights were won. A committee of safety was elected by the people, free men who owned no property were given voting rights, and representatives to the colonial government were elected by all voters.[50]

Although Leisler's regime was overthrown, a number of the democratic advances made during the rebellion continued. While the government was controlled by merchants, Crown officers, lawyers, and landowners, artisans and mechanics who purchased the right from the Common Council for a fee were able to vote. The possibility thus existed for a political movement of the artisans.

The opportunity presented itself during the 1734 campaign for alderman, when the Court party, representing Governor Cosby and the merchants, was determined to retain control of the city government by reelecting its alderman and councilmen. Arrayed against them was the Popular party, supported by the artisans and aided by John Peter Zenger's *New York Journal.* In a handbill distributed by the Popular party during the campaign, the workingmen of New York were urged "to choose no courtiers or trimmers; or any of that vain tribe that are more fond of a feather in their hats than the true interest of the City. Nor to choose any dependents on them." It reminded the voters that "*A poor honest man* is preferable to a rich knave." Toward the end of the campaign, the workingmen were rallied to the polls by this song:

> *Our country's rights we will defend,*
> *Like brave and honest men,*
> *We voted right and there's an end*
> *And so we'll do again.*[51]

The election was triumph for the Popular party. John Fred, laborer; Johannes Burger, bricklayer; William Roome, painter; Henry Bogart, baker; and other artisans were elected to the Common Council, which, by 1735, was completely controlled by the Popular party. Governor Cosby complained to the Lords of Trade in London of the "misled populace in this city," and another conservative commented that the city was "entirely at the beck of the faction and for the most part men of the low class."[52]

Infuriated by the victory of the people, Governor Cosby took action against John Peter Zenger. The songs, ballads, and several issues of the *Journal* were condemned by the Governor's Council and the Supreme Court. Zenger himself was arrested on a charge of seditious libel. He was defended by the prominent eighty-eight-year-old lawyer Andrew Hamilton of Philadelphia, without fee or reward. Stressing the issue of a free press, Hamilton said: "The question before the Court . . . is not of small nor private concern, it is not the cause of a poor printer, nor of *New York* alone. . . . It is the cause of Liberty; and I make no doubt that your upright conduct this day, will not only entitle you to the love and esteem of your fellow-citizens, but every man who prefers freedom to a life of slavery will bless and honor you."[53]

The verdict was "not guilty," and the precedent of a free press had been established in America.

Later, the conservatives in New York regained control of the city government, but the rich and the "well-born" in Colonial America never recovered from the panic created by the political upsurge of the people of New York City, especially by the role played by the artisans, mechanics, and laborers.

This role is of interest also because of the controversy among historians concerning the political status of the colonial artisans and mechanics. Historians of the Progressive era, especially Carl Becker and those scholars who followed him, believed that artisans, mechanics, and the underprivileged in general in the cities were disfranchised and deprived of a voice in the body politic, through property qualifications for voting. These requirements, they said, were steadily raised until the masses were effectively debarred from the franchise. In Philadelphia, Boston, and New

York City, according to these scholars, mechanics as a class were completely unenfranchised. Pressing this point further, the historians in the Progressive era argued that radical politics during the American Revolution consisted mainly of an attempt by the disfranchised and economically and socially deprived mechanics in the cities, and the yeomen in the countryside, to take possession of the body politic. This argument came to be known as the "internal revolution" thesis, according to which, after 1760, extralegal mass activities of the common man became the "open door" to political power. Thus, the Revolution became not only a struggle against Great Britain for "home rule," but also a contest over "who should rule at home." This much-quoted phrase is the final one in the introductory chapter to Carl Becker's seminal study, *The History of Political Parties in the Province of New York, 1760-1776*, published in 1909.[54]

All of these assertions came under attack after World War II by historians who saw more consensus than conflict in the Revolutionary movement. The consensus historians argued that there was widespread popular participation in politics in Colonial America and that most urban dwellers, including the majority of mechanics, were neither disfranchised nor otherwise institutionally excluded from politics. As for the "internal revolution" thesis, these historians insisted that Colonial America was actually a classless society — a land of unhampered opportunity; that a "propertyless proletarian class" never existed in this preindustrial society; and that, while there may have been some tensions in colonial cities, these were not an expression of conflict between "haves" and "have-nots," as the Progressive historians supposed.

In a 1952 article in the *New England Quarterly* and three years later in his book *Middle-Class Democracy and the Revolution in Massachusetts, 1691-1780*, Robert E. Brown set down the fundamental theories of the consensus historians. Drawing upon statistical methods and contemporary opinion, Brown concluded that practically all adult males in the Bay Colony had the vote. Massachusetts society before 1776, he argued, was "very close to a complete democracy." Scorning the idea of the "internal revolution," he insisted that "what applies to Massachusetts applies without too much change to other colonies as well." Nothing was more erroneous, he insisted, than to conceive of Colonial America as "undemocratic" or to believe that "property qualifications for voting eliminated a large portion of the free adult male population from participation in political affairs." Brown maintained that the qualifications were low enough and economic opportunities high enough to enable most men to meet them, and, moreover, that in practice they were often waived. Some free persons were indeed entirely propertyless—some seamen, tenant farmers, and town dwellers—but these were the exceptions. [55]

We have no electoral census for the colonial era, but sufficient evidence exists to indicate that the Progressive historians' picture of the suffrage in urban communities is indeed in need of revision. In Philadelphia, for example, most artisans were probably able to participate in politics for, even though the majority could not meet the voting requirement of ownership of fifty acres of land or fifty pounds of property, these requirements were rarely strictly enforced. [56] So far as New York City is concerned, we have already seen that artisans, mechanics, and laborers were an important factor in the victory of the Popular party in 1734. Actually, the qualification for the franchise for residents was simple enough. One had to purchase the freedom of the city from the Common Council for a fee ranging from £5 for a merchant or shopkeeper down to 20 shillings for an artisan. Apprentices were eligible for the freedom without fee after seven years' apprenticeship. Under these provisions, mechanics, who were generally propertyless, could gain the right to vote by becoming freemen. One student of voting in colonial New York concludes that in 1768 and 1769, 50 to 60 percent of the adult men in New York City were eligible to vote. [57]

On the other hand, to conclude, as a number of other scholars do, that virtually all mechanics and artisans could vote is not warranted. (The same is true of the assertion by some historians that disfranchisement did not matter anyway, since it was in the taverns that the colonial workers engaged in political action.) John Cary maintains that all of Massachusetts' artisan class was disfranchised by the property qualifications. [58] In his statistical work on Boston, James Henretta does not go that far, but he does reveal the existence of a propertyless proletariat comprising 14 percent of the adult males in 1687 and 29 percent in 1771, and

claims that at least these workers were disfranchised.[59] Alfred
Young and Staughton Lynd conclude that in New York City,
among "the poorer class of mechanics probably less than half
could vote."[60] Jackson Turner Main points to the existence of a
landless proletariat in Colonial America, comprising "nearly 40
percent of the population," and it is clear that few of these workers could vote.[61] In fact, it can be stated that most of the dockworkers, sailors, and unskilled or semiskilled wage workers could
not vote, and that their number increased in the eighteenth century as those without property in the colonial cities grew in number. When one adds to these the disfranchised Negroes, the
women who could not vote at all—not even those who were
printers, apothecaries, merchants, or tended their husbands'
shops—what becomes of the middle-class democracy of Colonial
America? Consensus historian Elisha P. Douglass defines
democracy as "a political system in which all adult males enjoyed equal rights."[62] Overlooking the fact that Douglass does
not even consider Negroes or women in his definition (they are
not even mentioned in his index), how democratic was Colonial
America?

Not very, says Jesse Lemisch in his study of the American
Revolution "from the bottom up." Taking sharp issue with the
consensus historians, he asserts that throughout Colonial
America, "property qualifications excluded more and more people from voting until a 'Jacksonian Revolution' was necessary to
overthrow what had become a very limited middle-class democracy indeed."[63] One does not have to agree with this sweeping
observation to realize that more workers voted in Colonial America than had previously been assumed, but not as many as the
consensus historians would have us believe. But one cannot
ignore the question Lemisch asks immediately afterwards:
"What if every single person could vote in the colonies? Would
that prove that the common man had come into his own?"[64] Or
to put it another way: was there no political exclusion of the
common people, even if we concede that there was a relatively
broad suffrage? "The suitability of mechanics for elective
office," Young and Lynd note, "the voter's inability to instruct
and control his representatives once they were elected, the administration of justice, the ability to elect officers who had tradi-

tionally been appointed, were as important as the right to vote."[65] To this statement should be added the voter's ability, or lack of it, to cast his vote without fear of intimidation by the wealthy and powerful, which was extremely difficult to achieve as long as *viva voce* voting, rather than the written ballot, was used. Writing in the January 8, 1769, issue of the *New York Gazette*, a mechanic complained that "many of the poorer people" had

> deeply felt the aristocratic power, or rather the intolerable tyranny of the great and opulent, who (such is the shocking depravity of the times, and their utter contempt of all public virtue and patriotism) have openly threatened them with the loss of their employment, and to arrest them for debt, unless they gave their voices as they were directed; and it being evident to all impartial men, that nothing else can preserve the freedom and independence of elections, and prevent for the future the like exorbitant influence of the rich over the poor, than a secret method of voting.

Recent scholarly studies indicate that in the six decades before the Revolutionary War began, lower-class elements in urban centers were involved in politics through the organization of political clubs, caucuses, tickets, and other devices.[66] Their effectiveness remains questionable, however, for the colonial governments were dominated by wealthy men of high status who formed a closely knit ruling oligarchy. In at least six pre-Revolutionary legislatures, the "economic elite," comprising the top 10 percent of the population,[67] held 85 percent of the seats, while the governor's councils, the bench, and even the bar were filled with men, or the relatives of men, who belonged to the ruling families.[68] If one substitutes the words "merchants and landlords" for "planters," what Josiah Quincy said of the South Carolina Assembly could be applied to each of the thirteen colonies: "'Tis true that they have a house of Assembly: but who do they represent? The laborer, the mechanic, the tradesman, the farmer, husbandman or yeoman? No the representatives are almost if not wholly rich planters."[69]

A Philadelphia mechanic who signed himself "A Brother

Chip" probably put it best when he complained in 1770, on behalf of his "brethren the tradesmen, mechanics, etc., the *useful* and *necessary* inhabitants of this province.":

> It has been customary for a certain company of leading men to nominate persons, and settle the ticket, for assembly-men, commissioners, assessors, etc. without ever permitting the affirmative or negative voice of a mechanic to interfere, and when they have concluded, expect the tradesmen will give a sanction thereto by passing the ticket; this we have tamely submitted to so long, that those gentlemen make no scruple to say, that the mechanics (though by far the most numerous, especially in the county) have no right to be consulted; that is, in fact have no right to *speak* or *think* for themselves. Have we not an equal right of electing, or being elected? If we have not the liberty of nominating such persons whom we approve, our freedom of voting is at an end, and if we are too mean a body to be consulted upon such a weighty occasion, our ballot is not worth throwing in on the day of election. . . . I think it absolutely necessary that one or two mechanics be elected to represent so large a body of the inhabitants. If merchants may be reasonably supposed to be best acquainted with commerce, millers and farmers with the situation and circumstances of farmers, consequently mechanics with those of mechanics.

The same observer continued:

> it is the great impudence to elect men of enormous estates; they are already our superiors, except in the point of election; but when they are elected, power is added to their wealth, which gives them such a superiority over us, as to render them our lords and masters, and us their most abject slaves, upon whom they will scarce vouchsafe to cast a friendly look, but at the approach of a new election.

Finally, he linked the struggle for "home rule" with the contest over "who should rule at home":

> Let us reflect on the distress our present country has

brought not only on herself, but on her American children, through the same misconduct, and what a noble struggle the citizens of London (chiefly mechanics) are engaged in, in order to retrieve that, which is *at present* in our power to prevent.

Not a few historians dismiss these and other letters in the contemporary press on the ground that there is no way of determining with any precision whether they were written by an "artisan" or "mechanic," as the anonymous writer claimed. While one cannot say that the writers spoke in every case for artisans and mechanics generally, it is clear from other contemporary sources that the views set forth in such letters did reflect thinking in artisan and mechanic circles.

The Philadelphia mechanic directed his main attack against the economic and political ruling class in Pennsylvania. At the same time, he was voicing another grievance of the colonial mechanics: the fact that, although they constituted a majority of the population in the cities and were "the *useful* and *necessary* inhabitants of this province," they were regarded as socially "mean, base and pitiful" and incapable, through lack of ability, to play any role in the political life of the colonies. He proclaimed that "we glory in the despicable name of mechanic," and he called upon his fellow mechanics to "act in union with spirit and integrity" to gain for themselves their rightful place in American society. [70] In short, the colonial workers were refusing to remain in the place to which a ruling class theory of deference and subordination had relegated them.

"A Brother Chip's" letter was published in the *Pennsylvania Gazette* of September 27, 1770. By this time, as we shall see in the following chapters, the artisans and mechanics had awakened to their common political and economic interests and had emerged for the first time as an independent force in politics. Through their participation in the numerous committees established to conduct public affairs and to police nonimportation agreements, mechanics became involved, as never before, in governmental operations and sustained political activity. This development was revolutionary indeed, but even more revolutionary was the politicization of the poorer artisans, journeymen, and laborers, not to mention the indentured servants and slaves.

2 ——— *The Sons of Liberty*

The decade preceding the actual outbreak of hostilities between Great Britain and her American colonies was marked by an ever-increasing resentment among Americans at what was commonly called "British tyranny." From the end of the Seven Years' War (1763) on, Americans became more and more convinced that they were being subjected to practices that threatened both their economic well-being and their future.

By 1763, a number of cities in the colonies had become commercial and manufacturing centers, although the manufacturers in these cities still had to await release from British mercantilist restrictions before they could develop in earnest. Under the British mercantile policy, the American colonies existed only for the purpose of increasing the profits of British manufacturers, merchants, and landlords. To assure that the colonies would not become an economic threat to the home industry, and to prevent the New World from becoming a power in its own right, the British rulers would not, for example, permit the colonies to set up furnaces or forges or to ship iron, wool, or woolen cloth from one colony to another. The colonies were forced to send their commodities either to England alone or, if they were destined for a non-British port, to England first. They could only import goods produced in England or goods sent to the colonies by way of England. After 1763, they were also forbidden to settle west of the Appalachian Mountains. By the Currency Act of 1764, they were deprived of the right to use legal tender paper money or to establish colonial mints or land banks—at a time when the absence of established paper money and banks was seriously retarding economic growth in all the colonies.[1]

Not all artisans, of course, suffered from British restrictions. The building trades, for example, had a natural monopoly over their craft. Moreover, mercantilism helped some artisans and mechanics. Hemp makers were given bounties; coopers were subsidized; manufacturers of potash were assisted by the removal of duties on that product upon its importation to Great Britain; and shipbuilders and producers of naval stores were encouraged with grants of money. Then again, the colonists often managed to circumvent mercantile restrictions by illegal production and smuggling, and some labor groups were able to obtain help from colonial governments to meet British competition.[2] Some scholars have cited these facts as evidence for dismissing mercantilism as a cause of the American Revolution, but more and more students of the period, following the lead of Richard Walsh, Jesse Lemisch and Charles Olton, have emphasized its significance in recent years.

Overall, the spirit of mercantilism pervaded in the colonies, and the small benefits any special group enjoyed were far outweighed by Parliament's favoritism for Englishmen over Americans. Illegal production and smuggling became increasingly difficult after 1763, when the complaints of English businessmen resulted in more rigid inspection and enforcement. A Bostonian stated in 1765: "A colonist cannot make a button, a horseshoe, nor a hobnail, but some sooty iron monger or respectable buttonmaker of Britain shall bawl and squall that his honor's Worship is most egregiously maltreated, injured, cheated and robbed by the rascally American republicans."[3]

The "bawling and squalling" intensified after 1763. During the Seven Years' War, commercial traffic between England and America had been disrupted, thereby fostering the growth of home manufactures. Furthermore, the British had been forced to rely on the colonies to supply many goods and services to support the American theater of war. Commenting on the prosperity that accompanied the campaigns of the French and Indian War, an Englishman reported from the colonies: "Cities flourish and increase by extensive trade, artisans and mechanics of all sorts are drawn thither, who teach all sorts of handiwork before unknown in the country, *and they soon come to make for them-selves what they used to import.*"[4]

Despite prohibitive legislation, up to that time colonial hats, shoes, finished ironware, and furniture competed profitably with English products in the colonies. Now, the London merchants, alarmed by reports of the great growth of these manufactures during the French and Indian War, began to dump large amounts of British manufactured goods on the American market, flooding the colonies with textiles, linens, hats, shoes, metal goods, and luxuries of all sorts. Daily, the artisans and mechanics of America "saw English-made furniture, silver, guns, iron, coaches, saddles, and shoes unloaded at their port for sale to the provincials."[5]

It was inevitable that, after 1763, these efforts to reestablish in America the antebellum mercantile model would exacerbate relations between the mother country and the colonies. The situation was aggravated further when the complaints from America counted for little when weighed against the profit motives of English manufacturers and exporters. An increasing number of colonial artisans, mechanics, and day laborers came to regard the importation of manufactured goods from Britain as a principal threat to their economic well-being. Many attributed the economic depression in their cities and towns following the French and Indian War to British mercantilist policies. They complained incessantly about the "ruinous" competition of foreign wares, which increased the burdens already weighing heavily on them.[6]

Adding to the misery of the colonial worker was the fact that when he sought employment in the already flooded labor market, he found himself competing with off-duty English soldiers who consistently undercut his wages. It was a long-standing practice in the British army to allow men to take civilian employment when they were free of military duties. Since the soldier would do for eighteen pence or two shillings what would normally cost the employer four shillings, the employer's preference for the soldier was understandable. To the day laborers, clerks, and seamen who came ashore looking for work, the soldiers laboring in stores and shops and along the docks as stevedores meant fewer jobs and a generally lower level of wages.[7]

Apart from seeing their job opportunities disappear and their wages undercut by off-duty soldiers, seamen were also the victims of the "cruel and tyrannical" institution of impressment. Since the end of the seventeenth century, impressment of seamen had become the customary method of maintaining a full complement of men in the British Navy. As Jesse Lemisch points out, "impressment and fear of impressment were constant facts in the lives of New York's seamen." They were also facts of life for seamen in other colonial ports, and, indeed, for other workers as well. Large numbers of lower class workers were often swept up to serve in the British Navy. In 1747, Commodore Knowles' press gang made a sweep of Boston's harbor, taking up ship carpenters, apprentices, and landsmen as well as seamen. Once impressed into the British navy, they were treated "little better than slaves."[8]

Except for the retainers of the Crown, all classes in America suffered from British policies and practices, but the artisans, mechanics, seamen, and day laborers suffered most intensely. The restraints on colonial trade and manufactures discouraged artisans who had to compete with their counterparts in England, intensified unemployment, and lowered the wages of all colonial workers. Journeymen and mechanics were particularly alarmed, for these restraints seemed to cut off both their employment prospects and their opportunity to rise into the shopowning class. The prohibition on paper money increased the pressue on the debtor, causing a rise in prices and making it difficult to carry on business. It was also not easy to conduct business in the face of the constant threat of invasions by press gangs to impress seamen and other colonial workers. To many colonial artisans and mechanics, it seemed that Britain was responsible for all their economic hardships. As one artisan put it, "A handful of English capitalists carried more weight at Westminster than the welfare of millions of Americans."[9]

The restraints on American economic development were intensified at precisely the same time that Americans were being subjected to a series of measures that were not only arbitrary and illegal, but that also threatened the very existence of their civil liberties.[10] The Sugar Act of 1764, the Stamp Act of 1765, the Townshend Acts of 1770, the Tea Act of 1773, and the "Intoler-

able Acts" of 1774—all were part of a series of "obnoxious measures" passed by Parliament which Americans believed were designed to fleece them and reduce them to a state of total dependence. They did everything they could to force the repeal of these
measures and to defeat what they came to view as a vast conspiracy against liberty in America.

As we shall see in detail below, the colonists used a wide variety of tactics and strategies in their resistance to the "obnoxious
measures." One which combined principle with economic benefits was the nonimportation of British goods. To a certain extent,
the importing merchants favored this response. Declining profits
in trade made the investment opportunities offered by domestic
industries appealing to them. Moreover, nonimportation permitted the merchants to dispose of their inventories at higher prices.

It was not in the merchants' interests to continue nonimportation beyond a certain point, however. When they had disposed of
their goods, the majority of them were ready to resume trade, regardless of whether the special grievance that had produced nonimportation was redressed. Not so, however, with the mechanics
and laborers. For them, nonimportation was not only one of several ways of pressuring Parliament to relieve the colonial complaints, but it also stimulated a revival of the domestic manufacturing that had brought them good times during the French and
Indian War and, with them, a considerable increase in local
employment. Hence, they were the most enthusiastic advocates
of initiating nonconsumption of British goods, and they continued to insist on maintaining nonimportation long after the
merchants were ready to resume importing.

The merchants had still another reason for curtailing resistance to British measures. As the urban artisans and laborers, in
unity with the seamen ashore in quest of employment, became
involved in the resistance movement, they began to emerge as a
political force of some importance. For some among them, the
nonimportation agreements marked their initial entry into
active political life; for others, the agreements made possible
a considerably enlarged participation. Furthermore, they began
to articulate other demands besides opposition to British tyranny—demands for the further democratization of colonial society. This new militancy frightened many of the merchants and

made them anxious to be done with movements that encouraged the emergence of the "lower orders" from out of the place to which the colonial ruling class had consigned them.

Analysis of the role of the mechanics, day laborers, and sailors in the resistance movement is not new. Most upper-class contemporaries and many modern historians have viewed their role as little more than that of an irrational, mindless, manipulated "mob," used by the wealthier elements in the resistance movement for their own ends and moved into action only after repeated sessions in the taverns. The contemporary view is summed up in the comment of Peter Oliver, a leading Tory, that "the people in general . . . were like the mobility of all countries, perfect machines, wound up by any hand who might first take the winch."[11] In describing the role of the mechanics, laborers, and seamen in the Revolution, many modern historians have described them as "the mob," "rowdies," "rough, loud, frequently intoxicated," "bully-boys," and "puppets whose ardor could be turned on or off to suit the policy of its directors." In fact, it would require a book just to list all the derogatory terms used for them.

Again, many historians today retain the term "mob," and some, like Pauline Maier, argue vehemently for its retention without quotation marks.[12] This insistence continues despite the view that has become increasingly common among a number of American historians since the writings of the British historians George Rudé, Eric Thompson, and Eric J. Hobsbawm began to have an impact on our scholarship.[13] A basic theme that has emerged on both sides of the Atlantic is that the popular uprisings, the riots that occurred in preindustrial France, England, and America, were largely directed by the rioters and consciously related to specific prevailing combinations of the economic, political, and social grievances, needs, and aspirations of the particular crowd. In other words, the actions of the crowd might be narrow reactions to relieve the effects of particular economic grievances, or they might be a combination of such factors with those of a broader nature.

Throughout the rest of this work, therefore, we shall not use the term *mob*, with its unfavorable implications, and instead use the word *crowd*.

Like the cities of Europe, colonial American cities had a tradition of crowd activity. The nature of this activity is the subject of
some controversy among historians. Some insist that it resulted
from genuine lower-class grievances and was aimed at social reform, while others argue that it was mindless, was often directed
by the ruling class elite for its own purposes, and had no links to
the Revolutionary movement launched in 1765.[14] While there is
some justification for the last interpretation, it ignores the fact
that many of the participants in the crowds of the Revolutionary
era had been involved in those of New York City, Philadelphia,
and Boston in the 1750s and early 1760s and that they came together because of deep-seated grievances—either against the
British or against the growing inequality of wealth in the colonies—and the power that the economic elite exercised over the
political process. Riots often took place on election days, when
small shopkeepers, artisans, and laborers would march to the
polls armed with sticks and stones, demanding the ballot. These
demonstrations were supplemented by literary protests, in prose
and verse, such as:

> Now the pleasant time approaches;
> Gentlemen do ride in coaches,
> But poor men they don't regard,
> That to maintain them labour hard.[15]

Certainly, the anti-impressment riots of the decades preceding
the Revolutionary movement were hardly "mindless," but
rather were provoked by genuine grievances. "The immediate
sufferers" of impressment, wrote one pamphleteer in 1747, "were
people of the lowest rank" whose resentment "grew up into rage
and madness." According to Thomas Hutchinson, royal governor of Massachusetts, "all orders resented [impressment], but
the lower class were beyond measure enraged."[16] The presence
in the crowds after 1765 of these very people of the "lower
class"—seamen, laborers, and other victims of impressment,
along with artisans and mechanics—provides a distinct link between the pre-Revolution crowds and those of the Revolutionary
era. As Jesse Lemisch succinctly puts it: "When Americans
finally took to arms to defend their natural rights, their act was

not without precedent, for in their midst were men with an ancient tradition of violent resistance to British tyranny."[17]

The direct action taken by crowds after 1765, however, was only one form of the activity of politically conscious revolutionists. In general, the resistance movement to British measures, from the 1760s right up to independence, utilized the threat of violence as a political weapon. In doing so, it acted on the popular notion that direct action against unjust or authoritarian official acts was legitimate. However, the movement relied primarily on an organized political struggle. As Bernard Bailyn notes, both as rioters and in their more orderly activities, the Revolutionary mechanics, artisans, seamen, and laborers represented a "full fledged political movement" which was "politically effective."[18] It was this politicalization that alarmed the perceptive conservative, Gouverneur Morris, at a mass meeting in New York in 1774, when he commented that "the mob begin to think and reason."[19]

Apart from the areas of tobacco cultivation in Maryland and Virginia, where the planters had their own special reasons for becoming involved, the protests against Britain centered in the cities. There, it was spearheaded by extralegal organizations generally known as the "Sons of Liberty." With its base among mechanics of all strata, the Sons of Liberty galvanized the crowds into action by means of demonstrations, handbills, and meetings. In several key cities, especially Boston, a highly organized command system was developed under the leadership of the Sons of Liberty which could bring crowds into being at a moment's notice.

The Sons of Liberty became a prominent agency of Revolutionary agitation in the fall of 1765, at the time of the Stamp Act. Its origin is somewhat obscure. It may, for example, have been taken over from the "True Sons of Righteous Liberty," formed as a political club in Connecticut in 1755 for the purpose of defending civil and religious freedom.[20] Or it may have been suggested by the Sons of Neptune, an earlier organization of mariners in New York City.[21] Colonel Isaac Barré probably gave the radical group its name "Sons of Liberty." In a speech before the House of Commons, Barré answered the argument that the people living in the American colonies were merely the offspring of the mother country and that they were therefore liable to any and all regulations she saw fit to impose upon them. In essence, Barré claimed that the American colonists were a separate people, defending a distant frontier of the British Empire—a noble set of men, true "Sons of Liberty." Jared Ingersoll, a special agent for the Connecticut Assembly in England, heard the speech and reported it to Governor Thomas Fitch.[22] As the opposition to the Stamp Act grew in America, those who opposed the act took up the name Sons of Liberty to distinguish themselves from those who were either neutral or favored the measure.

Apparently, the Sons of Liberty appeared first in eastern Connecticut and spread rapidly to Massachusetts and New York. Within a short time, associated bodies could be found in almost all the colonies. At first, they tended to operate anonymously, but they soon adopted the name Sons of Liberty, and by the beginning of 1766, the name was in common use.

While the Sons of Liberty included professional men, lesser merchants, and even local officials, the rank and file were mechanics, tradesmen, and artificers: carpenters, joiners, printers, shipwrights, smiths, caulkers, ropemakers, masons, and other members of the artisan community. In short, the craft element constituted the largest single unit in the group.[23]

The leaders of the Sons of Liberty were recruited from master craftsmen, merchants, and professional groups, a number of whom had once been mechanics and were accustomed to rubbing shoulders with craftsmen and laborers. In general, they were men of modest wealth who stood outside the merchant elite and exerted little political influence. In Boston, the Sons of Liberty was headed by Samuel Adams,[24] a one-time brewer, who has been called America's first professional politician, and the leading colonial protagonist of independence; William Molineaux, a lesser merchant; and Joseph Warren and Thomas Young, doctors. In New York City, the leaders were Alexander McDougall and Isaac Sears, ship captains; John Lamb, Francis Lewis, Marinus Willett, and Jacob Van Zandt, lesser merchants; and Egbert Benson and John Sloss Hobart, lawyers. Charleston's leader, Christopher Gadsden, a planter merchant, was called the Southern counterpart of Sam Adams, while in Philadelphia, the leader was Charles Thomson, master craftsman, referred to as the "Sam Adams of the Quaker City." In Boston, Ebenezer Mackintosh, a twenty-eight-old shoemaker, cordwainer, and leather-worker; in New York, Abraham Brasher, a writer of popular songs; in Charleston, William Johnson, a mechanic; and in Philadelphia, Timothy Matlock, a brewer, were also part of the Sons of Liberty leadership. It was on these mechanics that the leaders relied to mobilize the rank and file. Ebenezer Mackintosh acted as the link between the "Loyal Nine," the leading group of the Boston Sons of Liberty, and the crowd. He lived in the Southend, was a member of Fire Engine Company No. 9, and led the Southend crowd in a number of battles. He was apparently familiar with contemporary movements against tyranny, for he named his first son in honor of the Corsican Pascal Paoli, who was responsible for ending Genoese rule over Corsica and establishing enlightened rule and reforms. [25]

As the Sons of Liberty grew, they required a central directing body. The most famous one was Boston's above-mentioned "Loyal Nine," several of whom were mechanics, painters, printers, and jewelers. In 1767, when the "Loyal Nine" was transformed into the North End Caucus, its membership was still largely made up of mechanics. They were neither poor nor propertyless; they were engaged in a variety of occupations, ranging from housewright to goldsmith and leather dresser, which were typical of the city's artisan community. [26]

The relationship between the leadership and rank and file of the Sons of Liberty is a complex one, and we do not know all we need to about this aspect of the Revolutionary movement. It will become clear from what follows that the urban mechanics, far from being the "manipulated puppets" of the popular leaders, were fairly consistent in exerting pressure on and through the leaders for radical action. The rank and file workingmen were always more radical than the merchant-professional leadership and pushed both the leadership and the Revolution forward. "It was the [rank and file] mechanics," notes Alfred P. Young, "who in effect nullified the Stamp Act, provided the means of coercion to effect nonimportation, took the lead in direct action against the British army, provided the muscle for the 'Tea Parties,' and in the final crisis, exerted pressure from below for Independence." [27]

This pressure was to be expected. As we have seen, the Revolutionary movement offered the mechanic class the opportunity to influence the political movement of the day. At the same time, it opened the door to a brighter future for them through nonimportation and the accompanying development of home industry. The Revolutionary goals of the rank and file urban groups in the resistance movement were not, one historian argues, really "revolutionary" at all, since their aim "was not to remake, but to be incorporated more effectively within the existing social system."[28] This may be so, but the "existing social system" they envisaged was not the same as the one in operation when the Revolutionary movement got under way. They opposed not only the authority of a government three thousand miles away, but also the domination of "respectable and substantial merchants." Not all the leaders linked the two struggles, but to retain mechanic support they found it necessary to go along with the mechanics' more radical demands. Those leaders who refused were pushed aside. Indeed, in the final crisis, from 1774 to 1776, the mechanics assumed such an influential role in the group that they and the Sons of Liberty became practically synonymous. If the Sons of Liberty became too cautious and conservative, the mechanics exercised this influence outside the organization.

This development was partly the result of the mechanic class's rejection of the view that they were "mean, base, pitiful" and destined to remain subservient in American society. In 1776, John Adams, in rejecting the plea of his wife, Abigail, that the patriots should pay "particular care and attention" to the ladies, voiced the upper-class concern over the development of lower-class consciousness and wondered where it would stop: "We have been told that our struggle has loosened the bonds of government everywhere; that children and apprentices were disobedient; that schools and colleges were grown turbulent; that Indians slighted their guardians, and negroes grew insolent to their masters."[29]

Blacks had participated in a number of the urban crowd activities in the decades before the 1760s, including the anti-impressment riots, and they were to join in street crowd actions during the Revolutionary decade. All of the Revolutionary bodies remained closed to slaves and free blacks alike as well as to indentured servants.[30]

The Sons of Liberty, as the name implies, was an all-male organization. Associated with it was a kindred organization of patriotic women called "Daughters of Liberty." These women made
the nonimportation agreements effective by boycotting English
goods. They popularized homespun clothing with the slogan, "It
is better to wear a homespun coat than to lose our Liberty." As
the chief tea drinkers in the colonies, the women played an important role in the battle against the Tea Act; the Daughters of Liberty refused to drink tea under any circumstances. When a festival of the Daughters of Liberty was interrupted by a man who
denounced the Revolution, the women emulated some of the
crowd actions of the Sons of Liberty. They seized the intruder,
stripped him to the waist, and, in the absence of tar and feathers,
covered him with molasses and the downy tops of flowers.[31] The
Newport Mercury of December 9, 1765, reported in all serious-
ness that since marriage licenses required stamps, "the young
ladies of this place are determined to join hands with none but
such as will to the utmost endeavour to abolish the custom of
marrying with licence."

Although the Daughters of Liberty did not question the custom that a woman should not appear in a public gathering and
speak, they did challenge other customs. They passed spirited
resolutions condemning Parliament's interference with the liberties of Americans and commending the work of the Sons of
Liberty. The male organization welcomed their help. "With the
ladies on our side we can make every Tory tremble," they announced. On one occasion, the Boston Sons of Liberty passed a
resolution thanking its female associates in Providence, Rhode
Island, for their firm stand in defense of American rights.[32]

To all conservatives, especially the Tories, the Sons of Liberty
were always "the mob," "the mixed rabble of Scotch, Irish, and
foreign vagabonds," "descendants of convicts," "foul-mouthed
and inflaming sons of discord and faction."[33] Such epithets did
not intimidate the Liberty Boys. Before the hostile eyes of conservatives, the Sons of Liberty, armed with a variety of weapons
and determined to "fight up to their knees in blood" rather than
be ruled by tyrants, paraded to the Liberty Tree for public meetings, in military formation, with Liberty Tree medals suspended
from their necks. They held weekly educational meetings in inns

and taverns, at which the latest newspapers, pamphlets, and handbills were read aloud for the benefit of the illiterate.[34] At singing festivals, they raised their voices in revolutionary song, warning aristocrats that they "dared be free" from domestic as well as British tyranny. One of the songs went in part:

> *Come rally, Sons of Liberty*
> *Come all with hearts united*
> *Our motto is "We Dare Be Free"*
> *Not easily affrighted!*
>
> *Oppression's band we must subdue,*
> *Now is the time or never;*
> *Let each man prove this motto true*
> *And slavery from him sever.*[35]

A similar theme is struck in "An Excellent New Song for the Sons of Liberty in America." The last two stanzas read:

> With the beasts of the wood, we will ramble for food,
>   And lodge in wild deserts and caves
> And live poor as Job on the skirts of the globe,
>   Before we'll submit to be slaves; brave boys,
> Before we'll submit to be slaves.
>
> The birthright we hold shall never be sold,
>   But sacred maintain'd to our graves;
> Nay, and ere we'll comply, we will gallantly die,
>   For we *must not* and *will not* be slaves; brave boys,
> For we *must not* and *will not* be slaves.[36]

At their festivals, the Sons of Liberty drank toasts to "Taxation without Representation is Tyranny," "Natural Rights of Man," and other slogans of the Revolution. One of the most popular and most frequently repeated toasts was "Wilkes and Liberty." It was drunk in honor of John Wilkes, member of Parliament and editor of the *North Briton*. In that publication's issue of April 23, 1763 (No. 45), Wilkes had virtually called George III a liar for describing the peace ending the Seven Years' War as "honorable to my crown and beneficial to my people."

Attacking this statement as a falsehood, Wilkes implied that parliamentary approval had come only through general use of the Civil List as a form of bribery.[37]

The king and his first minister, George Grenville, reacted quickly, Wilkes was imprisoned briefly and later expelled from Parliament. With the support of London merchants, professionals, and workers, he was reelected by a decisive margin on March 28, 1768. He was forced to serve twenty-two months in prison for previous convictions. While in prison, Wilkes became the spokesman for all those in London who were dissatisfied with the government's American policy, as well as for other forces opposing the government, especially the workers.[38]

In May 1768, a crowd of workers gathered around King's Bench Prison, where Wilkes was held. Without the slightest provocation, the troops guarding the prison fired point blank into the crowd, killing six. Wilkes wrote a pamphlet charging the government with planning the "massacre of St. George's Field."[39] Expelled from Parliament, reelected, again expelled, again reelected, Wilkes was not only expelled again, but when he was overwhelmingly reelected, the Commons nullified the election and gave his badly beaten opponent the vacant seat. Parliament thus demonstrated that it could regularly disregard the wishes of the electorate by naming anyone it pleased to fill a vacancy.[40]

To assist Wilkes in continuing his agitation, a group of London radicals formed an organization in February 1769 called the "Society for the Supporters of the Bill of Rights." It included a number of prominent radicals, among them the popular pro-American historian, Mrs. Catherine MacCauley. Catherine Sawbridge MacCauley was a correspondent of Mercy Warren, and in her letters, she spoke strongly in support of the American cause against the British government. Her vigorous defense of Civil liberties in America was too radical even for most Whigs. Mrs. MacCauley is credited with being the first woman historian, author of an eight-volume history of England which became a republican classic. The February 15, 1770, issue of the *New York Journal* carried a letter praising the "History of England, written by Mrs. MacCauley, that celebrated Daughter of Liberty."

Through the influence of the radicals, a massive petition campaign was launched. The resulting document submitted to the king demanded the redress of such grievances as general warrants, the outlawing and imprisonment of Wilkes, excessive use of the military, violation of the rights of electors, and the mismanagement of the American colonies. It has been estimated that the total number of petitioners was sixty thousand—over a quarter of the entire English electorate. All of this activity was of no avail. The king refused to intervene, and the government was able to rely on comfortable majorities in both the Lords and Commons.[41]

There is an interesting resemblance between the pro-Wilkes movement and the Society of the Supporters of the Bill of Rights, on the one hand, and the Revolutionary movement and the Sons of Liberty in America, on the other. In both, the leadership was in the hands of the commercial middle class and professional people, while the rank and file was made up of mechanics and other workingmen. In both cases, too, the lower classes pushed the popular leadership in a more radical direction than it was prepared to go. In any case, the Americans identified Wilkes' plight with their own, and none more so than the Sons of Liberty. Were not Wilkes' opponents the same men who had enacted the Stamp and Townshend Acts? Not only did the Sons of Liberty identify their own cause with Wilkes, but they also felt he would be a staunch advocate of their cause in Parliament. As they wrote to him in April 1768: "May you convince Great Britain and Ireland in Europe, the British colonies and plantations in America, that you are one of those incorruptibly *honest men* reserved by heaven to bless and perhaps save a tottering Empire. . . . Your perserverance in the *good old cause* may still prevent the great system from dashing to pieces." In his reply, Wilkes demonstrated his support of the American grievances:

> As a member of the Legislature, I shall always give a particular attention to whatever respects the interests of America which I believe to be immediately connected with, and of essential moment to our parent country and common welfare of this great political system.
>
> I consider it as my duty no less strenuously to defend the rights of America than of England, and I feel an equal in-

dignation against the oppressors of our fellow-subjects, whether at home, or on the other side of the Atlantic.[42]

Wilkes' unswerving backing of America against the British government convinced many Americans that both struggles were identical. William Palfrey of Boston expressed this sentiment in a letter to Wilkes, on behalf of the Sons of Liberty, in which he exclaimed that *"The fate of Wilkes and America must stand or fall together."*[43]

Following his third expulsion from Parliament in March 1769, Wilkes reaffirmed his sympathy for the American patriots. He informed the Sons of Liberty that if he had been permitted to take his seat in the House of Commons, he would have been eager to move the repeal of the act which laid duties on paper, paint, and other articles. He called the Townshend duties "absolutely unjust, unconstitutional, a direct violation of the great fundamental principles of British liberties."[44]

The Sons of Liberty expressed their admiration for their comrade in arms in a variety of ways, including elaborate banquets to demonstrate their solidarity. Typical of these affairs was the civic celebration sponsored by the Sons of Liberty in Charleston, South Carolina, in April 1770 to commemorate Wilkes' release from prison. Bells were rung, colors displayed, cannons discharged, and over four hundred houses were illuminated to show, as the *South Carolina Gazette* commented, "the regard we pay to those who suffer in the cause of Liberty." Members of the Sons of Liberty were served a turtle weighing forty-five pounds, followed by forty-five toasts. The banquet broke up at forty-five minutes after twelve—all to commemorate the fateful issue No. 45 of Wilkes' paper.[45]

The Sons of Liberty showered Wilkes with gifts and raised funds to help him pay his debts. The Society of Supporters of the Bill of Rights, which received the funds, sent a letter of thanks to the Sons of Liberty of Charleston, where £1,500 had been contributed. The society pledged that "in this and every other constitutional struggle on either side of the Atlantic, we wish to be united with you, and are ready to give as well as receive assistance.[46]

A Sons of Liberty group was organized in Dublin, Ireland, which assisted the Americans morally and financially and drank

toasts hailing the "Sons of Liberty throughout the world."
Charles Lucas, who edited an Irish newspaper, the *Freeman's
Journal*, and who corresponded with the Sons of Liberty in
Boston, stressed the common plight of America and Ireland. [47]

In 1768, the Providence Liberty Tree was dedicated "in the
name and behalf of all the true SONS OF LIBERTY in America,
Great Britain, Ireland, Corsica, or *wheresoever they may be dispersed throughout the world.*" [48]

In England, the workers in particular responded and rallied to
their American brothers. "The Sailor's Address," a popular
British seamen's song of the 1770s, went in part:

Come listen my cocks, to a brother and friend,
One and all to my song, gallant sailors attend,
Sons of freedom ourselves, let's be just as we're brave.
Nor America's freedom attempt to enslave.

Firm as oak are our hearts, where true glory depends,
Steady, boys, steady,
We'll all be ready
To fight all our foes, not to master our friends.

True glory can ne'er in this quarrel be won,
If New England we conquer, old England's undone;
Our brethren we then should assist to fix chains,
For the blood of Great Britain flows warm in their veins. [49]

English weavers, seamen, tailors, and miners encouraged the
Sons of Liberty to continue the nonimportation agreements,
even though they had to endure unemployment and were in a
"starving condition." They urged the American Liberty Boys
on: "You have only to persevere and you will preserve your own
liberties, and England's too." [50]

And "persevere," as we shall now see, they certainly did!

*   *   *

In the following chapters, we will examine the urban working-
class movement, especially in the four cities which were to become decisive in the advent of the Revolution: Boston, New

York, Philadelphia, and Charleston. This movement will not be romanticized for in some communities, the Sons of Liberty were indifferent to the plight of other lower-class elements in the struggle. Nor was the political development of the organization a uniform one throughout the colonies, either numerically or ideologically. Some groups were more advanced than others, and some lagged behind for a long time.

Yet, despite any such qualifiers, there remains a fundamental truth: it was the Sons of Liberty, especially its mechanic and artisan component, supplemented by allies such as laborers and seamen, who pushed the struggle forward during the ten-year period and provided the apparatus and manpower for the transition from resistance to independence.

3_____ *The Stamp Act Crisis*

◻ The economic prosperity created by the French and Indian War began gradually to recede in most of the colonies after 1760. The seeds of economic crisis were being sown, and by 1763, they had developed into a full-grown business depression.

It was precisely at this time that the British government, through Prime Minister George Grenville, instituted a new policy of stricter imperial control. Confronted with the need to defend Britain's newly gained empire in America following the defeat of the French, the British government decided to station ten thousand regular troops in the New World. It was estimated that about £350,000 would be needed annually to support such an army. Grenville maintained that the colonies should contribute at least one-third of this amount, and he proposed the passage of two laws: the Sugar Act of 1764 and the Stamp Act of 1765.

The preamble to the new Sugar Act (which was to supersede the Molasses Act of 1733) stated that it was "just and necessary that a revenue be raised, in your Majesty's said dominions in America." It provided for an increased duty on all white sugar imported from the West Indies, banned the importation of rum from the same source, and only lowered the duty on foreign molasses from six to three pence a gallon, which was still considered prohibitively high.[1] While the sugar duty was relatively unimportant (since no great quantities were imported), the tax on molasses was a different matter. Millions of gallons of molasses were brought from the West Indies into the colonies, chiefly to New England. Once there, it was used to manufacture rum, which was then exchanged for slaves from Africa. The slaves were then carried across the Atlantic to the West Indies, where they were sold for specie and bills of credit, which in turn were used to buy English manufactured goods. The Sugar Act thus hurt the slave trade on which much of New England's economy was based. Many workers were employed in both the distilleries and the shipping industry. The act also reduced New England's already limited supply of specie and deepened the cloud of depression that had settled over these colonies.

To raise the rest of the money needed to support a military establishment in the colonies, Grenville secured the passage of the Stamp Act in March 1765, to become effective on November 1. The act required everyone in America to pay stamp duties, costing from a half-penny to twenty shillings, on periodicals, pamphlets, commercial paper, and legal documents. In addition, the act severely hampered the ability of a master craftsman to secure labor. It prescribed a tax of two shillings, six pence sterling, on all indentures and fixed a price of £7 currency on the stamp needed to negotiate agreements with apprentices. Apart from increasing the cost of doing business, the act drained still more specie from the colonies by requiring that the duties had to be paid in silver. Finally, it struck at a cherished political institution: the right of self-taxation. Most colonists believed, and many writers asserted, that the Stamp Act was unconstitutional.[2]

Another measure enacted by Parliament at this time was the Quartering Act of 1765. The act had been passed on the recommendation of General Thomas Gage, who was in charge of the British military in North America. It provided that, wherever possible, the Royal troops were to be garrisoned in colonial barracks at colonial expense, or, if necessary, in inns, livery stables, ale houses, empty dwellings, barns, and outbuildings, at the soldiers' expense. The troops quartered in barracks were to be furnished firewood, candles, vinegar, salt, bedding, and small beer, cider, or watered rum.

Grenville's financial program aroused practically the entire colonial population. The Sugar Act, wrote James Otis in his 1764

Rights of the Colonies Asserted and Proved, had "set people a-
thinking, in six months, more than they had done in their whole
lives before."[3] But the Stamp Act created such bitterness that it
became the focus of resistance to the entire Grenville program.
Opposition to the act took a variety of forms. Towns adopted
resolutions proclaiming that the constitutional rights of Englishmen had been violated. Nine provinces sent delegates to an
intercolonial Stamp Act Congress which met for a little more
than two weeks in mid-October 1765. Among the declarations it
drew up were the assertions that Americans were entitled "to all
the inherent rights and liberties of . . . subjects within the Kingdom of *Great Britain*"; that among the basic rights of Englishmen were freedom from all taxes imposed without their consent;
that Americans were not and could not be represented in Parliament; that the Stamp Act thus had a "manifest tendency to subvert the rights and liberties of the colonists"; and finally,

> That it is the indispensable duty of these colonies, to the
> best of sovereigns, to the mother country, and to them-
> selves, to endeavour by a loyal and dutiful address to his
> Majesty, and humble applications to both Houses of Par-
> liament, to procure the repeal of this Act for granting and
> applying certain stamp duties.[4]

While the towns and the Congress were petitioning, others
were acting. They boycotted English goods, stopped publishing
newspapers, and refused to do any business. This policy was
favored by the merchants and lawyers, who were mostly conservatives and moderates. The artisans, mechanics, laborers, and
seamen—the radicals—favored a consistent and persistent campaign against the officials appointed to administer the law and
urged the continuation of "business as usual," without stamps.
Moreover, they argued, if words did not produce results, then it
would become necessary to resort to violence. "The whole
people," reported General Gage to Secretary of State Conway,
"have been united to oppose the execution of the Stamp Act. . . .
They have differed only in the means to be pursued. One part
would set the Act aside by open force and violence, the better
sort by quibble that no stamps are to be had, and every other pre-

tence that could give some appearance at least of the legality of their proceedings."[5] Those who would "set the Act aside by open force and violence," if necessary, were the radicals, and the organization through which they acted in practically all of the colonies was the Sons of Liberty.

The Boston Liberty Boys set the pace on August 14, 1765, which was thereafter celebrated as "the happy day on which Liberty arose from a long slumber," on which, as Sam Adams commented, the "people shouted and their shout was heard to the distant end of the continent."[6] On the morning of that eventful day, an effigy of Andrew Oliver, the stamp distributor for Massachusetts, was hung on a tree in Newberry Street. That evening, a Sons of Liberty crowd, made up predominantly of artisans and laborers, paraded down the streets of Boston and destroyed a small building reported to be designated as a stamp office. It also beheaded Oliver's effigy and burned it under the tree—which a month later, on September 11, 1765, was dedicated as the first Liberty Tree in America. After some gentlemen—"persons of character"—had retired, the Liberty Boys, under the leadership of shoemaker Ebenezer Mackintosh, broke into Oliver's home and, according to one contemporary commentator, did "some damage but inconsiderable in comparison to what might have been expected." After seeing such tangible evidence of the people's feelings, Oliver declared his intention to resign his post, which he did the next day.[7]

The August 14 demonstration was merely a prologue to more vigorous action. On August 26, a crowd of turbulent sailors and dockyard workers tore down the customs house offices and destroyed the home of Lieutenant Governor Thomas Hutchinson. Hutchinson, a symbol of the aristocratic ruling clique of Massachusetts, was said to have encouraged the British to pass the Stamp Act, assuring them that it was "an easy method of gulling the people of their liberty and property."[8] Almost everything of value in Hutchinson's mansion was destroyed, and a number of costly articles were carried off.[9]

The conservatives were horrified by the violent behavior on August 26. Even the citizens of Boston passed a resolution at their town meeting, condemning the proceedings. Mackintosh was jailed for his participation in the demonstration, but was freed at once. Sam Adams informed the sheriff that no one would stand guard in Boston the next night unless Mackintosh was immediately released. Adams, of course, was speaking for the Sons of Liberty.[10]

After the terrified Hutchinson had fled, the Sons of Liberty assumed control of the town. On November 1, when the Stamp Act was to go into effect, courts and economic enterprises resumed normal operations without stamps. To Adams and the Liberty Boys, anything less than full resumption of business without stamps would constitute a tacit recognition of the Stamp Act's validity, and they were able to persuade the merchants and lawyers that this course was the most effective.[11]

On November 5, Guy Fawkes Day, crowds of workingmen, led by Mackintosh, demonstrated against the Stamp Act. A pageant with effigies of "Tyranny, Slavery, Oppression" paraded through the town, and the effigies were burned at night. On December 17, notices were posted all over Boston reading:

St—p! St—p! NO.

Tuesday morning Dec. 17th, 1765.

The true-born SONS OF LIBERTY are desired to meet under Liberty Tree at XII o'clock this day, to hear the public resignation under oath of Andrew Oliver, Esq., Distributor of Stamps for the Province of the *Massachusetts-Bay* . . .

A resignation? Yes.[12]

Since Oliver's first resignation was judged to be insincere, he would have to resign a second time. At the head of the crowd of Sons of Liberty, sailors, Negroes, and servants, Mackintosh marched the stamp master through the streets of Boston to the Liberty Tree. There, in the presence of two thousand people, Oliver resigned his office and swore that "he never would, directly or indirectly, by himself or any under him, make use of his deputation, or take any measures for enforcing the Stamp Act in America."[13]

Since the "cornerstone of Sam Adams's policy" was to "make farmers as zealous Sons of Liberty as were the North End mechanics and shipyard workers," the Boston Liberty Boys used the columns of local newspapers to familiarize rural radicals with what was happening in the capital. Despite the back country's long-standing suspicion of the Boston community, the city artisans and mechanics succeeded in forging an alliance with the Massachusetts farmers. Their success was demonstrated by the way rural Liberty Boys passed anti-Stamp Act resolutions in town after town, closed regular courts, and erected Liberty Trees.[14]

Some time later, the *Boston Gazette* boasted that the Sons of Liberty had "roused the Spirit of America" by demanding and obtaining the resignation of Andrew Oliver as stamp distributor, for their example was quickly followed by neighboring colonies.[15] In Newport, Rhode Island, on August 27, Liberty Boys paraded three effigies through the streets with halters about their necks and then suspended them from a newly erected gallows in front of the court house. The figures swinging in the wind were those of Augustus Johnston, who had been appointed distributor of stamps for Rhode Island, the collector of customs, and a newspaper printer who supported the Stamp Act.[16] Johnston quickly left town, but a crowd tore his house apart to remind him when he returned that he had better resign his post immediately. Johnston did resign, but not before he had the stamps placed aboard a man-o'-war, the *Cygnet*, for safekeeping. News of this action convinced the Newport Liberty Boys that Johnston intended to continue in office despite his public resignation. Therefore, a leaflet was posted in a conspicuous place in Newport warning the distributor that his life would "not be worth much in Newport, should he attempt to distribute the stamps," and should the collector of customs refuse to grant permission for any vessel to clear "without stamps . . . he shall be drove out of town with a high hand." Finally, any merchant using stamped papers "shall meet with our highest displeasure."[17]

The warnings sufficed. Johnston made it clear that he understood it would be "dangerous to his life and property" if he were to supply proper stamped paper. Business in Newport, as in Boston, was thereafter carried on as usual—without stamps.[18]

In Providence, as in Newport, the Sons of Liberty forced the resignations of officials suspected of preparing to distribute stamps. Moreover, the Liberty Boys of Newport and Providence jointly pressured the Assembly to adopt the most forthright stand against the Stamp Act of any Assembly on the continent. It resolved:

> That the inhabitants of this colony are not bound to yield obedience to any law or ordinance, designed to impose internal taxation whatsoever upon them, other than the laws or ordinances of the General Assembly. . . . That all the officers of this colony, appointed by the authority thereof, be, and they are hereby directed to proceed in the execution of their respective offices, in the same manner as usual: And that this Assembly will indemnify and save harmless all the said officers, on account of their conduct agreeable to this resolution. [19]

Trade without stamps continued uninterrupted in Rhode Island.

After hearing of the violent proceedings in Boston and Newport, James McEvers, who had been appointed stamp distributor for New York, did not wait to be asked to resign. McEvers was a storekeeper with close to £20,000 worth of such varied stock as wine, china, hose, and shoes. He promptly informed the British Treasury Department that the "populace would make sad havoc" of the entire store if he did not immediately relinquish his post. [20] After his resignation, the enforcement of the Stamp Act was left up to Lieutenant Governor Cadwallader Colden, a man already widely despised for his authoritarianism. [21] "I shall not be intimidated," Colden announced after he was informed of McEvers' resignation. [22] He immediately ordered Fort George reinforced with cannons, howitzers, and marines. He made sure that the people were aware of these reinforcements so that the Sons of Liberty would realize it would not be wise to try to emulate their brothers in Boston. Then, under cover of darkness, the stamps were removed from the vessel in the harbor and placed under guard in Fort George. Finally, Colden publicly took an oath to support the Stamp Act. [23]

The next day, broadsides were posted all over the city. [24] One copy hung all day in the Coffee House, and in the evening another was delivered to the fort. It was addressed to Lieutenant Governor Colden and was signed simply "New York." It called him the "chief murderer of the people's rights and privileges" because he took an oath to uphold the Stamp Act. His fate, the leaflet continued, was assured unless he declared that very night that he would do nothing to assist in the execution of the act. As for using the military to quell any disturbance:

> if you dare to perpetrate any such murderous act, you'll bring your gray hairs with sorrow to the grave, you'll die a martyr to your own villany, and be hanged, like Porter's [sic] upon a sign-post, as a memento to all wicked governors, and that every man that assists you shall be surely put to death.[25]

That very evening, November 1, a procession of five hundred seamen, three hundred carpenters, plus a host of other workmen, and hundreds who came from the neighboring country areas wound its way through New York's streets. At its head was a seaman carrying a chair on his head, and seated in the chair was a paper effigy of Cadwallader Colden. The crowd separated; one group went to the Fields and busied itself preparing a portable gallows for the effigy of Colden, "the grand deceiver of mankind," while the other went to Fort George. Upon arriving at the wall of the fort, the crowd taunted the authorities and demanded that the stamps be turned over. The garrison was ordered not to fire. This decision proved to be a wise one, for, as a writer in the *New York Gazette and Weekly Post-Boy* observed, the crowd, if it "had not been restrained by some humane persons, who had influence over them, would doubtless have taken the Fort, as I hear there were four or five hundred seamen and many others equally intrepid, and acquainted with military affairs."[26]

The crowd agreed not to attempt to take the fort and departed instead for the Fields to join the other group. After sacking Colden's coach house and seizing his coach and two sleighs, the two groups moved to Bowling Green where they used the vehicles to kindle a huge bonfire for Colden's effigy. Then they decided to pull down Vaux-Hall, the house of Major James, a British Officer who had publicly threatened to "cram the stamps

down [the people's] throats with the end of his sword." The
house was completely destroyed. Tables, chairs, desks, trunks,
chests, clothes, beds—"everything that would burn"—went
into a bonfire. When the crowd was finished, there was only a
shell where Vaux-Hall had stood. The reporter for the *New York
Gazette* wrote: "All this destruction was completed by about 2
o'clock, and every act of devastation on the goods of this unhappy gentleman was consider'd a sacrifice to liberty. . . . Many
military trophies, even the colours of the Royal Regiment, were
taken and carried off triumphantly."[27]

Most historians cite the November 1 riots in New York, cul-
minating in the destruction of Vaux-Hall, as an example of how
a "mindless mob" could be manipulated like puppets by men
behind the scenes to further a cause the "mob" hardly understood. While it is true that the "sudden eruption of violence"
shocked the merchants and landed gentry who opposed the
Stamp Act, and convinced most of them to have nothing to do
with "men who would endanger the safety of the city in order to
defeat the Stamp Act," [28] it was clear to most observers that the
crowd had been anything but "mindless" in its operation. As
Jesse Lemisch points out, when the leaders lost control of the
proceedings, "as all testimony agrees that they did on the night
of November first," the crowd did not "turn to aimless and un-
reasonable plundering," nor was anyone killed or wounded. Indeed, the crowd "had focused all its ire on the attainment of political goals":

> Although they were in the center of town, in the midst of an
> area rich for plunder, they chose to march, in a disciplined
> way, clear across town from the present City Hall to the
> Hudson River—in order to attack the logical political
> scapegoat, Thomas Jones. They considered their assault on
> his goods a "Sacrifice to Liberty," and indeed all the eve-
> ning's activities might be so described. The whole affair
> had been performed with what could rightly be described as
> "the greatest decency and good order." [29]

Impressive as the November 1 demonstration was, the stamps
were still in the hands of the authorities. The Liberty Boys were

determined to force the government to give them up. On November 2, Isaac Sears urged the people not to listen to those who preached reliance on peaceable conduct alone. "We must have the stamps," he insisted, adding with a note of confidence, "we will have them within four and twenty hours." He advised those who had contact with Lieutenant Governor Colden to counsel him "to send the stamp papers from the fort to the inhabitants."[30]

Meanwhile, notes began to be dropped at the fort gate and posted at the Coffee House, warning Colden that his life depended on the efforts he made to get the Stamp Act repealed and upon his clear declaration under oath that he would never, in any way, "countenance, or assist, in the execution of the Stamp Act, or anything belonging to it." When it appeared that John Holt, printer of the *New York Gazette and Weekly Post-Boy*, might "stop his press from the mere panic of the intended Act," a note was thrown into his doorway warning that "should you at this critical time shut up the press, and basely desert us, depend on it, your house, person, and effects, will be in imminent danger. We shall therefore expect your paper on Thursday as usual."[31]

Holt got the message and printed the *Gazette* on plain, unstamped paper. After the threat of a new crowd attack on Fort George, and upon the advice of General Gage, the City Council, lawyers, and merchants, Colden eventually acceded. He was finally forced to surrender the stamps to the municipal authorities, and on November 5, they were deposited at the City Hall. The ship that had brought the stamps to New York headed back to England with the news that the Liberty Boys had forced the lieutenant governor to give up the stamps after compelling the stamp distributor to resign.[32]

Although McEvers had resigned in August, news of it did not reach the stamp commissioners in England in time to halt their sending him a commission. And so, on November 30, a delegation of Liberty Boys visited McEvers to find out whether he intended to continue in office. A few days later, the terrified McEvers, in the presence of Isaac Sears and Joseph Allicocke, both leaders of the Sons of Liberty, resigned his post for the second time.[33] When Peter Delancey arrived, bearing an appointment as stamp distributor for Canada and Nova Scotia, a short conversation with the Liberty Boys sufficed to convince him, too, to resign. Meanwhile, Zachariah Hood, a Maryland stamp master, had fled to New York, where he had been promised protection by Colden. About a hundred Liberty Boys set out for Flushing, Long Island, where Hood had taken refuge. He hastily resigned his office and took the required oath of sincerity before a magistrate. The Liberty Boys' party returned to the city in triumph, carrying a flag on which were inscribed the words, "Liberty, Property, No Stamps." Before celebrating in the city, they forced the resignation of a stamp inspector who had been hiding on a recently arrived ship.

The Sons of Liberty in Baltimore publicly thanked the New York Liberty Boys for their action against Hood. John Holt's paper, whose columns were now freely open to the Liberty Boys, carried the following notice:

To the SONS OF LIBERTY in NEW YORK,

Greeting.

We your brethren on behalf of ourselves and many more, heartily return you our most greateful and sincere thanks for your vigilance in apprehending and bringing ZACHA-RIAH HOOD, Esq., Stamp Master for this Province, to a sense of his treachery to his country, and for causing him before a magistrate on his oath, to renounce the despicable employment. [34]

While there were no stamp officers left to attack, there were still the stamps themselves, though not for long: the forty militiamen guarding the stamps at the City Hall voted by thirty-five to five to burn the "detestable paper." [35]

Thus, the Sons of Liberty, with the substantial help of the crowd of workingmen, had succeeded not only in preventing the stamps from being used after they were landed, but also in destroying them and in guaranteeing that there would be no stamp distributors to carry out the law. Much of this activity had been conducted behind a nominal secrecy through use of names such as "Vox Populi," but it was generally known that the name represented the Sons of Liberty. Early in January 1766, the organization surfaced, and its meetings were announced regularly in the press.[36]

Meanwhile, the lawyers and merchants were proceeding with their own cautious method of combatting the Stamp Act, relying on the policy of nonimportation and a cessation of business in order to pressure Parliament to repeal the Stamp Act. The wealthy importers could afford to sit and wait—"or even could profit from the artificial monopoly which the situation created." Retailers with less capital, however, were in danger of losing their businesses, while the artisans, mechanics, day laborers, and seamen found themselves without employment. New York had not yet shaken off the effects of the postwar business slump when the Sugar and Stamp Acts plunged it into a depression. The mechanics, laborers, and seamen simply could not afford to wait for Parliament to act; they had to have work. Therefore, they urged the Sons of Liberty to do something to restore business as usual. They were not the only ones to appeal to the Sons of Liberty. Since trade was continuing uninterrupted in Rhode Island without stamps, the Providence Sons of Liberty were able to chide their New York comrades: "It is to be lamented that in some of the colonies, who had the same sentiments with us, a suspension of public business hath not found place."[37]

On November 26, the New York Sons of Liberty acted. A meeting of the Freeholders, Freemen, and Inhabitants was called, the "great design" of which "was to put business in motion again." After trying unsuccessfully to prevent the meeting by pulling down the notices (which the Liberty Boys just as quickly replaced), the conservative and moderate forces schemed to gain control of it. The meeting's sponsors had drawn up an address to the city's assemblymen in which they expressed the highest respect for Parliament. Nevertheless, they considered themselves bound "by every sacred obligation to oppose and reply to the injury for we act not only for ourselves, but for all succeeding generations." Citing the need for united effort against the Stamp Act, the address concluded by calling on the representatives to sanction business as usual without stamps: "Business without Stamps. Now or never is the time."[38]

By means of a skillful maneuver, the representatives of the

wealthy merchants and lawyers substituted for the proposed action one which called for the repeal of the Stamp Act through petitions to the king and Parliament. This demand, however, "was defective in the grand point, it contained nothing to remove the present obstructions to business and therefore is not the thing now most wanted." The "thing most wanted" by the Sons of Liberty was not what the men of wealth wanted. Moreover, the latter were incensed by what they considered the presumptuousness of Sears and his Liberty Boys in attempting to dictate to those who had long had a free hand in ruling the province. [39]

The initial sponsors of the meeting noted that while their proposed address was "laid aside," there "are many hundreds in the city who approve and are ready to subscribe to it." [40] Some had the opportunity to demonstrate this approval through public letters. On December 19, "Freeman" complained in Holt's paper: "Our business of all kinds are stopped, our vessels, ready for sea, blocked up in our harbours, as if besieged by an enemy, great numbers of our poor people and seamen without employment and without support." Why then, the writer asked, should they continue to submit to the Stamp Act, whose very unconstitutionality everyone acknowledged? Would not Parliament think Americans "a herd of mean, despicable wretches" who lacked the courage to defend their rights? On December 27, "Philoluthetus" developed this theme further in a letter covering the entire front page of Holt's paper. While the boycott agreement was useful as a "temporary expedient," he argued, it was not a wise policy to prolong it, for "if we are to continue doing no business, 'til the Stamp Act is repealed, or we hear the issue of our petitions at the Court of Great Britain, it is evident that nothing can be more absurd, for it is pregnant with the most harmful consequences in whatever light we view it." This way of combatting the Stamp Act constituted not only "slavish abjection" to a clearly unconstitutional law, but was also inconsistent. First the Americans forced the stamp distributors to resign; then they contradicted themselves by stopping business, thereby tacitly acknowledging the law's authority. This was not only the "basest cowardice," but it was useless as well: "We have been blustering for liberty for some months, but put to the trial, we shrink back in a most dastardly manner, and all our courage evaporates in smoke."

The British, the writer went on, must be shown that "nothing will ever execute it, but downright force," which they would not dare to use. Yet, this approach could be used only by considering the law "absolutely null and void in itself and behaving ourselves in all things, as though it did not exist":

> Let us pay a due regard to the parliament of Great Britain, but not one moment seem to give up or liberties, by allowing she has a right to enslave us. Let us no longer desist in a course so evidently shameful and ruinous, but push on all kinds of business as usual. If we are but unanimous, we have no difficulty before us but we can easily surmount. [41]

Since the advocates of nonimportation and no business operations refused to yield, however, unanimity was out of the question. The Sons of Liberty promised to protect anyone who carried on business as usual. However, the Royal Navy complicated the situation for the Liberty Boys by turning back vessels without properly stamped papers. The Sons of Liberty responded by parading an effigy of Lord Colville, commander of the Royal Navy in American waters, and burned it on the Commons. Meanwhile, the failure to resume business activities was aggravating an already depressed economic situation, and hundreds of idle men, especially seamen, were discussing among themselves the need to take matters into their own hands. [42] It did not take long before this news brought results. In late December 1765, the New York Customs House began issuing unstamped clearances. Explaining this action, the collector and comptroller wrote to the commissioner of customs in England: "This step, we thought the more advisable as we understood the mob (which are daily increasing and gathering of strength, from the arrival of seamen, and none going out and their whole dependence for a subsistence is upon trade) were soon to have a meeting." "From such a meeting," write Edmund S. and Helen M. Morgan, "the officers knew what to expect." [43]

Although the port was open, the Liberty Boys had not succeeded in forcing the lawyers and merchants to continue to do business, and the royal officers still suspended court functions. On January 1, 1766, the Sons of Liberty met and adopted a series of resolutions which served both as the formal articles of association for the group and also a warning that the battle against the Stamp Act would continue. First, they pledged their lives and fortunes to "go to the last extremity" to prevent the operation of the Stamp Act. Next, they warned that anyone who delivered or received stamps would "incur the highest resentment" and be "branded with everlasting infamy." They promised protection to those who did business without stamps. They also explained that individuals or groups were attacked only because they promoted the Stamp Act, and not for any personal reasons. Finally, they assured the public that they would do all in their power to "maintain the peace and good order of this city, so far as can be done consistently with the preservation and security of our rights and privileges."[44]

At another meeting on February 18, 1766, the organization reported that its promise of protection for those who did business without stamps was producing results, and it added another article to its association. It promised to help its friends in other colonies "to repel every attempt that may be made, to subvert or endanger the liberties of America."[45]

As this meeting was taking place, supporters of the Sons of Liberty in the rural areas of the province were engaged in defending their "liberties" against the aristocrats. If the organization and assumption of extralegal power by the mechanics, laborers, and seamen and their leaders in New York City were not enough to frighten the aristocrats and cause them to envisage the end of civil society, then the events elsewhere in the province certainly were. A rebellion of tenant and small farmers started in Westchester County in the fall of 1765 and by the spring of 1766 had spread to the great landed estates of the northern counties, particularly Albany and Dutchess. The farmers had many grievances against the land barons. They had to sign long-term leases that generally operated in favor of the proprietors. In some areas of Albany County, farmers had purchased tracts from shady operators, only to find later that their lands were already claimed by others. Naturally, they resisted attempts at eviction, especially after they had performed the backbreaking work of clearing and cultivating the fields.

In the fall of 1765, an antirent movement swept through upper Westchester County. Under the impact of the anti-Stamp Act agitation, the tenants organized both to resist sheriffs who were enforcing eviction orders and to free their leaders from the up-country jails. By May 1766, under the leadership of a small farmer named William Pendergast, the tenants' rebellion against "manorial tyranny" was coordinated, and they did not hesitate to use direct action. Soon there were seventeen hundred anti-renters under arms at Poughkeepsie, and three hundred more at Pawling. Attempts by the landed gentry to put down the revolt were generally unsuccessful. The enraged farmers had no intention of obeying officers whom they considered agents of the manor lords. The farmers even assaulted Sheriff Hermanus Schuyler of Albany.

Frightened by their inability to control their tenants, the landowners, like the Livingstons and others who rented thousands of acres to small operators, appealed to Generals Gage and Moore for military assistance. The intervention of the troops saved the aristocrats. The rural crowds were finally dispersed and their leaders arrested. Pendergast was brought to trial, and within twenty-four hours, he was found guilty and condemned to death. [46]

Unlike the Sons of Liberty in Massachusetts, the organization in New York did nothing to form a united front with the discontented, militant farmers, who publicly cast themselves as "rural Sons of Liberty." [47] To be sure, the Liberty Boys had welcomed the farmers when they came into New York City to participate in the November 1 demonstration, and were proud that "some returned home satisfied with our firmness, and determined to maintain their freedom in their respective places of residence." [48] When they asserted this determination "to maintain their freedom" in the up-country, however, the leaders of the Sons of Liberty joined the great landlords and merchants in deriding them as "Levellers." (The epithet "Levellers" stemmed from the Levellers' movement which emerged during the Puritan Revolution in England among the soldiery of Oliver Cromwell and was directed against the clergy and church and, of course, against the aristocrats.) [49] When a number of antirenters were seized by the authorities and jailed in New York City, the tenants marched to the city, confident that they would be both welcomed and supported by the metropolitan Sons of Liberty. Instead, after waiting in vain at the outskirts, they returned home, disappointed. Staughton Lynd maintains that the failure of the Sons of Liberty to join the farmers on this occasion "spurred the sending of British troops."[50]

It is difficult to explain why the Sons of Liberty were indifferent, and even hostile, to the tenant-farmers. A British captain observed wryly that "they are of the opinion that no one is entitled to riot but themselves."[51] The historian Roger Champagne is probably closer to the truth: "Perhaps men like Sears and Lamb were too urban-minded to be concerned about rural matters and the mechanics were undoubtedly ignorant of the nature of agrarian complaints.[52] In any case, another historian, Herbert Morais, was undoubtedly correct when he observed that the failure of the New York Liberty Boys to "forge an alliance between the urban masses and rural peasantry . . . was indeed a grave mistake."[53]

While Boston, Newport, and New York were exploding with opposition to the Stamp Act, in Philadelphia and Charleston there was little overt crowd violence over the act. The reasons differ for each of the two cities. The mechanic-dominated Sons of Liberty of Charleston, under the leadership of Christopher Gadsden, did employ force to compel stamp inspector George Saxby and stamp distributor Caleb Lloyd to sign a declaration that they would suspend the duties of their office, and to make Justice Skinner drink "Damnation to the Stamp Act."[54] But when nearly fourteen hundred seamen, who were unemployed and confined to Charleston because the customs officials refused to clear their vessels on unstamped paper, called upon the Sons of Liberty to "get the port open upon the same terms as they are in many places to the northward," their plea was rejected. Moreover, when they became "licentious" and "formed a mob," it was the Sons of Liberty who "suppressed them instantly, and committed the ring-leaders to gaol," a Charlestonian wrote in the *Boston Gazette*.[55]

A major reason for the absence of violence in Charleston was the resistance movement's fear that activities like those in Boston, Newport, and New York would unleash a slave insurrection. With the slave population of South Carolina outnumbering the whites by two to one—90,000 to 45,000—the whites lived in

constant fear of conspiracies. "His [the Negro's] presence meant
that any lapse in vigilance, any failure of government, appeared
to threaten the white community with annihilation. South
Carolinians were therefore notoriously wary of any disorders."[56]
When it became clear that the libertarian ideas unleashed by the
resistance to the Stamp Act could trigger a slave insurrection, it
was inevitable that the movement would refrain from any mass
pressure tactics. In January 1766, some blacks paraded through
the streets of Charleston, calling out "Liberty," and "the town
was under arms for a week while messengers scanned the province for evidence of a slave insurrection."[57] If the mechanics,
who made up the bulk of the Charleston Sons of Liberty showed
little sympathy for the unemployed seamen, one can imagine
what their attitude was when blacks raised the cry of "Liberty."
Charles Woodman, a spokesman for the rural South Carolina
back country, may have gone too far when he condemned the
Charleston Sons of Liberty for "not caring who may starve so
they can eat—who sinks so they swim—who labour, and are
heavy laden, so they can keep their equipages."[58] Nonetheless,
Charleston seamen and blacks alike would certainly have echoed
his sentiment.

In Philadelphia, on the other hand, the resistance to the Stamp
Act was complicated by a split in the artisan community. While
all Philadelphia mechanics hated the act, the nature of the forces
involved in the struggle against it caused a different reaction
from that among the mechanics in other cities.

On the eve of the Stamp Act controversy, Benjamin Franklin
and his political associate, Joseph Galloway, were engaged in a
campaign to replace the Penn family's proprietorship with a direct royal government. In the process, they sought to overthrow
the control of "a narrow, privileged minority, whose power and
policies were maintained in a political structure that had changed
little since 1701." The Penn family, proprietors of Pennsylvania,
occupied the roles of both chief executive and chief landowners in
the province. Governor Thomas Penn, although resident in Britain, had appointed a lieutenant governor to represent him while
he lived off his vast Pennsylvania estates. His followers established the Proprietary party, utilizing the governor's power to
appoint judges, sheriffs, and other officials. The Assembly, on

the other hand, was controlled by the Quaker party, based in Philadelphia and Chester County. Originally a closely knit group dominated by wealthy Quaker merchants of Philadelphia, the party, under the leadership of Benjamin Franklin, had been broadened in the 1750s to include able professional men from a variety of religious backgrounds. It won strong support from the Philadelphia artisans, who generally followed Franklin's political lead. However, in the election of 1764, both the Proprietory and Quaker parties made unprecedented efforts to gain popular support in the city. The artisan community of Philadelphia was split, with a minority voting with the Proprietary group, while most remained loyal to Franklin and the Quaker party.[59]

The cleavage was intensified by the passage of the Stamp Act. In order to discredit Franklin's idea of royal government, the Proprietary party took the lead in opposing the act, while Franklin, from his position as Pennsylvania representative in London, supported the act and even arranged for his friend John Hughes to be appointed stamp commissioner in Philadelphia. When it became evident that the act was provoking a violent response from the mechanics in various urban centers, Franklin counseled his artisan supporters in Philadelphia to use "prudence and moderation" in their Stamp Act activities.[60] He was concerned that the Stamp Act crisis should not eclipse the anti-Proprietary campaign.

Thus, the Philadelphia mechanics, while hostile to the Stamp Act, had to choose between organizing violent opposition to it or remaining loyal to their mentor. They split, with one group moving into the Sons of Liberty and the other remaining on the sidelines. When a Sons of Liberty crowd threatened Franklin's home, the artisans loyal to him gathered to defend it, and the threat evaporated. It is not surprising, therefore, that while a crowd organized by Sons of Liberty printer William Bradford and some of the Proprietary leadership did prevent stamp commissioner Hughes from enforcing the law, it was unable to compel his resignation.[61] Writing from New York in late November, Alexander Colden, son of the lieutenant governor, informed his father that "the Sons of Liberty of this place have wrote to Philadelphia that if they do not make Hughes resign as fully as the other distributors, they will disown them and hold no longer correspondence with them."[62] The warning did no good. With the mechanics split, the Philadelphia Liberty Boys were too weak to satisfy their New York brothers' demand.

The defense of Franklin's home is the subject of an interesting scholarly dispute between James H. Hutson, on the one hand, and Jesse Lemisch and John A. Alexander, on the other. Hutson identifies those who protected Franklin's home as the "White Oaks" ship carpenters and argues that this indicates that not all workingmen followed the lead of the seamen in expressing "the inarticulate's penchant for revolutionary violence." Indeed, he sees the ship carpenters acting as a "conservative constabulary." Lemisch and Alexander question whether the "White Oaks" ship carpenters were workingmen at all and note that even if they acted in a "conservative" manner, this would apply only to the period of 1765-1766 and certainly not to that after 1770. There is a good deal more to be said in criticism of Hutson's article, but insofar as the resistance to British policies is concerned, Lemisch's and Alexander's is the essential point. Curiously, they do not complain that Hutson stretches the "White Oaks" element to include all Philadelphia mechanics. He writes that while elsewhere the mechanics "swelled the ranks of the Sons of Liberty," in Philadelphia, they "were all on the other side." *All*? One section of the mechanics did move into the Sons of Liberty.

While the Philadelphia mechanics were split over putting their opposition to the Stamp Act into action, the seamen remained united and, as in the other colonies, they asserted their rights militantly. It was probably seamen who issued a Stamp Act broadside, "The Lamentation of Pennsylvania, on Account of the Stamp Act," containing the following curse on John Hughes:

If J—n H— —es, don't the Stamp refuse
I wish he may be thus abus'd
Grant Heaven, that he may never go without
The Rheumatism, Itch, the Pox, or Gout,
May he be hampered with some ugly witch,
And dye at last in some foulsome Ditch
Without the benefit of Psalms or Hymnes

And Crowds of Crows devour his rotten limbs
May wanton Boys, to Town his Bones convey,
To make a Bonfire on a Rejoicing Day. [63]

The refusal of the Philadelphia customs men to clear ships
without stamped paper created both unemployment and discontent among the sailors. "Our city," wrote Benjamin Rush, Philadelphia's distinguished physician and reformer, "is full of sailors
who cannot procure berths, and who knows what the united resentment of these too numerous people can accomplish?" The
customs officials were equally aware of the threat. "People will
not sit quiet," they wrote, "and see their interests suffer, and
perhaps ruin brought upon themselves and families when they
have it in their power to redress themselves." It was therefore
decided to reopen the port of Philadelphia and permit clearances
without stamps. A customs officer explained the reopening in
these words:

> Nothing is more certain than that so great a number of sea-
> men, shut up for that time in a town destitute of all protec-
> tion to the inhabitants . . . would commit some terrible mis-
> chief, or rather that they would not suffer themselves to be
> shut up, but would compel the officers to clear vessels
> without stamps—This would undoubtedly have the conse-
> quence of a few days longer delay. [64]

The mechanics played no role in this decision. In fact, Philadelphia's mechanics were quite content to have the opposition to
the Stamp Act rest on the nonimportation agreement adopted by
the Philadelphia merchants. They felt that the sealing off of the
American market from English goods would foster the growth of
home manufactures and that, soon enough, Philadelphia workers
would find employment in manufacturing "many articles which
they would otherwise always be enabled, and would choose, to
take from England." Thus, the artisans would find it much easier
to gain "independence" as manufacturers for the home market. [65] It is significant that while elsewhere the nonimportation
movement was organized primarily by merchants with little participation by mechanics, in Philadelphia, at least 34 of the 236

subscribers to the nonimportation agreement were mechanics. Moreover, Charles Thomson, probably Philadelphia's most prominent Son of Liberty, was convinced that it was the nonimportation policy, and not the broader political and constitutional issues, that was responsible for developing the mechanics' opposition to the Stamp Act, and kept that opposition confined within a moderate framework, under the complete control of the merchants. [66]

Thus, for a variety of reasons, the Sons of Liberty had less impact in Philadelphia than in any other urban center. Early in 1766, William Bradford wrote gloomily to the Sons of Liberty in New York: "Our body in this city is not numerous, as unfortunate dissentions in Provincial politics keep us rather a divided people." [67] The New York Liberty Boys sent their leader, John Lamb, to Philadelphia to spur the lagging movement there, but nothing was accomplished. [68] It was to take several years before the Philadelphia mechanics would emerge as a united, powerful, independent force in the Revolutionary struggle.

John Lamb's mission to Philadelphia was only one of many examples of the fact that, during the resistance to the Stamp Act, the Sons of Liberty did not devote all of their attention to affairs within their own colony. From almost the beginning of the resistance movement, they kept in touch with sympathizers in other colonies. They formed their own committees of correspondence which enabled them to exchange information with their brethren in the neighboring provinces. On February 17, 1766, the Boston Sons of Liberty wrote to those in Portsmouth:

Enclosed you will find a portion of that detestable paper mark'd with America's oppression, it being half that we obtain'd of a brother of ours from another colony which we intend to exhibit with chains, etc. next Thursday in a public manner on Liberty Tree—The occasion of our delaying is, that we may have them exhibited at one time—It will be taken down at 12 o'clock by a common executioner and burnt—Let us show as much abhorrence as possible—After which we propose to have the following toasts drank—George the third, our gracious, rightful and lawful sovereign—Succession to the Royal House of Hanover—Confusion to its enemies—Success to the foes of the Stamp Act—

A perpetual itching without the benefit of scratching to the
friends of the same — Long life health and prosperity to all
the Sons of Liberty on the Continent. [69]

It was the New York Sons of Liberty who took the initiative in
transforming this toast into an intercolonial organization of the
Sons of Liberty. Apart from the greater effectiveness such a
close association would achieve, the New York Liberty Boys
were motivated by the fear that the British Ministry would attempt to enforce the Stamp Act with military power. Early in
1766, they learned of a letter from Secretary of State Conway to
all colonial governors, instructing them not to hesitate to apply
for military assistance in order to maintain the authority of the
civil government. The leaders and members of the Sons of Liberty were well aware that there were men in the colonies so frightened by the "levelling" tendencies of the resistance movement
that they would welcome the troops to force the tax upon Americans, and, in the process, preserve both "law and order" and
their own dominant position in colonial society. [70] Secretary of
State Conway had concluded his circular letter by justifying the
use of coercion to maintain the dignity of the Crown and the authority of Parliament against "force and violence, and . . . an
avowed attempt of all order, duty and decorum." [71] Conservatives in the colonies felt that the military power would be useful
in quelling the lack of "decorum" on the part of mechanics,
laborers, and, of course, seamen.

On Christmas Day 1765 at New London, the New York and
Connecticut Sons of Liberty ratified a plan for mutual military
aid against the expected attack by a British army. After paying
homage to George III and denying that they desired "any alteration or innovation in the grand bulwark of their liberties," they
declared that they would not be "enslaved by any power on earth
without opposing force by force." They agreed "to march with
the utmost dispatch, at their own proper costs and expence," to
each other's assistance with their entire force. The pact also
pledged to protect anyone who went about his business, whether
public or private, in the face of the penalties for violating the
Stamp Act. It went on to warn that persons "who from the nature of their offices, vocations, or dispositions, may be the most

likely to introduce the use of stamped papers" would be watched carefully and treated accordingly if they tried to subvert "the British constitution and American liberty."[72]

Reaction to the "New London, Connecticut Agreement" revealed an almost total unanimity of support among Sons of Liberty from New Hampshire to Virginia. (Pennsylvania was the sole exception.) Groups in New Hampshire, Massachusetts, Rhode Island, Connecticut, New York, Maryland, and Virginia agreed to prevent the operation of the Stamp Act, even if it meant armed resistance. Resolutions adopted by the Liberty Boys in dozens of towns expressed a willingness to oppose the Stamp Act "to the last extremity, even to take to the field," and, as in the case of the Sons of Liberty of Newport, declared that it was their "indispensable duty . . . to . . . unite with the Sons of Liberty throughout America in every reasonable measure, to prevent the execution of the Stamp Act."[73]

By the spring of 1766, the Sons of Liberty groups in New Hampshire, Rhode Island, Massachusetts, Connecticut, New York, New Jersey, and Maryland had joined in a military alliance. Pennsylvania alone of the middle and northern colonies was not represented; the Philadelphia Sons of Liberty could not put across the idea of an intercolonial organization.[74]

As the union of the Sons of Liberty spread throughout the colonies, the leadership of the New York group began to envisage a general congress which would draft a common plan of action for all Sons of Liberty and would "mobilize for putting more pressure upon Great Britain." "Perhaps the time is drawing near," Isaac Sears argued, "when all commercial intercourse must cease, as the only means of retaining our freedom."[75] Artisans and laborers, who saw in this development the growth of home industry and consequent employment for more workers, welcomed the suggestion.

The Sons of Liberty of Maryland, Rhode Island, and Massachusetts were asked for their opinion, but before the idea could materialize, the news arrived that a bill to repeal the Stamp Act had passed the House of Commons on March 4, the Lords on March 12, and by March 18, had been signed by the king. The cry, "The Stamp Act is repealed!" rang through the colonies as the news was carried from city to city by the Sons of Liberty's correspondence machinery. As the news spread, the plans both to bring the Southern Sons of Liberty into the military association and to convene a general congress were abandoned. By May 1766, whatever military association already existed had collapsed. Although a few men tried to keep the union alive, the repeal of the tax, for the time being at least, removed the common bond of the association, and the effort proved futile.[76]

The military associations of the Sons of Liberty may have been held in contempt by General Gage. Even so, they did reveal that as early as 1766, despite their toasts to "George the Third, our gracious, rightful and lawful sovereign," the Liberty Boys in a number of colonies were prepared to resort to military measures against the king's army if it should be used to enforce the Stamp Act. Moreover, the Liberty Boys were confident that the colonists were a match for the British army, and that, "even if the seaports fell into the enemy's hands, the patriots could take refuge in the inland country where the British army could never penetrate." Over and over again, the Sons of Liberty voiced the need for intercolonial union to preserve "those privileges and immunities which God and nature seem to have intended us."[77] It was only the repeal of the Stamp Act that prevented the formation of an intercolonial union of the Sons of Liberty from New Hampshire to New Jersey and from Maryland to Georgia.

Although no central organization was effected, almost every independent unit of the Sons of Liberty had its committee of correspondence. These committees served both to unite the opposition to the Stamp Act and to lay the framework for further resistance until independence was finally achieved. One need not accept Pauline Maier's repeated emphasis on the "ordered resistance" of the Sons of Liberty and its opposition to the crowd violence which emerged in the resistance movement to agree with her observation that "by institutionalizing the colonists' new commitment to a resistance of a defined type, and by implementing it with a new type of organization, the Sons of Liberty durably established a pattern for further opposition to Britain."[78]

Conservatives and moderates in the colonies praised the British merchants and manufacturers for bringing about the repeal of the Stamp Act. There is no doubt that these latter groups, dependent as they were on trade with the colonies, had been hurt by the legislative policies of the Grenville ministry and had sought the repeal of the Stamp Act. But the Sons of Liberty were convinced that it was their firmness and unity alone that had brought about repeal. As a Connecticut Son of Liberty expressed it in a letter to Isaac Sears after news of the repeal was received: "America's glorious Sons of Liberty have at last obtained a settlement."[79] In Providence, Rhode Island, during the early morning of March 18, 1767, the first anniversary of the repeal of the Stamp Act, a paper appeared on the Liberty Tree and another in the most public part of town. It read in part:

To the SONS OF LIBERTY

Dearly Beloved,

Revolving time hath brought about another anniversary of the repeal of the odious Stamp Act—an act framed to divest us of our liberties, and to bring us to slavery, poverty and misery. The resolute stand made by the Sons of Liberty, against the detestable policy, had more effect in bringing on the repeal, than any conviction on the Parl— —t of G— — B— — —n of the injustice and iniquity of the Act.[80]

4___ The Townshend Program

☐ As news of the Stamp Act repeal was confirmed, celebrations were staged throughout the colonies, and illuminations and fireworks were set off everywhere. These celebrations were organized, in the main, by local groups of Sons of Liberty — and appropriately so, for it was the Liberty Boys who "had united the country as it had never been united before,"[1] and it was their special correspondence mechanism that had carried the good news through the colonies.

Amid such rejoicing, the Bostonians, headed by the Sons of Liberty, each with a Liberty Tree medal suspended from his neck, marched to the Liberty Tree, where a temporary obelisk, designed by craftsman Paul Revere, was erected. The tree itself had been specially pruned for the occasion by carpenters who refused to accept any money for their work on the ground that "they were always ready to serve the true-born Sons of Liberty, whenever occasion call'd for it."[2]

When New York City learned of the repeal, bells were rung, and hundreds of boys ran through the streets carrying poles topped with handkerchiefs. A celebration held on May 21, 1766, organized by the Sons of Liberty, featured a sermon entitled "A Congratulatory Discourse on the Joyful Occasion" by the rector of Trinity Church; the raising of the Liberty Pole on the Commons; the firing of a twenty-one gun salute; and a huge dinner at which twenty-eight "constitutional" toasts were drunk. At night, the city was completely illuminated, except at the military and naval officers' residences, and two great bonfires were set —

one for the Sons of Liberty and another for the City Corporation. When the morning dawned, New York City had its first great Liberty Pole erected by the Sons of Liberty.[3] As we shall see, it was to have an interesting history.

For the next twelve months, the colonies remained relatively quiet. This outward calm was deceptive, for after the repeal of the Stamp Act, the situation in the colonies never turned to normal. To be sure, the intercolonial union of the Sons of Liberty had collapsed, and most of the organization's separate groups, if they did not go out of existence, no longer held meetings. In New York, British officer Montressor happily recorded in his journal on July 16, 1766, that there were "no more caballing and committees at every corner of the street, nor even at present the name of Sons of Liberty mentioned or one to be heard of."[4]

A few weeks later, the first of many battles over the Liberty Pole erupted between the New York Liberty Boys and the royal troops garrisoned in the city. The friction had actually been brewing since the Fort George incident the previous November 1. It was exacerbated daily by the practice of the soldiers, as well as sailors from the wintering warships, of taking jobs in the city at lower wages than other workers. Now, however, it burst out into the open.

On August 16, 1766, the city awoke to find the Liberty Pole lying on the ground. Instantly, the Liberty Boys were in an uproar. The next day, the Sons of Liberty, led by Isaac Sears, and followed by two or three thousand people, gathered in the Fields where a group of soldiers were going their daily exercises. Sears demanded an explanation of the destruction of the Liberty Pole, but the troops ignored him. An exchange of bitter words was followed by the throwing of stones at the soldiers. A more serious outbreak seemed imminent between the Red Coats, who had drawn their bayonets, and some of the Liberty Boys, who were armed with pistols. At this point, however, two officers intervened and assured the crowd that any soldiers responsible for the Liberty Pole's destruction would be punished. The crowd, temporarily appeased, dispersed.

The next day, the Sons of Liberty erected another Liberty Pole and vowed to defend their sacred symbol with their lives, if necessary. A passing drummer made an obscene remark, and when a mariner resented it, the drummer drew a weapon. Thereupon, the crowd, led by the Liberty Boys, chased both the drummer and a corporal who had come to his aid into the city barracks. The soldiers charged into the crowd with drawn bayonets and wounded Isaac Sears slightly. Again the officers intervened and prevented a bloodier confrontation by assuring the crowd that the soldiers would be punished if they were found guilty of having started the fight.

From then on, tension between the Sons of Liberty and the royal troops kept mounting. When the 28th Regiment held a review parade for General Gage, using the Commons, the Sons of Liberty and many others were again present, yelling catcalls at the soldiers and demanding that they leave the "hallowed ground of liberty." When it was learned that the British officers who had promised that the soldiers would be punished if found guilty had done nothing, the Sons of Liberty went into the courts. Evidence was assembled against the soldiers for their conduct on August 16, and two writs were served on Major Brown, each for £ 5,000 in damages. When nothing was achieved in the courts, the Sons of Liberty decided to force the troops out of the city and to end the era of living "as in a military or conquer'd town." They proposed that inns and taverns stop serving the military, that stores refuse to sell them goods, and that all homes be closed to them. Finally, the Liberty Boys drafted a petition demanding that the garrison get out of town. Mechanics, laborers, and sailors circulated the petition through the town, gathering signatures. "The great object here is that of not having any troops at all," Governor Moore acknowledged.[5]

While this "great object" was cherished by the mechanics and laborers of New York, it was not regarded with any relish by the merchants, traders, lawyers, and landed aristocrats. If the troops were removed, they reasoned, what would keep the mechanics, laborers, and seamen under control? Moreover, would not the transfer of the garrison spur a revival of the tenant-farmer uprising, which the royal troops had crushed in the spring? To these privileged groups, "the only barrier to anarchy was General Gage and the two regiments stationed in Fort George."[6] So the garrison remained in New York.

Although the Sons of Liberty had suffered a setback, they continued to display publicly their hatred of the troops. Their bitterness increased when the second Liberty Pole was destroyed on the night of September 23. A new one was promptly erected by the Liberty Boys, and it lasted until the following spring, when it, too, was destroyed. The next pole, again erected immediately, stood until January 1770.

The Sons of Liberty had made their presence felt during the attacks upon the troops, but the group had actually ceased to exist as a formal organization. When Nicholas Ray, New York's agent in London, suggested that the Liberty Club be reorganized as it had been during the Stamp Act crisis, Sears, Allicocke, Lamb, and a few others replied in October 1766 that "as it is imagined that some inconveniences would arise should such a club be established, just at this time," it had better be postponed.[7]

Elsewhere in the colonies, too, the reorganization of the groups was being postponed—except for Boston, where the Sons of Liberty continued to function just as it had from its formation. Skeleton organizations remained in most cities, for the Liberty Boys had good reason to feel that the situation was still ominous, despite the universal rejoicing over the repeal of the Stamp Act. They knew that incorporated in the repeal was the Declaratory Act, passed by Parliament "for the better securing the dependency of his Majesty's dominions." Couched in the same sweeping terms as the Irish Declaratory Act of 1719, it proclaimed the American colonies subordinate to and dependent upon the Crown and Parliament. Thus, the American contention that the Stamp Act was an unconstitutional extension of power was denied, and Parliament's absolute sovereignty over America was reaffirmed.

Meeting with the mechanics of the Charleston Sons of Liberty under the Liberty Tree, Christopher Gadsden pointed out that the repeal of the Stamp Act had come at a price for Americans, and that it would be folly to rejoice while Parliament "still asserted and maintained the absolute dominion of Great Britain over them." He urged continued vigilance so that they might be in a position "to break the fetters whenever again imposed upon them." The mechanics then "joined hands" and swore "their defence against tyranny." They pledged themselves "to resist" in the event of a new contest with Britain.[8]

In other cities, too, Sons of Liberty were meeting, although informally, with the same objective in mind. As the Newport Liberty Boys put it, they were "more ready to unite, in any emergency, in defence of their natural and Constitutional rights."[9]

The second contest with Britain, anticipated by the Sons of Liberty, was precipitated by the Townshend Program. In 1767, Charles Townshend, chancellor of the Exchecquer, proposed, and Parliament passed, a series of acts intended to raise revenues to support the British military and civilian establishment in America, thus freeing them from dependence upon colonial legislatures. The Townshend Revenue Act levied new duties upon tea, lead, paper, and painters' colors. In order to make sure that they were collected, the act authorized the use of writs of assistance which gave customs officials broad authority to search for contraband on the mere suspicion of wrongdoing. The Restraining Act, another part of the Townshend Program, suspended the power of the New York Assembly until it complied with the Quartering Act and provided British troops within the province with certain specified articles.

Like the Stamp Act, the Townshend laws evoked a wide storm of protest in the colonies. As was the case before, the first response was a petition to Britain for relief. The artisans, mechanics, and laborers, knowing from past experience that petitions alone would bring no relief, sought other measures to achieve the result. During the first resistance movement, the Philadelphia mechanics had been the only group to support nonimportation. Now artisans, mechanics, and laborers everywhere placed their main emphasis on nonimportation of British goods as the means of persuading the mother country to repeal the new taxes. In an address to all "in no ways conceived in the importation of British manufactures," a mechanic wrote in the *South Carolina Gazette* that it was necessary to act to halt the depressing economic effects caused "by several late acts of P— — — for raising a revenue in America":

Our monies have been taken from us, without our consent, and we are deprived of our best inheritance, a trial by jury and the law of the land . . . while the deepest scheme of systematical slavery is preparing for us, to which the acts now complained of seem only the mere preludes. Can we then hesitate one moment longer, to unite with our brother sufferers in the other colonies, in the only probable means of averting so horrid a train of evils as are staring us in the face, namely, that of coming into a general resolution, not to consume one farthing more of British manufactures than we can possibly avoid?[10]

The reason for excluding from the address those "conceived in the importation of British manufactures" is quite clear. The importing merchants were not greatly disturbed by the Townshend duties; they simply passed the cost along to their customers. The artisans and laborers, however, were in a far different position. Painters, cabinetmakers, builders, and others in related trades, who owned their own tools and produced for the local market, had to absorb the additional cost of the tax on painters' colors and white lead. Moreover, the act would further drain specie from the colonies (as in the case of the Stamp Act, duties had to be paid in silver) and would only deepen the economic crisis.[11] Artisans and laborers saw only one real solution for their continuing distress: the creation of a viable home industry—and nonimportation was the means for achieving that goal. When the artisans of Charleston celebrated the repeal of the Stamp Act, it was noted that "everywhere, the joy seem'd to be in some measure damp'd by the existence of the late Revenue Act." Spirits lifted when one of the toasts went: "That we will encourage and promote to the utmost of our power, the use of North American manufactures."[12] Nonimportation appealed especially to Charleston mechanics (and to others elsewhere, to a lesser degree) for still another reason. It usually included the prohibition of the import of slaves from Britain, and "mechanics who competed with slave labor were joyful over any halt in the commerce of slavery."[13]

"Encouragement to American Manufacturers" became a popular slogan during the resistance to the Townshend measures, and societies were formed among artisans called "Lovers and Encouragers of American Manufacturers."[14] Advertisements appeared in the press announcing homespun products for sale, and items such as "Liberty umbrellas" were advertised as the produce of home craftsmanship. American-made clothing now became the fashion. Harvard graduates agreed to take their degrees clothed "in the manufacture of the country."[15]

While in some colonial cities the merchants were pressured to initiate the nonimportation agreements, in others it was the artisans, mechanics, and laborers of the Sons of Liberty who launched the campaign, and in all cases, they were the ones who made it a reality. The denial of British trade was a boon for artisans, who found a greater market for their goods, while the resulting increased employment for journeymen and laborers strengthened their support for nonimportation. The Daughters of Liberty reappeared and devoted themselves to spinning and weaving. They passed resolutions pledging women not to patronize merchants who broke the nonimportation agreements. In Boston, William Molineaux, a leading member of the Sons of Liberty, organized the women into spinning bees. The contests he organized created "remarkable records." When the Daughters of Liberty of Connecticut, Rhode Island, and New York engaged in a contest to see who could show more "dexterity at the spinning wheel," the *New York Journal* expressed the hope that "the same spirit would spread thro' the continent. That the ladies, while they vie with each other in skill and industry in this profitable employment, may vie with the men, in contributing to the preservation and prosperity of their country and equally share the honour of it."[16]

The Daughters of Liberty of Newport were willing to make whatever sacrifices were needed for "the preservation and prosperity of their country," provided their husbands and lovers gave up "their dear and more beloved punch, renounce going so often to tavern, and be more kind and loving sweethearts and husbands." One put the idea into verse:

Most gladly we our tea wo'd lay,
Could we more pleasure gain some other way.[17]

At times, the Sons and Daughters of Liberty acted jointly. A broadside posted in Boston read:

WILLIAM JACKSON
an importer, at the Brazen Head,

North Side of the Town House, and opposite the town-pump, in Corn-Hill, Boston.

It is desired that the *SONS AND DAUGHTERS OF LIBERTY*, would not buy any one thing of him, for in so doing they will bring disgrace upon themselves, and their posterity, for ever and ever.   *AMEN.* [18]

One can agree with John C. Miller that "the Daughters of Liberty did much to make [the nonimportation campaign] a success." [19]

Some historians contend that, during the period of relative quiet that followed the repeal of the Stamp Act, the Sons of Liberty was rendered completely ineffective, both in numbers and influence, and that the organization never actually revived. [20] The truth is that, while some local bodies did not continue, the majority did. Under the impact of the Townshend measures, the organization sprang to life again. Where it reappeared, it became the leading supporter and enforcer of nonimportation. In Boston, the Sons of Liberty persuaded the merchants to adopt a policy of nonimportation as early as August 1768, and, under the leadership of William Molineaux, it soon prevented practically every importer in town from ordering or selling English goods. [21] Among the measures employed against those who refused to join the movement for nonimportation, or, having joined, decided to resume the sale of imported goods, were street demonstrations, crowd marches to the offenders' homes and businesses, hanging of signs and effigies before these places, defacing of shop windows, and intimidation of customers seeking to enter the offending establishments. On one occasion, an attempt to remove an effigy resulted in bloodshed. The importer involved fired into the rock-throwing crowd and hit an eleven-year-old boy. The merchant was dragged through the streets with a rope around his neck, and only the intervention of Molineaux himself saved him from being lynched. Importer Patrick McMasters was actually banished from Boston for refusing to abide by nonimportation. [22]

In Philadelphia, the Sons of Liberty convinced hesitant Quaker merchants to join the nonimportation campaign. The Liberty Boys of Wilmington and Brunswick, North Carolina, made their own agreement, and the colonial assembly extended it to the province. In Charleston, the merchants were loath to act; indeed, when circular letters were received from Boston in September 1768, calling for concerted opposition to the Townshend Acts, they were treated with "silent neglect." The mechanics were anything but silent. They paraded through Charleston wearing their Liberty Tree symbols and praising the Bostonians for their opposition to British authority.

In June 1769, the Charleston mechanics announced that they were going to "follow the laudable example of those in other cities who espoused nonimportation." At the same time, they allied themselves with the planters against the merchants. (The planters complained that the revenue duties, by decreasing the amount of specie in the colony, were causing them economic distress.) In order to isolate the mechanics, the merchants themselves tried to establish an alliance with the planters which would exclude the mechanics. The mechanics angrily exposed this maneuver and forced the merchants to abandon the plan. The nonimportation agreement adopted was the one drawn up by the mechanics and planters. It included the mechanics' major demands, such as the need to encourage American manufacturers and the prohibition of the importation of Negroes from Great Britain. While the mechanics favored the latter demand mainly to eliminate slave competition, the planters went along out of fear that continued slave importation, by increasing the number of blacks in a colony where they already vastly outnumbered the whites, would intensify the danger of slave revolts. [23]

The mechanics received equal representation with the planters and merchants on the committee to enforce the boycott—each group had thirteen representatives. [24] This established a tradition which was to continue. "The committee, being an extra-legal body," notes Richard Walsh, "the mechanics' persistent agitation was to find them on every such organ of revolution to the convening of the Provincial Congress of 1775." [25]

It was the mechanics' representatives on the Committee of Enforcement who urged harsh measures to compel obedience and who introduced the "Sign or Die" motto. Sons of Liberty mechanics went about the streets of Charleston distributing boycott notices and threatening violence against those who refused to sign. In a few instances, more than threats was employed. Usually, however, nonsubscribers were simply boycotted; their names were advertised as men "inimical to American rights," they were denied the use of wharves "for shipping or landing goods or rice," and they were generally subjected to "great inconveniences."[26]

In New York, the Sons of Liberty were at first conspicuous by their absence in the agitation against the Townshend Acts. The society had split into two factions which spent most of their time attacking each other. One faction, called the "Genuine Sons of Liberty" and sometimes the "Friends of Liberty and Trade," was led by Sears, Lamb, Allicocke, and John Morin Scott. The other, which took the name "True Sons of Liberty," and sometimes "Friends to Liberty," was led by Alexander McDougall. [27] The roots of the split went back to the conflict over the use of nonimportation or of resuming business without stamps as weapons in the assistance to the Stamp Act: McDougall supported the moderate position of the lawyers, while Sears and Lamb insisted on the radical course of resuming business without stamps.[28] The split finally became public during the spring elections of 1768 and 1769 in New York City, when the Sons of Liberty divided over support of rival assembly candidates. Sears and Lamb and their followers supported James DeLancey (who won), while Alexander McDougall and his group backed Philip Livingston.[29]

So the two factions continued on their separate ways, holding their own celebrations on the anniversary of the repeal of the Stamp Act. On that occasion, toasts were drunk to "the ever memorable 18th of March, 1766, and Unanimity, and Fidelity, and Perserverance to the Sons of Liberty in America." Whatever "unanimity" existed among the Sons of Liberty in New York was confined to toasts.[30]

As a result, opposition to the Townshend Acts in New York was practically nonexistent. While a merchants' and traders' nonimportation agreement had been adopted in August 1768 to become effective the following November, it was a paper boycott only, without any real enforcement.[31] Faced with this disheartening situation, the two factions of the Sons of Liberty came together on July 7, 1769, and organized the "United Sons of Liberty." In a broadside announcing this step, they said:

It must appear to every unprejudiced mind that supineness would prove as fatal to us as a disunion; and therefore, the more effectually to guard against both — a number of the inhabitants of this city have determined to drop all party distinction that may have originated from a difference in sentiments in other matters — to form ourselves into a Society, under the appelation of the UNITED SONS OF LIBERTY.

The main purpose of the reorganized body was to support the nonimportation agreement, and the members vowed not to "engage in any other matter whatever."[32]

Thus, the two groups overcame their differences in order to defend their common rights.

Once reunited, the New York Sons of Liberty really enforced nonimportation. While there was now a committee of inspection made up of merchants, it was the Sons of Liberty who did the enforcing through mass meetings, effigy burning, and crowd action. A scaffold erected near the Liberty Tree brought the submission of recalcitrants, together with their public pledge to uphold the agreement. On September 21, 1769, the Sons of Liberty inserted a notice in the *New York Journal* recommending New York's "method of proceeding with non-importation delinquents" to the Bostonians: "It would have a more powerful effect in reducing . . . such culprits to reason than the most convincing arguments that could be used."[33]

The Boston Liberty Boys took this advice seriously. When Nathaniel Rogers, an importer, attempted to flee from the crowd in Boston, the Sons of Liberty sent an express rider to their New York brethren "to give him a warm reception" if he came their way. When Rogers reached New York, he was hunted down, hung in effigy before a crowd of five thousand people, and barely got out of town in time to escape a coat of tar and feathers. When it was reported that the terrified Rogers was proceeding to Philadelphia, a letter was sent to the Sons of Liberty of the Quaker City, advising them to give him a similar reception.[34]

All of these events took place during the period when the Sons of Liberty were carrying signs in praise of John Wilkes as they paraded through the streets and were drinking toasts to "Wilkes and Liberty." Even as the Liberty Boys were honoring the man who went to jail in London for libeling the king and his ministry, they were also identifying Wilkes' plight with one of their own. For in New York City, Alexander McDougall—the "Wilkes of America"—was in prison, charged with seditious libel.

It will be recalled that one of the Townshend laws was designed to punish the New York legislature for refusing to contribute to the support of the British army. It provided for the suspension of the Assembly's right to pass legislation until it fulfilled its obligations under the Quartering Act of 1765. Under Parliamentary threat, the New York Assembly agreed in 1767 to a quartering bill, but it was not until December 15, 1769, that it actually passed by a close vote, over the bitter opposition of the Sons of Liberty, who took to the streets in protest.

The supply bill enraged the taxpayers of New York City, where the main British force was garrisoned, and where, as we have seen, friction between the townspeople and the soldiers was almost a daily occurrence. The Sons of Liberty took immediate action. Protest meetings were organized on the Commons, circulars were distributed, and the legislators were condemned for betraying their trust by voting money for the troops. On Saturday, December 16, 1769, a broadside addressed "To the Betrayed Inhabitants of the City and Colony of New-York," appeared. Under the pseudonym of "A Son of Liberty," its author, Alexander McDougall, attacked the supply bill as another example of British tyranny and despotism. Calling attention to the fact that both the Massachusetts and South Carolina Assemblies had refused to supply the king's troops stationed on their soil, McDougall insisted that the New York Assembly was guilty of "betraying the common cause of liberty" in failing to take a similar stand. "And what makes the Assembly's granting this money the more grievous," he continued, "is that it goes to the support of troops kept here not to protect but to enslave us." He called on his countrymen to rouse themselves: "Imitate the noble example of the Friends of Liberty in England; who, rather than be enslaved, contend for their right with k——g, lords and Commons. And will you suffer your liberties to be torn from you, by your representatives? Tell it not in Boston; publish it not in the streets of Charleston."

The public, he wrote, had a means at its disposal "to prevent the accomplishment of the designs of tyrants." A mass meeting should be held in the Fields, and a public vote taken on the important issue. Once this was done (he took it for granted that the vote would be overwhelmingly against the Fund), the meeting should visit the city's representatives and insist that they join the opposition. "If they dare refuse your just requisition," then he urged the appointment of a committee to send explanatory letters to the other American assemblies and "to the friends of our cause in England." Such action, McDougall was confident, "will defeat the enemies of American liberty."[35]

On the following day, a Liberty Boy who signed himself "Legion" also urged a meeting. Early on Monday morning, another handbill appeared, calling upon the people to meet at noon and reminding them that they must choose between "UNION, ACTIVITY AND FREEDOM" and "DIVISION, SUPINE-NESS AND SLAVERY."

By noon, more than fourteen hundred people had gathered in the Fields. John Lamb, a leader of the Sons of Liberty, was appointed chairman. He noted that the soldiers were the cause of high taxes, inflation, and unemployment, and were a constant menace to the workingmen by competing with them for jobs. "The providing of these necessaries will increase the burden on the poor," he declared, and he asked the audience, "Do you approve of the vote?" "No!" "Are you for giving money to the troops, on any consideration whatsoever?" "No!" "Will you appoint a committee to communicate the whole of this transaction to your members?" "Yes." A ten-man committee, including Lamb, Sears, and McDougall, was appointed. They received a hostile reception when they visited assemblymen to convey a "sense of the inhabitants" on the recent bill. In spite of the evidence of the mass meeting, they were told that theirs was a minority opinion, and Lamb was accused of being a trouble-maker.[36]

On December 19, 1769, the Assembly condemned the anonymous broadside as a "false, seditious and infamous" libel, and Lieutenant Governor Colden approved a reward of £100 for information leading to the discovery of its author. Under great pressure, and having been promised immunity from criminal charges, the printer, James Parker, named Alexander McDougall as the author. Judge Horsmanden then issued a bench warrant for McDougall's arrest and offered him the choice of putting up bail or going to jail. "Sir, I will give no bail," McDougall replied. [37]

McDougall spent almost three months in prison. He issued a statement "to the Freeholders, Freemen, and Inhabitants of the Colony of New York," giving the details of his arrest and the history of the Assembly's actions, and closed:

> I rejoice that I am the first sufferer for liberty since the commencement of our glorious struggles; and if my sufferings shall in the least conduce to promote this cause, I shall esteem my confinement a singular felicity, and my very bonds (however I abhor even the momentary loss of my personal liberty) glory and triumph. . . . Let it be tried, let it be fairly tried, whether freedom of speech and freedon of writing are not the natural effect of the freedom of our excellent Constitution, and whether on suppressing that freedom, the Constitution can possibly survive. I should therefore be sorry that any of my friends should give themselves the least pain or anxiety on account of my imprisonment: For myself I feel none. The cause for which I suffer is capable of converting chains into laurels, and transforming a gaol into a Paradise. [38]

Just as Wilkes' address to his Middlesex constituents carried the notice that it was written in jail, so McDougall signed his "From the Gaol in New-York." And just as Wilkes had invited his constituents to see him in prison, so McDougall invited the public to see him, setting visiting hours from three to six. A daily procession began, which included "female lovers of liberty."

The magic number "forty-five" associated with John Wilkes was also applied to McDougall, especially after it was learned that the action of the Assembly which led to his imprisonment was printed on page 45 of its journal. On the forty-fifth day of the year (February 14), forty-five men, "real enemies to internal taxation by, or in obedience to external authority, and cordial friends of American liberty, went in decent procession to the New Gaol" and dined with McDougall on "forty-five pounds of beef steaks, cut from a bullock forty-five months old." On March 14, forty-five virgins marched in procession to the jail where the imprisoned leader of the Sons of Liberty entertained them with tea, cakes, chocolate, and "conversation adapted to the company. After the repast, was sung the second part of the 45th Psalm."[39]

The Sons of Liberty were particularly active in publicizing one of their leaders as the "American Wilkes," pointing out, among other things, that he, like Wilkes, had worked to democratize elections. In fact, shortly before his imprisonment, McDougall had led a movement to replace *viva voce* voting by the secret ballot. Boston Liberty Boys, celebrating the anniversary of the repeal of the Stamp Act, joined in a toast that the "pigmy apes of Mr. Wilkes's oppressors be confounded and defeated in their attempts on the brave Captain McDougall." In New York, the reunited Sons of Liberty, its membership swelled as a result of McDougall's courageous stand, held a dinner where forty-five toasts were drunk, including salutes to McDougall, Wilkes, "the Liberty of the Press," "the Freedom of Elections," "A Continuation of the Nonimportation Agreements, until the Revenue Acts are Repealed," "Prosperity to the Trade and Manufactories of America," and "Unanimity among all the Sons of Liberty in America, and Perseverance in the Glorious Cause."

> A little before sunset, the company from Hampden-Hall, joined by a number of people in the Fields, went with music playing, and colours flying, to the New-Gaol, where they saluted Capt. McDougall, with three cheers, which were answered in like manner by the company within. He thanked them for this mark of their respect, in a short address thro' the grates of the window of the middle story.[40]

The Sons of Liberty made it clear that only the common people, especially the mechanics and laborers, could free McDougall: "Trust not the rich, they trust in their wealth and will sneak in an hour of distress." If the common people did not act, they warned, "perdition is just before us." The common people responded. On the way to court to appear before the Grand Jury, McDougall was escorted by what a conservative New Yorker described as a "mob . . . consisting of two or three hundred of the rabble of the town, headed by some of the most zealous partisans of the republican faction." [41]

On April 25, the Grand Jury, after describing McDougall as a "person of a turbulent and unquiet mind and seditious disposition," indicted him for libel. The trial was set for October 1770. The demand that the case be dropped was so great, however, that the trial never took place. Amid much rejoicing, the "John Wilkes of New York" was released from prison. [42]

Just before the celebrated McDougall case made its way through the courts, armed clashes were taking place in New York and Boston between British regulars and the citizens, especially the working people. The first open fighting between Americans and the British army led to the first shedding of American blood.

5__ The Battle of Golden Hill and the Boston Massacre

On January 8, 1770, General Thomas Gage wrote from New York to Lieutenant Colonel William Dalrymple in Boston: "People seem distracted everywhere. It is now as common here to assemble on all occasions of public concern at the Liberty Pole and Coffee House, as for the ancient Romans to repair to the Forum. And the orators harangue on all sides."[1]

The Liberty Pole mentioned by Gage had been raised in the Fields on a spot near the British soldiers' barracks, and had already, it will be recalled, been the cause of several fights between the soldiers and the civilian population. This was the fourth Liberty Pole erected by the Sons of Liberty, the other three having been demolished by the soldiers. On the night of March 18, 1767, after New Yorkers had celebrated the first anniversary of the repeal of the Stamp Act, a few soldiers destroyed the third Liberty Pole. The immediate replacement was larger and more substantial than the previous three. It was reenforced by iron bars, laid lengthwise, and the carpenters and iron workers had wedged iron hoops between the bars and hammered them in with nails.

On the same night that the fourth Pole was erected, soldiers tried to undermine it. They failed, as did an attempt a few nights later to blow it up with gunpowder placed in a hole bored in it. After five other unsuccessful attempts, the British army staff and city magistrates finally took action to prevent further assults on the symbol sacred to the Sons of Liberty.[2]

During the tenure of the fourth Liberty Pole, relations between the soldiers and the citizenry deteriorated daily. New Yorkers, especially those city workers whose jobs were being taken away by the soldiers, increasingly resented having to pay to support the garrison. The same was true of the sailors who, upon their return to the city seeking employment, found that their places had been taken by off-duty soldiers. Still, the fourth Liberty Pole had been free of attacks by the soldiers for nearly three years, and the authorities hoped that the brawls between the troops and the Sons of Liberty over the patriotic shrine were a thing of the past. It was a vain hope.

During the evening of January 13, 1770, about forty soldiers of the 16th Regiment tried to blow up the Pole. They set about sawing its supporting braces, drilling holes and filling and plugging the borings with powder charges and fuses. John White, a cordwainer, observed the soldiers at work, and rushing into Abraham Montayne's tavern, which was frequented by the Sons of Liberty, gave the alarm. When two of the Liberty Boys in the tavern went out and returned with a confirmation of the report, the entire crowd in Montayne's Tavern rushed out. Once discovered, the troops tried to finish their work quickly and lit the fuse, but the fuse failed. To alert the rest of the town, the onlookers shouted "Fire!" and then hissed at the soldiers. The soldiers, enraged, chased the civilians into Montayne's Tavern and promptly wrecked the place. In the process, they broke eighty-four panes of glass, insulted and drove the patrons out of the windows, beat up the waiter, and threatened to kill Montayne himself if he raised a cry for help. By this time, some of the citizens had warned the officers, who ordered all soldiers to their barracks and posted a sentinel to guard the Liberty Pole. The sentinel promptly disappeared, but the Pole was not menaced again during the night.

Two nights later, the soldiers were back again, trying to blow up the Pole. Before any damage could be done, an alderman reported it to their officer, and the second attempt also ended in failure. On January 15, a broadside, undoubtedly written by John Lamb but issued in the name of "Brutus," alerted the public to what was taking place. Voicing the grievances of the poor and unemployed who were forced to compete for jobs with British soldiers, Lamb-Brutus wrote: "Whoever seriously considers the impoverished state of this City, especially of the many of the poor inhabitants of it, must be greatly surprised at the conduct of such as employ the soldiers, when their are a great number of the former that want employment to support their distressed families." Was it not enough, he asked, that New Yorkers had to pay taxes "for billeting money to support the soldiers, and a poor tax, to maintain many of their whores and bastards in the work house, without giving them the employment of the poor who you must support if you don't employ them, which adds greatly to swell your poor tax?"

The writer expressed the hope that upper-class New Yorkers, and particularly the "employers of labourers," would refuse to hire any more soldiers, especially after the "atrocious wickedness" of attempting "to blow up the Liberty Pole" and the wrecking of Montayne's Tavern. He warned the soldiers — "a set of men who are enemies to liberty, and at the beck of tyrants to enslave" — must go, or the city would earn "the just reproaches of the poor." The closing lines of the broadside summoned "All the friends of liberty" to gather at the "Liberty Pole, at twelve o'clock on Wednesday next" — January 17.

Before the meeting at the Liberty Pole could take place, the soldiers achieved their objective. Actually, they had been scared off early in the night before by Sons of Liberty who were meeting to plan the resolutions for the next day's affair. After the Liberty Boys went home, however, the vindictive Red Coats crept back, cut down the Pole, sawed it and split it into small pieces, and dumped the whole mess in the doorway of Montayne's Tavern.

At noon the next day, "not less than three thousand" people, fighting mad, met at the spot where the Liberty Pole had stood. As one observer noted, even before the meeting got under way, they "could hardly be restrain'd from proceeding to some acts of violence." A substantial number of those present were "men likely to be affected by the employment of soldiers." The chairman of the meeting, who was most probably John Lamb, pointed to the vacant place in front of the platform. He cited the destruction of the Liberty Pole, which he called "a Memorial of Freedom," as proof "of the impropriety of contributing to support such a set of people" who were determined to destroy every "least monument, raised to show the laudable Spirit of Liberty, that prevails among the inhabitants." He appealed to the audience "to drop all party differences, and unite in supporting their liberties." He then read the resolutions which the Sons of Liberty had drawn up the night before:

> RESOLVED, That we will not employ any soldier, on any terms whatsoever; but that we will treat them with all that abhorrence and contempt which the enemies of our happy Constitution, deserve. And whereas many of them have repeatedly travelled the streets of this City; in the night, with arms, with which they have attempted to take the lives of many of the citizens, and notwithstanding made their escape, and thereby eluded the laws, and passed with impunity: THEREFORE, that the inhabitants may not for the future be insulted, and put in peril of their lives,

> RESOLVED, That if any soldier shall be found in the night having arms, (except sentinels and orderly serjeants) or out of the barracks after the roll is called such as are found even without arms, and behave in an insulting manner, shall be treated as enemies of the peace of this City: And we do hereby solemnly engage, to and with each other, that we will to the utmost of our power, strictly adhere to the above resolutions, and if possible bring the transgressors of them, to condign punishment.

The crowd cheered and, with Sears, Lamb, and McDougall leading the way, signed the resolutions. Then William Lisk, a carpenter, pointed to the house facing the Commons which had been used as a guard house by the soldiers the night before. "It must come down!" he shouted. The soldiers, hearing the cry, drew swords and bayonets and dared the crowd to approach. The challenge was accepted, but through the intervention of magistrates and officers, the crowd appointed a committee to demand that the Corporation have the house destroyed.

Meanwhile, a party of seamen decided to carry out the first part of the first resolution. They patrolled the streets armed with clubs, "entering houses and vessels, and forcibly turning out and driving away, all the soldiers whom they found at work in either, denouncing vengeance against any inhabitants, who should presume to employ them again." One of the employers threatened blamed the Sons of Liberty for having sent "a set of lawless men to patrol the streets with great clubs in their hands."

On Friday, January 19, the soldiers struck back with a broadside signed by the 16th Regiment of the Foot. "WHEREAS," it began, after four lines of verse lamenting the plight of the soldier, "an uncommon and riotous disturbance prevails throughout the city," caused by those who "style themselves" Sons of Liberty, but would better "be called the real enemies to society." While the Sons of Liberty were the real enemies of society—"murderers, robbers, traitors"—who stirred up "the minds of his Majesty's good subjects to sedition," the king's soldiers had made the city safe for women and children and were the real defenders of English liberty. Finally, the soldiers gave notice that they refused to "tamely submit" to the attacks on their character and were ready to "stand in defence of the rights and privileges due a soldier."

As several soldiers were posting this attack on the Sons of Liberty, Sears and Walter Quackenbos, a baker, saw them. Sears seized a soldier and asked him "what business he had to put up libels against the inhabitants," and told him he was going to bring him before the mayor. When another soldier drew his bayonet, the Sons of Liberty leader threw a ram's horn at him, which struck him in the head. The rest of the soldiers ran off to alert their barracks, while Sears and Quackenbos grabbed two of them and brought them before the mayor, who was asked to arrest them for posting libels against the people.

Meanwhile, a crowd had gathered outside the house of Mayor Hicks, and suddenly twenty soldiers marched up with swords and bayonets drawn to free their two companions. At this point, Captain Richardson, an unemployed provincial soldier, led a small group to the door to stop the soldiers. While heated words were being exchanged, Mayor Hicks and an alderman came out and ordered the soldiers to their barracks.

The soldiers retreated sullenly, followed by the crowd. When the soldiers, still brandishing their swords, arrived at Golden Hill on John Street, between Cliff Street and Burling Slip, they turned up Golden Hill instead of proceeding toward their barracks. When they reached the summit, the soldiers turned on the

people, and one—"suspected of being an officer in disguise"—
shouted: "Soldiers, draw your bayonets, and cut your way
through them." The other soldiers obeyed, cutting and slashing
their way through the crowd, some shouting, "Where are your
Sons of Liberty now?" At the same time, soldiers from the barracks who had arrived at the bottom of the hill joined the attack
from the rear, shouting to the soldiers at the summit "to cut their
way down, and they would meet them half way."

Although several in the crowd had sticks and clubs, and one or
two had sleigh-rungs, the vast majority "were naked." A number of them received sword wounds. One seaman was run
through the body with a bayonet and died shortly afterward, the
day's only fatality.

The terror did not stop with Golden Hill. The soldiers chased
the people up the streets, yelling and waving swords. When citizens came out of their houses to see what the shouting was about,
the soldiers pounced on them, too—including women and children. Before the fighting could spread further, the city magistrates and military officers put an end to the attacks on the civilian population.

The soldiers returned to their barracks. They had taught the
Liberty Boys two lessons now. To make their point clearer, late
that evening they sauntered through the town, harassing townspeople. They attacked two lamplighters: they cut one in the
head, "and drew the ladder from under another, while he was
lighting the lamps."

The next day—Saturday, January 20—the seamen, Liberty
Boys, and townspeople got their revenge. According to one version, "sailors with clubs [out] to revenge the death of their
brother" attacked soldiers on Nassau Street, who retaliated
"with great rage," bringing Liberty Boys and citizens in general
to the defense of the sailors. Another version charged a group of
drunken soldiers with starting the fight by attacking some
sailors. In any case, the seamen, Liberty Boys, and others pursued the soldiers to the gates of the barracks, where, nursing
their wounds, the Red Coats were saved from further punishment.

So ended the two days of battle. Mayor Hicks announced a
partial victory for the townspeople when he reported that Gen-

eral Gage had ordered that no soldiers were to leave their barracks when off duty, except under the command of a noncommissioned officer, who was to be accountable for the "orderly behaviour" of his men. But the workers' complaints against unfair competition from off-duty soldiers continued to be ignored.[3]

So far as the Liberty Pole was concerned, the victory over the Red Coats was complete. Two weeks after the Golden Hill incident, a committee of Liberty Boys, headed by Isaac Sears, John Lamb, and Alexander McDougall, applied to the Common Council for permission to erect a new Liberty Pole on the Commons. After it was built, it would be presented as a gift to the City Corporation. To the committee's astonishment, the Corporation rejected the offer—an action which the Sons of Liberty felt could not be "paralleled by any act of any Corporation in the British Dominions, chosen by the suffrages of a free people." Sears and a few other Liberty Boys purchased a strip of private land twelve feet wide and one hundred feet long, near the place where the former Pole had stood. There, a hole twelve feet deep was dug, "and a large pitch pine mast erected. The mast was cased round with iron bars, laid lengthwise, riveted thro' with large flat rivets, and laid close together, so as entirely to cover the mast for about two thirds of its length, and over these bars were driven large iron hoops, near half an inch thick, at a small distance from bottom to top." On the top of the forty-six-foot Pole was a twenty-foot mast, topped with a gilt weathervane inscribed with the word LIBERTY. As the Liberty Pole was constructed like a ship's mast, it was probably built by seamen. The seamen's role is not surprising, since they had been fully involved in the Battle of Golden Hill and had good reason to hate the working soldiers.

On February 6, 1770, the new Liberty Pole "was drawn through the streets from the ship yards, by six horses, decorated with ribbands, three flags flying, with the words Liberty and Property, and attended by several thousands of the inhabitants." It was raised "while the French horns played *God Save the King*."[4]

This Liberty Pole was strong enough to stand until October 28, 1776, by which time many of those who had fought in the Battle of Golden Hill were enlisted in the Continental Army, fighting for American independence. Indeed, Michael Smith, a twenty-year-old chairmaker's apprentice, fought with the musket, belts, bayonets, and cartridge box he had seized from a British grenadier when he charged up Golden Hill with a chair leg to defend the "naked" citizens.[5]

In *The Sons of Liberty in New York* (1859), Henry B. Dawson gave the title "The Battle of Golden Hill" to the two days of fighting in January 1770, and he called it *"the first conflict of war of the American Revolution."*[6] In most historical accounts of the events leading up to July 4, 1776, the Battle of Golden Hill, if mentioned at all, does not loom as large as the Boston Massacre, which took place six weeks later. Yet, both were rooted in the same problems—resentment against an arrogant occupying army and the growing antagonism between colonial workingmen and British troops because of the competition for jobs and the cutting of wages. Before turning to the fatal March 5, 1770, in Boston, it should be noted that the Battle of Golden Hill solidified the unity of the Sons of Liberty, and, as Roger Champagne notes, "the shoulder-to-shoulder camaraderie of Sears, Lamb, and McDougall dated from the battle."[7]

On March 12, 1770, the *Boston Evening-Post* carried on its front page a report of a "bloody massacre" in the city a week before, which it described as "the destructive consequences of quartering troops among citizens in a time of peace."[8] Four persons had lost their lives:

> The dead are Mr. Samuel Gray, killed on the spot, the ball entering his head and beating off a large portion of his skull.

> A mulatto named Crispus Attucks who was born in Framingham, but lately belonged to New-Providence and was here in order to go for North Carolina, also killed instantly, two balls entering his breast, one of them in special goring the right lobe of the lungs and a great part of the liver most horribly.

> Mr. James Caldwell, mate of Capt. Morton's vessel, in like manner killed by two balls entering his back.

> Mr. Samuel Maverick, a promising youth of 17 years of age, son of the widow Maverick, and an apprentice to Mr. Greenwood, ivory-turner, mortally wounded; a ball went through his belly, and was cut out at his back: He died the next morning.

A fifth victim was Patrick Carr, who died of his wounds on March 14.

All five were workers. Crispus Attucks, a runaway Negro slave, was a seaman and stevedore; Samuel Gray, a ropewalk worker; James Caldwell, a young seaman; Patrick Carr, an employee of a leather breeches maker; and Samuel Maverick, a joiner's apprentice.

The "Bloody massacre" of March 5, 1770, was the culmination of a series of disturbances that began in 1768 when two regiments of British regulars arrived in Boston. From the outset, General Gage had been seeking the opportunity to place Boston, the hotbed of radicalism, under military domination. In January 1766, he wrote to Secretary of War Barrington that he was seeking "a legal pretext" to achieve this objective.[9] But it took more than two years to achieve it. The "legal pretext" finally presented itself when the Sons of Liberty led a crowd against the notoriously corrupt customs commissioners, who, in addition to operating a flagrant system of bribery which raised the cost of products, were also accused of bribing someone to cut down the flagstaff of the Liberty Tree. The commissioners were forced to flee to Castle Williams for safety. Since it was clear that customs operations, and the bribery and other forms of corruption that went with it, could not survive without armed support, two regiments were sent from Halifax to Boston.[10] Paul Revere wrote in his journal:

> On Friday, Sept. 30, 1768 the schooners transports etc., came up the harbour and anchored round the town; their cannons loaded, a spring on their cables, as for a regular siege. At noon on Saturday the fourteenth and twenty-ninth regiments and a detachment from the 59th regiment, and a train of artillery landed on Long Wharf; there formed and marched with insolent parade, drums beating, fifes playing, up King Street, each soldier having received sixteen rounds of powder and ball.[11]

The soldiers were there, Governor Bernard said, "to rescue the Government from the hands of a trained mob and to restore the activity of the civil power." In short, the troops occupied Boston, not for any military purpose, but solely as policemen.[12]

Boston's Sons of Liberty had met just before the troops landed in order to decide whether to offer armed resistance. A policy of "dignified non-cooperation" was decided upon, but it was not long before this passive stance yielded to an implacable hatred of the Red Coats. Nor was this hostility surprising. In 1766, Benjamin Franklin had told Parliament that troops sent to America "will not find a rebellion; they may indeed make one." Two years later, a writer in the *Boston Gazette* observed that in "a free country . . . a standing Army rather occasion[s] than prevent[s] them [conflicts]."[13] Events soon justified these predictions.

"Eighteenth-century British armies were composed in large measures of scourings and scrapings," notes John C. Miller, "but the Twenty-ninth Regiment, which the Ministry had sent to tame the Bostonians, seems to have had more than its share of its gallow birds."[14] Not that Bostonians could not see for themselves the terrible conditions under which the soldiers were forced to exist. In his study of the British army in the American colonies, James Shy points out that there was a popular revulsion in Boston against the harsh discipline in the army, and that many townspeople actually gave shelter to deserters. He concludes that the Bostonians had "a certain humanitarian feeling for these poor creatures who seemed worse off than slaves."[15]

The offensive conduct of the soldiers, however, was an everyday reality to Bostonians—if not to the many historians who have dismissed this charge as propaganda[16]—and it far outweighed their sympathy for the troops. The soldiers would amuse themselves by jabbing civilians in the ribs with bayonets and hustling them off the sidewalks. The presence of sentries in the streets, continually challenging passersby, was "more than most Bostonians could bear." In truth, the entire town seemed to be converted into a garrison, for the troops were everywhere— even in Faneuil Hall and the Town House. The increase in drunkenness, petty theft, and prostitution, as well as the practice of Sunday horse racing on the Commons, further deteriorated relations between soldiers and citizens.[17]

An additional factor in the worsening relations, was the British army's practice of allowing off-duty soldiers to take civilian employment at wages which undercut Americans by as much as 50 percent. Competition for work was, as we have seen, one of the causes of the Battle of Golden Hill. It was inevitable that when this competition for jobs was added to the harassment of civilians, a similar, and even more tragic, outcome would result. "This sharp competition," Richard B. Morris reminds us, "must be kept in mind in understanding the events leading to the Boston Massacre."[18]

On March 2, 1770, a pitched battle was fought between British troops and ropewalk workers over this very issue of competition for work. It started when one of three British soldiers looking for work at the ropewalk belonging to John Gray was told by one of the employees to "go and clean my s[hi]t house." This insult led to a fistfight, in which the British soldiers came out the losers. They then ran back to their barracks and returned with several companions. When they were driven off, they, in turn, came back reinforced by thirty or forty Red Coats, armed with clubs and cutlasses. Other workers in the neighboring ropewalks joined the thirteen or fourteen workers at Gray's ropewalks, and, though armed only with sticks, they routed the soldiers.

The workers' jubilation was tempered somewhat when the ropemaker who had insulted the soldier was discharged at the insistence of the military. The soldiers, however, were both angry and humiliated, and vowed revenge. On the evening of March 5, Sam Gray, one of the ropemakers involved in the earlier encounter, and a crowd of workers who had suffered from the competition of off-duty soldiers approached the garrison where the soldiers were on duty, fully armed. "Come on, you rascals, you bloody backs, you lobster scoundrels," Gray taunted, "fire if you dare, G[o]d damn you, fire and be damned, we know you dare not." But the soldiers did dare; three of them who had participated in the fight at the ropewalks, along with the others, opened fire. When the smoke cleared, three workers were dead and several were wounded, two of whom died later.[19]

Conflicting testimony makes it difficult to determine whether the troops fired deliberately at workers whom they recognized as having fought with them for jobs. (Indeed, Hiller B. Zobel may be correct in his otherwise slanted "Tory account" of the Boston Massacre when he concludes that "no one yet knows what really happened."[20]) But there is no doubt, even though Zobel neither sees nor understands it, that a real relationship existed between the earlier fight at the ropewalk and the later massacre.[21] Moreover, it was Crispus Attucks, the fugitive slave from Framingham, who John Adams later said was mainly responsible for leading the charge against the British soldiers, that led to the massacre. Attucks, one of three or four in the crowd who were black or Indian, was a seaman who supported himself while in Boston as a stevedore. He had good reason to resent the constant "moonlighting" of the British soldiers, since it cut into his job opportunities and reduced his wages in these hard times.[22]

After the massacre, some soldiers sallied out of the barracks and beat up a number of civilians. "An apprehension of a settled plan for a general if not universal massacre, from such barbarous outrages, in conjunction with their former attacks, justly alarmed the people: — The bells were set a-ringing, and great numbers assembled." While some were taking care of the dead and wounded, William Molineaux and others were asking Lieutenant Governor Hutchinson to order the soldiers back to their barracks. When Hutchinson refused, the Liberty Boys themselves drove the troops back.[23]

All five victims of the Boston Massacre, black and white alike, were buried in a common grave, and ten to twelve thousand people marched in the funeral procession. Two of the soldiers involved were convicted of manslaughter; they had their thumbs branded and were discharged. Six others were acquitted. The judges and others involved in the proceedings received monetary rewards for their efforts in freeing the accused.[24]

Although popular feeling had never been so strong in Boston as it was after the massacre, the soldiers who were released were never molested. Bostonians insisted, however, that the troops be removed immediately, and when the authorities were evasive about evacuating them, the Sons of Liberty set up a watch to see that the removal was carried out. They announced that the troops would be removed by force if necessary. This action won the support of the Portsmouth (New Hampshire) Sons of Liberty, who sent word that they would march, ten thousand strong, "to help drive the redcoats into Boston Bay." Salem's Liberty Boys promised a force of thousands to help Boston destroy a "licentious and blood thirsty soldiery." In fact, armed men began to march on Boston, but Bostonians stopped them at the outskirts of the city. [25] One scholar has written that popular feeling over the massacre was so great that "the Revolution might well have started in 1770 had not the British removed their troops from Boston." [26] Even at that, when the troops finally left, it was necessary for William Molineaux to walk alongside them from their barracks to the wharf to save them from the wrath of a thoroughly aroused citizenry. [27]

In 1770, the citizens of Boston voted to commemorate March 5 with speeches, followed by a public exhibition in King Street, where the massacre took place, depicting the scene of the murder, the troops, and the slaughtered victims. Until the end of the War for Independence, the memory of the five workers, including the black seaman, was kept alive by means of commemorative exercises at which leading Sons of Liberty delivered orations. Each year, huge crowds witnessed the exhibition, and collections were taken for surviving victims. In 1774, a "very generous collection" was taken up for Christopher Monk, one of the young workers wounded on the night of March 5, 1770. [28]

*   *   *

General Thomas Gage, who witnessed both the Battle of Golden Hill and the Boston Massacre, stated that the Sons of Liberty in New York had conspired to stir up the people against the troops "to have a pretence to desire the removal of the troops," and that "this plan of getting the troops removed by quarreling with them was soon transmitted to Boston." Cadwallader Colden expressed a similar opinion, speaking of "the similarity of the proceedings of the faction in this place and in Boston." [29] Many historians agree, attributing the events in New York and Boston early in 1770 to the reckless determination of the Sons of Liberty to find "some kind of incident" in which to move their puppets—"the lower class mob"—against the soldiers. From the material presented here, however, it should be clear that no one had to incite the workers against the troops. Except for the conservatives, who needed the troops to keep the people in check, the entire populace had sufficient grievances against the troops. The workers, on the other hand, had all these and more, for in addition to sharing the popular resentment against the soldiers' arrogance, they suffered from competition with them for work.

In the 1772 exhibition commemorating the Boston Massacre, the following inscription was posted above the panorama depicting the slaughter on King Street: "The fatal effect of a standing Army posted in a free City."[30]

6 ——— *Struggle over Nonimportation and the Tea Parties*

☐ The merchants in the seaport towns reacted to the Townshend Acts of 1768 by agreeing to suspend the importation of English wares until the colonial grievances were redressed. In most cases, however, they acted hesitantly and only under pressure by the mechanics and their allies in the Sons of Liberty. Eventually, the nonimportation agreements were sealed, but many of the signers remained reluctant and looked for the first chance to abrogate them. One reason for their reluctance was their concern over the mechanics' and artisans' increasing role in enforcing the nonimportation agreements. As members of the ruling class, the merchants "had come to realize that the increasing political power of the mechanics and artificers was as much a threat to their control of the provincial government as it was to the British government."[1] The unity achieved by the Sons of Liberty in New York; the emergence of a more effective Sons of Liberty movement in Philadelphia, under the leadership of Charles Thomson; the organization of a mechanics' political party in Charleston—all these intensified the merchants' desire to be finished with nonimportation, which they considered the catalytic agent responsible for these unprecedented developments.[2] Small wonder, then, that the nonimportation associations formed by the merchants usually provided for their own dissolution once the Townshend Revenue Act was repealed. Had it not been for the pressure of the Sons of Liberty, the merchants would have discarded the policy of nonimportation even before the repeal.

The merchants' opportunity came in the spring of 1770, when Parliament repealed all the Townshend duties except the one on tea. The merchants immediately took steps to scuttle the nonimportation agreements, but the Sons of Liberty insisted that the agreements remain in force until *all* of the Townshend duties had been repealed; otherwise the right of Parliament to levy the tax would be conceded. This policy had the enthusiastic support of the mechanics. Nonimportation, which gave them a monopoly over the local market, had been a boon to them, and they naturally became its most ardent champions, hoping to extend it as long as possible.

The Boston Sons of Liberty acted swiftly to insure the continuation of nonimportation despite Parliament's partial concessions. When a number of Boston merchants called a meeting to adopt a resolution permitting the importation of all British goods except tea, the Liberty Boys decided to attend and demanded that the resolution be changed to require that nonimportation continue until all taxes were removed. The merchants hastily adjourned the meeting, but the Sons of Liberty took over the Merchants Club, where it was held, and turned it into the "Body of the People" which, by its own authority, passed resolutions extending nonimportation and forming separate committees of inspection. Street parades were then organized to force importers to deliver their goods to the inspection committees. A merchant who refused to comply was run out of town and warned not to return.[3]

The Boston Liberty Boys made it clear that they would take "recourse to the sword before they will suffer the agreement to be broke."[4] Even the sword would be of little avail, however, if British goods flowed freely into other seaports. Shortly after the news of Parliament's action reached Rhode Island, the Newport merchants, over the vigorous protests of the Sons of Liberty, broke the unity of the colonies by rescinding nonimportation. Soon afterwards, rumors began reaching Boston that disaffection was growing in New York and Philadelphia. If these cities followed Newport's lead, the attempt to maintain the agreement in Boston was doomed to fail. This was precisely what happened.

The New York City merchants announced that they alone had the right to determine whether the agreement should be continued. They specifically did not want the mechanics to have a voice in the matter which, according to the merchants, only involved the economic well-being of the mercantile community. Of course, the welfare of the mechanics was intimately connected with the future of nonimportation, but the merchants used the argument as a cover for their real complaint: that the mechanics were becoming too active in affairs which did not concern the "lower class."

As might be expected, the Sons of Liberty rejected the merchants' argument. A New York Liberty Boy issued a brilliant Swiftian broadside entitled "For Erecting and Encouraging a New Manufactory." He proposed that as "the mechanic (it is difficult to define these animals), or in other words the two legged pack horse, was created solely to contribute to the ease and influence of a few importers," the government should establish a tannery in order to compensate the importers for their defense of American rights:

> First, the proper methods be fallen upon to encourage the breed of such mechanics as are inured to the severest bodily labour.

> Secondly, that upon the demise of said mechanics, their wives, and children, a committee of these importers be appointed to flea them; and transport their hides to the company's tan-yards.

> Thirdly, that a manufactory be established at the expence of the province for dressing, curing, and tanning the said hides.

> And fourthly, that the profits arising from the sale of the leather be applied to the company's use.[5]

On May 30, 1770, the New York Sons of Liberty held a mass meeting to "deliberate on measures to support the liberties of this country which had been invaded by a tyrannical ministry." Resolutions adopted "by a great majority" denounced the Newport merchants "for their inglorious defection from the interests of their country." They and all others who followed their example were "declared enemies to the liberties of North

America." They declared further that the Sons of Liberty and their supporters would:

> to the utmost of our power, by all legal means, preserve the Non-importation Agreement inviolate in the City and Colony, until the Townshend Revenue Act aforesaid is totally repealed, and that we will not buy any goods from any portion or persons who shall transgress that salutary Agreement, and that we will use our utmost influence to prevent others from purchasing goods from them.

The meeting also resolved that a shipment from Scotland, just arrived, should be returned immediately and that the consignees should make a public pledge that it would be returned.[6]

The Sons of Liberty's actions drew immediate fire from the merchants, who insisted that they alone had the right to decide such matters. The Liberty Boys responded with a warning that importers in other colonies who took their position were "so odious and contemptible, that they are generally shunned as if infected with the plague, so that they live most unhappy and miserable lives, and most of them apprehend they shall be obliged to leave the Colony."[7] Undaunted by these threats, the merchants proceeded with a scheme to poll the city on nonimportation. They set up a committee composed, said the Sons of Liberty, of "selfish, mercenary importers and a few mechanics, the tools of a party,"[8] to canvass the people on whether they wanted the old association or a new one which would permit the importation of all goods from Britain except tea. Should the vote be in favor of the latter, it would not go into effect unless Boston and Philadelphia concurred. If, however, these cities rejected the New York proposal, another poll would be taken in the city to determine whether New York should "go it alone."[9]

The merchants conducted their poll over the bitter objections of the Sons of Liberty. Thereupon, Isaac Sears and Peter Van Bevoort, two Liberty Boys on the committee of inspection, resigned their positions in protest. They would not, they stated, associate "with men who are using every effort to counteract the very design of our appointment."[10] The merchants completed the poll, and on June 16, 1770, they informed Boston and Philadelphia that the people of New York were in favor of importing everything but dutied items—that is, tea. [11]

The Sons of Liberty promptly informed Boston and Philadelphia that the poll had been a fraud, and that 1,180 signers, a mere fragment of the entire population, had either been bribed or so confused that they did not know what they were signing. To demonstrate graphically what would happen if the merchants did abrogate the agreement, the Sons of Liberty began seizing and burning merchandise imported from England. The merchants announced their determination to proceed with their plans, regardless of what the "lawless ruffians" did. [12]

When the replies from Boston and Philadelphia revealed that these cities had rejected the New York proposal, the Sons of Liberty demanded that the letters be published and the plan to revoke nonimportation be dropped. The merchants refused; instead, they went ahead with a second poll and announced publicly that they were sending orders for British goods by the mail packet scheduled to leave within a few days. [13]

Sears, Lamb, and McDougall responded by inserting an advertisement in the name of the Sons of Liberty, calling for a mass meeting to inform the people that "no private set of men have a right to determine on a mode, by which the citizens are to give their voices, on a question pregnant with the most dangerous consequences to the freedom of Americans." [14] Sears and Lamb presided at a City Hall mass meeting on July 7. Alexander Colden, son of the lieutenant governor, reported that Sears told the people that if any merchant presumed to break his pledge not to import British goods, "he would lose his life in the attempt, or the goods imported should be burnt as soon as landed." The crowd roared approval and demanded continuation of the old agreement. [15]

The merchant polltakers went about the city again, but this time the Sons of Liberty trailed along, explaining the issues to the people who were approached and hooting and hissing those who signed in favor of eliminating nonimportation. That afternoon, a gang of toughs hired by the merchants and accompanied by Elias Desbrosses, a city magistrate, attacked the Liberty Boys on Wall Street and beat them with clubs. Sears and

McDougall, two of those assaulted, tried to lodge formal complaints against Desbrosses for assault and battery, but the court refused to entertain the complaint. [16]

Even though this time the merchants obtained only eight hundred signatures to end nonimportation, they proclaimed the question settled once and for all. They sent letters to Philadelphia and Boston, informing the merchants of these cities that orders were being sent to England on the packet the next day. The merchants of the Quaker City were asked if they wanted to avail themselves of the same opportunity. The Sons of Liberty published a "Protest" signed by John Lamb and Isaac Sears. It denounced the merchants' decision to import after

> only 794 persons in this populous City, including all ranks, and both sexes, declared in the affirmative of the question, and upon this slender voice, (will posterity whose liberties are in our hand believe it!) the glorious and salutory Union of so many Colonies, has been rescinded in this City, without the privity or consent of the other numerous inhabitants of the Colony.

Since repeal of nonimportation would be "attended with consequences, the most dangerous to American liberty," the public would be given the opportunity to sign the "Protest," and thereby give testimony of their abhorrence of the end of nonimportation. So that "no fraud may appear," the public was urged "to set down along with their *names* their occupations and places of residence." [17]

There were many signers of the protest, but since the majority were mechanics (as indicated by their occupations and residences), the merchants simply ignored it. Nonimportation had ended, and nothing the Sons of Liberty or the people in New York in general could do about it made any difference to the merchants. The merchants had at last succeeded in gaining complete control of affairs, a goal they had sought since the beginning of the resistance movement. Despite the Liberty Boys and regardless of whether the other colonies approved, they had ended nonimportation in New York.

It would appear that the merchants' victory would humiliate

and discredit the Sons of Liberty in New York. The exact opposite occurred, however. For one thing, in the eyes of the public, the Liberty Boys were now "permanently identified as the defenders of American rights in New York,"[18] and, indeed, in many ways, their only defenders. Then again, the Sons of Liberty would never again rely on merchants, aristocrats, or others in the ruling circles as allies in carrying through a persistent struggle against Britain. Here, as we shall see, were laid the seeds of the independent mechanics' resistance movement.

Boston publicly burned the July 16 letter from the New York merchants, and Philadelphia replied scathingly: "We cannot forbear to tell you, that however you may color your proceedings we think you have in the day of trial, deserted the cause of liberty and your country."[19] The wealthy merchants of Philadelphia would have followed the lead of their New York colleagues, had it not been for pressure from the Sons of Liberty. The importing merchants who traded with Britain did, in fact, raise a demand that nonimportation be ended, but the less wealthy "wet goods" merchants, whose commercial dealings with the West Indies had continued as usual, united with Philadelphia's mechanics in opposing a resumption of trade with Britain. With the purchase of American manufactures considered a patriotic virtue, and with outside competition cut off, the mechanics of Philadelphia were experiencing good times. As "Tradesman" wrote at that time, Philadelphia's mechanics supported nonimportation unanimously because those who suffered were "but few, when compared to the number of those who have received great benefit from it."[20]

When the merchants appeared to be leaning toward New York's example, the mechanics broke completely with the Quaker-merchant party and allied themselves as one with Charles Thomson, a small merchant and a strong advocate of home manufactures, and John Dickinson, a Presbyterian lawyer. Dickinson's *Farmer's Letters*, published in 1768, rejecting the right of Parliment to tax colonies, had won wide support in the artisan community throughout the colonies. Together, Thomson and Dickinson exerted strong pressure on the merchants to stand firm after the importers of Newport and New York had repudiated the nonimportation agreements. They were aided in this effort by a letter from Franklin to Thomson, his political associate, urging adherence to nonimportation until all duties were repealed. [21] When the merchants called meetings to consider rescinding nonimportation, the mechanics, under Thomson's leadership, attended, and they were able to prevent such action. Then in late June 1770, they organized a "Mechanics Committee" to help police the nonimportation agreement. When word circulated that some merchants wanted to abrogate it, a meeting of "Artificers, Manufacturers, Tradesmen, Mechanics and Others" was called to define the position of the artisan community. The meeting resolved to encourage the continuation of nonimportation and to promote American manufactures. When several merchants broke the agreement, they were warned that they would be "dealt with by the Mechanics Committee" if they refused "to make ample satisfaction." Most of these merchants made a confession of wrongdoing, but only after they were threatened with tarring and feathering. [22]

Despite the mechanics' efforts, the Philadelphia merchants eventually rescinded their nonimportation agreement and resumed commerce with Britain. The action was taken at a meeting on September 20 (which was boycotted by the mechanics and lesser merchants). [23] Still, the mechanics refused to concede defeat. One mechanic proposed in the *Pennsylvania Journal* of October 1, 1770, that since the merchants had defaulted as the protectors of American liberties, "Let the powers of patriotism be drawn from their proper source. Let the landholders, artificers, and independent freemen of this province take upon themselves the defense of those liberties in which they have the greatest and most substantial interest." He went on to suggest that citizens boycott importing merchants and undertake further efforts to promote home manufactures.

While it was too late to undo the merchants' action, the mechanics showed their anger at the polls in the election held in October 1770. They completely deserted the Quaker party, which was associated with ending nonimportation, and cast their ballots for the party led by Charles Thomson. This ticket, which was elected, was headed by John Dickinson and Charles Thomson, and included Joseph Parker, an artisan tailor. All of these men were fervent advocates of nonimportation. [24]

Thus, while nonimportation was rescinded in Philadelphia, the controversy over it had transformed the city's political alignments. The mechanics had entered the struggle as an independent power and had become "a force to be reckoned with."[25] Under the leadership of Charles Thomson, they provided the Philadelphia Sons of Liberty with what the organization had lacked until then—the united support of the most numerous and influential artisan population in the colonies. Neither its internal politics nor the struggle against Britain in Philadelphia were ever to be the same again.

After Newport, New York, and Philadelphia all had yielded to the merchants over mechanic opposition, it was inevitable that Boston would follow suit. The Sons of Liberty tried, however, to stave off the inevitable. Committees headed by Molineaux visited Newport and Providence in an effort to stir up sufficient resistance to force the "gentlemen of trade" to live up to the agreements, but it was of little use. Eventually, the mechanics and their associates in Boston were forced to give way, as had their brethren in other colonies. The merchants emerged victorious and nonimportation was rescinded in the Bay City as well.

In Charleston, the Sons of Liberty were able to maintain nonimportation despite merchant opposition, but the end of nonimportation in the Northern colonies finally forced them to yield as well. The merchants made effective use of the argument that the Carolina radicals had been deserted by their brothers in the North, and that to cling to nonimportation under these circumstances would only prove that the Sons of Liberty were determined to destroy Charleston's commerce. Nonimportation ended in Charleston early in 1772, but Christopher Gadsden, leader of the Sons of Liberty, was able to boast that the Charleston Liberty Boys were "the last to desert the cause."[26]

Historians have called the years following the Nonimportation Association (1770-1773) the "quiet period," and some have claimed that, during this period, the Sons of Liberty all but vanished from the scene. It is true that an apparent calm settled over political affairs, but the appearance was deceptive. That calm was restored to the streets of Boston after the removal of the troops is quite understandable, since the presence of the Red Coats was the major cause for that city's turbulent events early in 1770. The fact is that the Boston Sons of Liberty were building for the future. In the spring elections of 1771, they waged a successful campaign to keep their radical leaders — Adams, Otis, and Hancock — in the General Court, the Massachusetts Assembly. It was during the "quiet period" of 1772, moreover, that the Boston Committee of Correspondence was organized to rouse the people of Massachusetts and inform them of their rights. It, in turn, initiated the use of local committees of correspondence. Eighteen of the leading members of the Boston Committee of Correspondence were Liberty Boys. In addition, special messengers were employed to establish contact with other colonies. Paul Revere, a Son of Liberty, and John Marston, "a high Son of Liberty," were used for this purpose. During these "years of inactivity," Liberty Boys in other parts of America were in touch with their associates in Boston.[27]

The New York Sons of Liberty was one of the organizations which continued to maintain contacts with its brother societies. In 1771, it showed it was still alive by celebrating the repeal of the Stamp Act, hailing the day that had redeemed America "from the yoke of slavery and oppression." Tribute was paid to all who had stood firm for nonimportation to the end, and two of the toasts were "May Elections be by Ballot, and no Representative of the People Excluded but by the known Law of the Land," and "May the American Colonies Fully Enjoy the British Constitution." Before the celebration was adjourned, the participants informed the public that they could still be counted on to lead the battle to achieve the principle enunciated in the last toast.[28]

The "quiet period" was also one in which the first shots were fired in the Revolution. The violence erupted on June 8, 1772, during the burning of the *Gaspée*, which, in turn, had resulted from the resentment in Rhode Island over the British attempt to enforce the revenue laws. The American schooner *Hannah*, under the command of Captain Lindsay, having reported her cargo at Newport, was proceeding up the river to Providence, when the *Gaspée* gave chase. The *Hannah* succeeded in crossing the shallow water at Namquit Point, but the *Gaspée* ran aground attempting to follow. On the evening of the same day, citizens of Providence, led by the Sons of Liberty, having learned of the

Gaspée's plight from Captain Lindsay, set out in boats for Nanquit Point, six miles away. They boarded the vessel at night, removed the crew, and set fire to it. Upon their approach, William Duddingston, in command of the *Gaspée*, fired shots and was wounded by a return shot.

Governor Wanton issued a proclamation offering a reward for the discovery of those involved; the British government subsequently offered larger rewards. A court of inquiry was appointed, but in vain. A ballad, "A New Song, Called the Gaspée," made the rounds of the colonies and was sung wherever the Sons of Liberty gathered. It told the story of the burning of the *Gaspée* and predicted in its concluding stanza that those who were involved would never be discovered. Pointing out that the public peace was continually being disturbed by British ships interfering with trade, creating a condition "the sons of liberty could not bear," the ballad concluded:

Then set the men upon the land,
And burnt her up we understand,
Which thing provokes the King so high,
He said those men shall surely die.

So if he could but find them out,
The hangmen he'll employ no doubt;
For he's declared in his passion,
He'll have them tri'd, a new fashion.

Now for to find these people out,
King George has offer'd very stout;
One thousand pounds to find out one
That wounded William Duddingston.

One thousand more he says he'll spare
For those who say they sheriffs, were:
One thousand more there doth remain,
For to find out the leader's name.

Likewise five hundred pounds per man
Of any one of all the clan,
But let him try his utmost skill,
I'm apt to think he never will
Find out any of those hearts of gold,
Though he should offer fifty fold.[29]

In 1772, the Philadelphia mechanics founded a permanent political organization known as the Patriotic Society. In its articles, the members said they would "endeavour to promote . . . and preserve, inviolate, our just rights and privileges, to us and our posterity, against every attempt to violate or infringe upon the same, either here, or on the *other side of the Atlantic.*" They would promote candidates and policies in accordance with the best interests of the province as interpreted by the majority of the club. "Clearly," writes Charles S. Olton, "class-related sentiment was at work in Philadelphia in the early 1770's." Clearly, too (though Olton, like many other consensus historians, refuses to recognize the significance of the evidence), the struggle over who should rule at home, as well as over home rule, was in operation in Philadelphia in the early 1770s. Joseph Reed, an acute contemporary observer, noted that "the frequent appeals to the people must in time occasion a change, and we every day perceive it more and more difficult to repress the rising spirit of the people."[30]

In 1769, the mechanics of Charleston had formed their own political party; they had nominated and elected a ticket in the fall elections, and had completely transformed South Carolina politics. In 1770, the first political meeting specifically restricted to mechanics was held in Philadelphia, and two years later, mechanics formed a permanent political organization—the Patriotic Society—to promote artisan candidates and policies. In Boston, they engaged in political action and, as we have seen, in creating a new form of revolutionary organization—the Boston Committee of Correspondence. In New York, the mechanics had vowed never again to place their confidence in the merchant class in the struggle for American rights.

By 1773, when the Tea Act sparked a new round of popular protests, the mechanics had emerged as a conscious, aggressively anti-British element in colonial politics. It was with the passage of the Tea Act in May of that year that the Revolutionary movement came fully alive again. This time, however, instead of dying down as it had in 1770, the resistance became a rebellion that led inexorably to independence.

The Tea Act was initiated on behalf of the East India Company and permitted that company to export tea directly to the colonies. It also provided it with allowances to repay the customs duties which would be collected in America. The company and its factors were thus able to sell tea at lower prices than other merchants, even while the existing duty on tea was maintained as a matter of principle. The act gave the East India Company an effective monopoly over the American tea trade. Not only did the refunded English tea duties undercut smugglers, but the company's ability under the law to ship the tea directly to America and avoid wholesalers enabled it to undersell competitors as well.[31]

In a circular drafted by Samuel Adams and Joseph Warren, leaders of the Boston Sons of Liberty, it was pointed out that the issues raised by the Tea Act were the same as those that had been fought over since 1765. The Stamp Act had been repealed. All of the Townshend duties had been repealed except that on tea. The tax on tea had been retained as proof that Parliament had the right to tax the colonists. The colonists must therefore never consent to pay the tax, for to do so would constitute an admission that the power of taxation rested in Parliament, a body in which they were not themselves represented. The Tea Act created a giant monopoly power that would destroy colonial trade while increasing Britain's unconstitutional revenues. It had to be confronted with united colonial resistance.[32]

The standard anti-Tea Act arguments generally stressed the points set forth in the Massachusetts Circular Letter. Occasionally a mechanic would add the note that the tea monopoly would also drive local merchants out of business, thereby destroying colonial commerce, and, with it, job opportunities for mechanics and laborers. Hence, mechanics as well as merchants, and mechanics alone, if necessary, had to resist the parliamentary measure.[33]

In October 1773, seven ships set sail from England, destined for Boston, New York, Philadelphia, and Charleston. They had on board hundreds of chests of tea consigned to the agents of the East India Company in those cities. The question of the hour was: Would the tea be landed and the duty collected?

The answer came first from Boston. As early as October 23, the mechanics and their allies in the North End Caucus—headquarters of the Sons of Liberty—voted to "oppose the vending of any tea, sent by the East India Company to any part of this continent, with our lives and fortunes."[34] On November 2, the Caucus resolved that the East India tea absolutely "shall not be landed." It went on to make plans for a mass meeting to be held at the Liberty Tree to force the resignation of the tea agents. Should the agents fail to give "satisfaction," it warned, they would feel the "just resentment" of the Caucus and of all others who had gathered at the Tree.[35]

At the Liberty Tree gathering on November 3, the commissioners refused to resign their posts, and only after additional pressure was exerted were they persuaded to change their minds.[36] In the meantime, three ships had arrived in the harbor with tea aboard. Plans were laid to prevent the landing of "the . . . ministerial tea." The Sons of Liberty, "back in full stride," went about Boston, posting the historic notice:

Friends! Brethren! Countrymen! The worst of plagues, the detested tea shipped for this port by the East India Company, is now arrived in the harbour; the hour of destruction, or manly opposition to the machinations of tyrants, stares you in the face; every friend to this country, to himself, and to posterity, is now called upon to meet at Faneuil Hall, at nine o'clock this day, at which time the bells will ring to make united and successful resistance to this last, worst and most destructive measure of administration. Boston, Nov. 29, 1773.[37]

That same day, a large crowd of people heard the fiery Dr. Young suggest that the tea be thrown overboard. Members of the Sons of Liberty, especially Paul Revere and William Molineaux, hailed the suggestion.[38] It was not until December 16, however, that a considerable number of traders, mechanics, and laborers acted on it. After gathering at the Green Dragon Tavern, they disguised themselves as Indians and went on board the tea-laden vessel. Within a short time, they had dumped into the Boston harbor 342 chests of tea valued at £18,000 sterling.[39] Rural Liberty Boys worked alongside the Bostonians in dumping the taxed tea into the harbor, an indication of the effectiveness of recently created Boston Committee of Correspondence. Even before the tea had landed, the Boston Committee had in-

vited its counterparts from five neighboring towns to meet with
it at Faneuil Hall, and all voted "to use joint influence to prevent
the landing and sale of the tea expected from the East India Company." [40] The Boston Tea Party was a product of this "joint
influence."

Benjamin W. Labaree, in *The Boston Tea Party*, assigns
"final responsibility" for the destruction of the tea to the Boston
Committee of Correspondence, but it is likely that the actual
direction and execution were carried out by the North End Caucus. In any event, it was the Boston Sons of Liberty, and the mechanics and their allies who made up the bulk of the movement,
who planned and carried through the Boston Tea Party. [41]

With the tea at the bottom of the harbor, North End Mechanics and day laborers were able to rejoice and sing:

> Rally, Mohawks, bring out your axes,
> And tell King George we'll pay no taxes
>   On his foreign tea!
> His threats are vain, and vain to think
> To force our girls and wives to drink
>   His vile Bohea!
> Then rally, boys, and hasten on
> To meet our chiefs at the Green Dragon!
>
> Our Warren's there, and brave Revere,
> With hands to do, and words to cheer,
>   For liberty and laws;
> Our country's "braves" and firm defenders
> Shall ne'er be left by true North Enders,
>   Fighting Freedom's cause!
> Then rally, boys, and hasten on,
> To meet our chiefs at the Green Dragon! [42]

Soon the mechanics and laborers in Philadelphia, New York,
and Charleston, where public protests against the tea tax had
already begun, were in full concert with their Boston brothers.

A mass meeting in Philadelphia, called for October 18 by the
Sons of Liberty, appointed a committee to see the merchant to
whom the tea was consigned and induce him to resign his position. When he made "*a decent renunciation* of his dangerous and

disgraceful office of tea commissioner," the *Pennsylvania Gazette* congratulated him for being "now despised somewhat less than he used to be."[43]

When the news reached Philadelphia that the ship carrying the tea was arriving, the Sons of Liberty distributed a handbill to the "Delaware Pilots," informing them: "A SHIP loaded with TEA is now on their way to this port, being sent out by the Ministry for the purpose of *enslaving* and poisoning ALL the AMERICANS." Pointing out that the ship could not be brought to Philadelphia's harbor "without your assistance," the Sons of Liberty asked the pilots to turn the ship back.[44] What happened was described by Henry Laurens in a letter to his son, John, on January 21, 1774:

> The river pilots were properly addressed and admonished not to take charge of any ship having such tea on board, and accordingly, when the ships arrived in the Bay of Delaware, every pilot refused his assistance. The Bay is a more dangerous navigation than the open sea. The captains of such ships were therefore necessitated to put to sea again.

The very next day after the ship was approached by the "Delaware Pilots," the captain turned around and sailed back to England—with the tea still aboard.[45]

When news of the Tea Act reached New York, a debate over it raged in the press. Some claimed that the act itself represented no danger to American liberties, especially since it offered plenty of tea at a cheap price. The Sons of Liberty immediately attacked this argument as "a shameful falsehood." As for the prospect of cheap tea, it urged, "let the world see, that your palates are not yet so depraved" that you will give in to "alluring temptations."[46]

While the debate went on, the Sons of Liberty came forward with a definite program. First, it took steps to make the tea agents resign their commissions. After a visit from a committee of Liberty Boys experienced in such activities from the Stamp Act days, the tea agents expressed a willingness to resign their posts because of the "general opposition" to the sale of tea.[47] Next, on November 29, 1773, the Sons of Liberty published Ar-

ticles of Association, calling upon members who signed a pledge
to boycott anyone who should introduce, store, or use tea imported under the act. Such individuals were to be condemned as
"enemies to the liberties of America," and members were to
promise not to "deal with, or employ, or have any connection"
with those who either ignored or violated the articles. [48]

Meanwhile, the tea ship arrived in New York harbor. When
Governor Tryon ordered the ship convoyed to the wharf by His
Majesty's sloop, *Susan*, [49] the Sons of Liberty went into action
to prevent the tea from being removed from the ship. A notice for
a mass meeting read:

THE MEMBERS OF THE ASSOCIATION of the SONS
OF LIBERTY, are requested to meet at the CITY-HALL,
at one o'clock TO-MORROW, being Friday, on business of
the utmost importance: — And every other friend, to the
liberties, and trade of America, is hereby most cordially invited, to meet at the same time and place.

The COMMITTEE of the ASSOCIATION. [50]

On December 17, though "the weather was bad," two to three
thousand people met at the City Hall. John Lamb, the presiding
officer, read letters from other cities on the need for unity against
the Tea Act and called for the appointment of a Committee of
Correspondence to establish regular contacts with other colonies
on the subject of the tea duty. [51] The idea for such a committee
grew out of a letter from the Boston Committee of Correspondence to Isaac Sears and Alexander McDougall, requesting that
they use their "influence with your fellow citizens at any future
meeting to appoint a similar Committee of Correspondence" to
the one in Boston, in order to facilitate a swift, reliable exchange
of news on issues of concern to all the colonies. [52]

At this point in the meeting, the mayor appeared and delivered
a message from Governor Tryon that the tea would be landed
and placed in the fort until a final decision was made as to what
should be done with it. "Gentlemen is this satisfactory to you?"
the mayor asked. The answer came swift and loud: "No, No, No."
The Tea Act was then read by Lamb, and two resolutions were

adopted by a large majority, with only the merchants and other conservatives present voting in the negative. One resolution pointed out that the "patriotic inhabitants" of Boston and Philadelphia had determined that no tea should be landed in either of these cities. The other approved the "spirited and patriotic conduct" of their brethren in Philadelphia and Boston "in support of the common liberties of America." Before the meeting closed, Lamb posed the question: "Is it then your opinion, gentlemen, that the tea should be landed under this circumstance?" As the conservatives had left by this time, the vote "was carried so generally in the negative, that there was no call for a division."[53]

Four days later, conservative men of property circulated a petition pledging signers not to resort to force in imposing the importation of tea. Except for the merchants, there were few signers.[54]

Reinforced by this popular support, the Sons of Liberty began meeting regularly at the tavern to plan for any new arrival. At the same time, the New York Committee of Correspondence wrote to committees in Boston, Philadelphia, Baltimore, and Charleston, proposing a boycott of all English tea until the Parliament repealed the Tea Act. They also promoted a plan by William Goddard, a Philadelphia printer and Son of Liberty, for an independent postal system for the colonies. The system would provide secure privacy for communications between the colonies, and it would cut off the revenue which the existing post office raised for the ministry. When Goddard arrived in Boston, he carried with him a "vigorous recommendation" from the New York Committee of Correspondence in favor of his plan.[55]

Meanwhile, the Liberty Boys urged New Yorkers to be on guard and help "their sister colonies, in establishing the freedom of their country." The conservatives were confident that the presence of Governor Tryon, the conqueror of the Regulators (the enraged farmers of North Carolina who had banded together to end the taxes and other inequities forced upon them), would deter the Liberty Boys from resorting to force to prevent the tea from landing.[56] But the Sons of Liberty announced to the public that no power—not the governor, and certainly "no monopolizing company"—would sway them from their course:

We trust with God's blessing, to stand our ground, and
as the day of trial is near come; that we shall convince the
whole American world that we are not slack and indolent,
nor in the least degree unworthy, of being registered as a
genuine sister province; fully persuaded, that RESOLU-
TION AND UNIVERSAL HARMONY, will ever be the
firm bases of UNIVERSAL SUCCESS.[57]

The first tea ship was never able to land its cargo. Then, during
April 1774, two vessels carrying tea made their way to New
York. The Sons of Liberty immediately organized a group of
"Mohawks" "prepared to do their duty." One of the ships was
returned to England without unloading or landing its cargo. On
April 21, while the "Mohawks" were preparing to leave for the
vessel, the crowd boarded the ship, seized the tea, and, "in the
manner of the redskins of Boston," dumped it into the harbor.
The captain barely escaped with his life. Escorted by a sloop
commandeered by the Sons of Liberty, the ship was put to sea—
tealess.[58]

Paul Revere had written to John Lamb from Boston, informing him that he had news of the New York tea ship nearing port,
and that "by the next post, I expect to hear a good account of it."
His expectations were fully realized. After the tea party in New
York harbor, Lamb wrote: "We are in a perfect jubilee. Not a
Tory in the whole community can find the least fault with our
proceedings. . . . The spirit of the people throughout the country
is to be described by no terms in my power."[59]

Lamb was either naive or overoptimistic. The merchants and
conservatives in general were in anything but a "perfect jubilee." On the contrary, they were furious over the popularity of
the Sons of Liberty, over the growing influence of the mechanics
in affairs which the upper classes felt were not their concern, and,
of course, over their own failure to steer the resistance to the Tea
Act into "safe and sane channels."[60] Five days after the departure of the tea ships, a merchant writing in the conservative *Rivington's Gazetteer* denounced the Sons of Liberty and expressed
outrage that "cobblers and tailors" should take "upon their everlasting and unmeasurable shoulders, the power of directing the
loyal and sensible inhabitants of the city."[61] The mechanics did

not take such slurs lightly. One of them, who described himself as a Liberty Boy "with his Liberty cap on," accused the writer of having lost his head, and charged him with voicing the opinions of aristocrats both in England and the colonies, whose viewpoint could be summed as follows:

> That the voice of the people, is the voice of the mob, and the voice of the devil.
>
> That the people have no right to expect their constituents to consult, or be influenced by their inclinations.
>
> That the asserters of constitutional freedom, are disrespectful to the Governor.
>
> That the late proceedings in this and the neighboring colonies, for the preservation of their rights, were unjustifiable on constitutional principles; and that the persons most active in those important transactions, were actuated by rebellious principles, and deserved blame, rather than the thanks of their country.[62]

Even as the Tea Act was being nullified in New York City, a new confrontation was shaping up between the merchants and the mechanics — between the conservatives and the Sons of Liberty.

Charleston's "tea party" was late in coming and, in a sense, was an effort by the Sons of Liberty to atone for the "shame" that the consignments of East India Company tea had not been landed anywhere but "*here.*"[63] To be sure, they had mobilized to prevent the landing of the tea when the first ship arrived carrying 257 chests. At a meeting on December 20, 1773, the mechanics and planters joined together to overcome the opposition of the merchants, who wanted to accept the tea, and a resolution was adopted to prevent the tea from being landed. The resolution was prepared by the mechanics, who urged the planters to support their position and to abandon their original stand, which had condemned the Tea Act but was silent about the landing of the tea.

While the debates were going on, the vessel remained in the harbor. After it had been there for twenty days, the collector was empowered to seize the cargo and store it for nonpayment of customs. With the aid of the sheriff and his men, the tea was landed and placed in the Exchange. Thus, Charleston, the last city to rescind the nonimportation agreement, was the first in which the hated tea was landed.[64]

Charleston's Sons of Liberty were called to account. "It was an evil hour for America," the New York Sons of Liberty wrote. South Carolina's receiving the tea, it claimed, would "delay the repeal of the Revenue Act."[65] Goaded by the criticism of their brothers in the North, the Sons of Liberty redoubled its efforts to prevent further landing of tea. In November 1774, when another cargo of tea arrived, the chests were thrown into the Cooper River while crowds cheered from the wharves.[66] The reputation of Charleston's mechanics had been redeemed.

Throughout the colonies, the Sons of Liberty were so effective in preventing the landing of tea that no tea was even smuggled in, and the Liberty Boys boasted that "there was no longer need of the 'tide-waiters, pimps or informers' of the customhouse."[67] Indeed, so effective was the vigilance of the Sons of Liberty, and so complete the cooperation of the Daughters of Liberty, who pledged "never to drink another cup," that tea disappeared from the colonies. "You may ride days, nay weeks," a traveler observed, "and never get a drop."[68] John C. Miller comments: "Coffee drinking became patriotic in the colonies and Americans were weaned from the teacup to the coffee cup, where, for the most part, their devotion still rests."[69]

7_ The Rise of the Mechanics

Colonial opposition to the Tea Act enraged the British government. The focus of this ire was Boston, the "Metropolis of Sedition." In March 1774, a law was passed closing the port of Boston until such time as compensation was paid to the East India Company for tea destroyed during the Tea Party on December 16, 1773. In May, Parliament, acting on the initiative of Prime Minister Lord North, changed the charter of Massachusetts so as to give the Crown the exclusive right to appoint the provincial council; to prevent the calling of town meetings unless approved by the governor; to allow sheriffs to select jurors; and, if "fair courts" were not available in the colony, to hold trials in England. Finally, British troops were returned to occupy Boston.

The result of this action was that soldiers, magistrates, and customs house officers who acted against the people could not be tried by "juries [made up] of Sons of Liberty."[1] It also meant that leading Liberty Boys could be sent to England for trial. After the bitter struggle to remove the troops, they were to be again imposed on the people. Small wonder that these measures were known as the "Intolerable Acts."

By making an example of Boston and Massachusetts, the Crown hoped that the lesson would be clear to all resisting colonies. It seemed to many in England that the government appeared determined to goad Americans into rebellion.

Since Boston was wholly dependent on trade, the closing of the port until "full satisfaction" was given to the East India Com-

pany for its losses meant that the city's principal source of live-
lihood was abruptly cut off. In effect, Boston was blockaded. The
result was that by the end of May, some fifteen thousand people
were, according to one estimate, "poverty struck" and on the
verge of starvation. A pamphlet signed "A Bostonian" described the situation facing the workers of Boston in graphic
terms:

> The people here are almost universally laborers or artificers
> of this or the other denomination, who, by this act which
> has stopped the course of trade, are totally deprived of the
> only means of their subsistence. This is the case of our ship
> builders, ship joiners, mast makers, riggers, caulkers, rope
> and sail makers; whose occupations once gave them and
> their dependents a comfortable maintenance. This is the
> case of our house carpenters and masons, who have now
> little to do, either in the way of building or repairing houses,
> as timber, boards, shingles, brick and lime are not permit-
> ted to be brought into the town in any vessel whatever from
> any part of the province or elsewhere. This is the case of our
> distillers and sugar boilers; who are at once incapacitated
> for carrying on that business which was their support, as
> neither molasses nor sugar are suffered to come into Boston
> Harbor. This is the case with our coopers; who, if they could
> procure staves and hoops could make little or no use of
> them, as the work of trimming imported casks and making
> others for exportation, has at present, an unhappy period
> put to it. This is the case also of our truckmen, porters, and
> a numerous train of day laborers, who will now be necessi-
> tated to become idlers, and must suffer hunger and be
> clothed in rags.[2]

Under these circumstances, the city made an urgent appeal for
help, which was forthcoming in the form of food, clothing, and
money from American, Canadian, West Indian, and even British
sources.[3] Typifying the solidarity felt by the mechanics and laborers in other cities was a resolution introduced by Alexander
McDougall, on behalf of the New York mechanics, at a public
meeting in that city. It urged:

> That a subscription should be immediately set on foot for the relief of such poor inhabitants of *Boston* as are, or may be deprived of the means of subsistence, by the operation of the Act of Parliament for stopping up the port of *Boston*. The money which shall arise from such subscriptions to be laid out as the city Committee of Correspondence shall think will best answer the end proposed.[4]

To receive and distribute these gifts, it was necessary to establish a coordinating agency. In September 1774, therefore, a Donations Committee was organized in Boston with about 80 percent of its personnel drawn from the Sons of Liberty and "mostly mechanics."[5] The committee went into action at once. It announced its intention to create work by repairing public streets, constructing a brickyard, and distributing wood to carpenters, flax to spinners, and leather to shoemakers.[6]

Those who applied to the committee for relief were mainly "mechanics and laborers" whose meager resources were insufficient to sustain them through months of unemployment. Aware of the economic distress of these workingmen, the British authorities tried to win them over by hiring them to build barracks for the four regiments which had arrived in Boston in August 1774 and were encamped on the Commons. Even though most Boston workers were unemployed, few accepted such work, and those who did did so out of ignorance. As soon as they realized what they were doing, they promptly laid down their tools. They proved so "mulish" by firmly refusing to return to work that General Gage wrote to Lord Dartmouth, Secretary of State in England: "I was premature in telling your Lordship that Boston artificers wou'd work for us. This refusal of all assistance has thrown us into difficulties."[7]

Gage was obliged to send to New York and Nova Scotia for carpenters and bricklayers. When two New York mechanics agreed to do carpentering work for Gage, the Sons of Liberty visited them, and, after dissuading them, issued a stern warning: "Should any miscreant be found amongst us, who will aid the enemies of this country to subvert her liberties, he must not be surprised if that vengeance overtakes him, which is the reward justly due to parricides." On September 24, 1774, the mechanics of New York met and voted thanks to those among them who had refused to give aid to General Gage.[8] Thus, New York workers "fully cooperated with the striking Bostonians."[9]

Gage, therefore, had to depend primarily on Nova Scotia. Governor Francis Legg in Halifax was eager to help. As he explained to Lord Dartmouth:

> The disorders in the colonies have arisen to the greatest height, and require coercive measures; I am in hopes this single example, made of the town of Boston, will be a means to convince the Americans that it is their interest as well as duty to be amenable to the laws of Great Britain.[10]

Fifty carpenters and bricklayers were sent from Nova Scotia to Boston, and a few additional mechanics came from New Hampshire. But only a few. The Sons of Liberty in Rochester, New Hampshire, found Nicholas Austin guilty of acting as labor contractor for the British army in Boston. He was made to pray for forgiveness on his knees and to pledge that in the future he would never act "contrary to the constitution of the country."[11]

As soon as news of the Port Act reached Boston, the Boston Committee of Correspondence—a Sons of Liberty organization—began immediately to press for a merchants' agreement to countermand their orders for full imports. This, it was felt, would serve as a stimulus to other colonies to join in an intercolonial agreement to suspend trade with England and would quickly force Parliament to reopen the port. But, as in the past, the merchants resisted. Some proposed raising funds to pay for the tea, thereby freeing Bostonians from the commercial blockade. Others were willing to consider nonimportation if the other colonies first agreed to do so. The Committee of Correspondence thereupon developed a strategy to force the merchants to cease their imports. Drawing up a "Solemn League and Covenant respecting the disuse of British Manufactures," they proposed suspension of *all* commercial intercourse with Great Britain as the only alternative to "the horrors of slavery" or "the carnage and desolation of a civil war." In short, nonconsumption would be substituted for nonimportation. By eliminating themselves as consumers of British imports, the signers would compel merchants to cease their imports.

All adults of both sexes were urged to sign the "Solemn League and Covenant" by August 31, 1774, and the Sons of Liberty posted notices informing the public that a successful boycott of British goods instituted by that date would prove to be "the salvation of North America."[12] Although the merchants still balked, insisting instead on paying for the tea, the Boston town meeting endorsed the plan with only one dissenting vote. The Committee of Correspondence was empowered to write to the other colonies, urging them to enter "into a Non-Consumption Agreement."[13] In the end, despite continuing grumbling, the merchants had to accept the new tactic of resistance initiated by the Sons of Liberty. The Liberty Boys were confident that, once this plan was adopted by all thirteen colonies, it would become a powerful weapon against the Intolerable Acts.

Although this vision finally did become a reality, it did not come easily, despite the storm of protest that rose from one end of the colonies to the other over the measures taken against Boston. Even in Boston, there was no certainty that the merchants would not sabotage nonintercourse. In describing the situation in that city to the absent Sam Adams, Joseph Warren wrote on June 15, 1774: "If the *timidity* of some and the *treachery* of others in this town does not ruin us, I think we shall be saved." Not only was he apprehensive about Boston, but he also feared what was happening in New York. Still, there was some hope amidst the gloom: "I fear New York will not assist us with a very good grace," he wrote, "but she may be ashamed to desert us: at least, if her MERCHANTS offer to sell us, her MECHANICS will forbid the auction."[14]

When Warren referred to "mechanics," he meant the Sons of Liberty, for by the summer of 1774, the two terms had become synonymous, and the Liberty Boys openly referred to themselves as "the mechanics."

On May 12, 1774, New York learned of the Boston Port Bill, the first of the Intolerable Acts. Two days later, Isaac Sears proposed to the merchants that a general meeting of the trade be called on May 16 to "deliberate on the expediency of a non-importation agreement . . .[and] . . . also to determine on a nomination

of a committee of correspondence, to bring about a congress" of
delegates from all colonies to achieve a unified nonimportation
program. [15] The next day, the Sons of Liberty's program was ex-
panded to include nonexportation as well. Writing to Boston on
May 15, Sears and McDougall explained that they had already
felt the "pulse of the inhabitants upon some means to extricate
you out of your distress," and had found the way to defend American rights:

> A great number of our citizens wish our port to be in the
> same state as yours. And as the ministry have put it out of
> your power, to continue your trade with Great Britain, we
> have stimulated the merchants to appoint a meeting tomor-
> row evening at 7 o'clock, to agree upon a general nonimpor-
> tation, and nonexportation agreement of goods, to and
> from Great Britain, until the American grievances are re-
> dressed, under such regulations as may be agreed upon by
> committees from the provinicial towns of the continent, to
> meet in a general congress to be called here for that purpose.

The Liberty Boys suggested that Boston approach all the
towns north of New Haven, and they promised that New York
would take the responsibility of writing to New Haven, Philadelphia, Charleston, and other towns south of New England. In
this way, a congress could be speedily convened. [16]

McDougall had notices posted in the Merchants' Coffee Exchange outlining the above proposal, urging its adoption by the
merchants and assuring the suspicious businessmen that the
Sons of Liberty would not seek to dominate the proceedings.
This move may have allayed the conservatives' fears somewhat,
for at the meeting, the Liberty Boys' suggestion for a committee
of correspondence with the other colonies on steps to support
Boston was adopted by a large majority. When the question of
the size and composition of the committee came up, however, a
split occurred between the Sons of Liberty and the conservatives. The Liberty Boys favored a small committee of between
fifteen and twenty-one members, while the conservatives, fearing that the mechanics' leaders in the Sons of Liberty might dominate a small body, opted for a fifty-man committee, the mem-

bers of which were to be approved later by the people. The merchants not only put across their fifty-man committee, but also packed it with their leaders and henchmen.[17]

The Sons of Liberty then met separately and nominated their own committee of twenty-five mechanics. Their names would be put before the public the following day, and the people would have the opportunity to determine which of the two committees should represent New Yorkers.[18]

The meeting was announced for May 19—at "a most inconvenient hour for mechanics and laborers," notes one historian, "and hence the best time for shrewdly calculating merchants who were playing the political game for all it was worth."[19] Despite this maneuvering, a large number of workingmen attended the meeting. Sears, pointing out that these men could lose a whole day's work if the meeting did not proceed quickly, urged swift action on the issues that had brought the people together. This suggestion was ignored, and the proceedings dragged on interminably, with the result that many of the mechanics and laborers had to leave before any decisions could be reached. With the meeting under their control, the conservatives were able to shout down any Sons of Liberty proposal. When Sears started to read letters he had received from Boston in which nonintercourse was recommended for New York, he was silenced by loud jeers. Likewise, when he suggested that the nominees for the committee of correspondence be selected by a city poll, he was again shouted down. The conservatives finally endorsed the Committee of Fifty. However, Frances Lewis, one of the leaders of the Sons of Liberty, was added to the committee as a gesture to the Liberty Boys, and the name changed to the Committee of Fifty-One. "Most if not all" of the Committee of Fifty-One were merchants and lawyers.[20] In a letter to Lord Dartmouth in England, Colden reported happily that it was made up of "the most prudent and considerate people of the place." Some of its members, he wrote, had been induced to suspend their business activities so that the committee would not be dominated by "many . . . of the lower rank, and all the warmest zealots of those called the Sons of Liberty."[21]

In a famous letter of May 20, 1774, the young conservative Gouverneur Morris described the public meeting at which the list of fifty nominees was presented to the general populace for approval. "I stood on the balcony," Morris wrote, "and on my right were ranged all the people of property, with some few poor dependents, and on the other all the tradesmen, etc., who thought it worth while to leave their daily labour for the good of the country." Morris explained how he interpreted the meaning of the Sons of Liberty and their "mechanic" party:

> These sheep, simple as they are, cannot be pulled as heretofore. In short, there is no ruling them; and now, to leave the metaphor, the heads of the mobility grow dangerous to the gentry; and how to keep them down is the question. While they correspond with other colonies, call and dismiss popular assemblies, make resolves to bind the conscience of the rest of mankind, bully poor printers, and exert with full force all the other tribunal powers, it is impossible to curb them.

Morris blamed the aristocrats for the rise of the mechanics. They had talked so often and so long about constitutional principles and the rights of man, he maintained, that it was inevitable that the people would become politically educated. Although the aristocrats were still in control, the future was uncertain: "The mob begin to think and to reason. Poor reptiles: It is with them a vernal morning, they are struggling to cast off their winter's slough, they bask in the sunshine, and ere noon they will bite, depend on it. The gentry begin to fear this."

Morris's only answer to the problem was immediate reconciliation with the mother country, through which the popular leaders would be deprived of opportunities to arouse and lead the common people down the democratic road: "I see, and I see it with fear and trembling, that if the disputes with Great Britain continue, we shall be under the worst of all possible dominions; we shall be under the domination of a riotous mob."

Morris believed that the one issue between the "people of property" and the "mob" was domestic: "they fairly contended about the future forms of government, whether it should be founded upon aristocratic or democratic principles."[22] He was referring to the fact that the Sons of Liberty "claimed equal rights for the classes hitherto excluded from voting." This was a logical extension of the campaign the New York Liberty Boys had waged since 1769 for the abolition of *viva voce* voting and for the use of ballots instead to make "the suffrage of the people for places of trust . . . conducive to the preservation of liberty." [23]

Gouverneur Morris's reflections were being discussed by other conservatives in New York. In addition to their alarm at the rise of the mechanics, they were concerned that the Sons of Liberty's proposal to cut off all trade with Britain threatened their fortunes. They were determined to dominate whatever resistance was decided upon in answer to the Intolerable Acts. So far as they were concerned, Boston could fend for itself; the city by its radicalism had brought its plight upon itself. However, a general congress might be a good idea, for the endless debating at such a gathering would provide innumerable opportunities for delay, with the likelihood that the congress would adjourn without reaching any decision. [24] In any event, the mechanics must not be allowed to play any further role in the resistance movement. The conservatives were so frightened by the rise of the mechanics that when effigies of British Prime Minister Lord North and two of his henchmen were carried through the town by the mechanics and burned on the Commons, the merchants circulated a petition to ban effigies in New York. This proposal brought the response from the Sons of Liberty that "the true design of it was to discourage and prevent any effectual opposition to the ministerial measures now vigorously pursued with an openly avowed intention of reducing America to slavery." All freemen were urged to ignore the proposal to ban effigies. [25]

Meeting on May 20, the mechanics decided that they "would try the Committee of 51 and if they misbehaved, they would be removed." Three days later, the Committee of Fifty-One met, and a delegation "from the body of the mechanics," headed by John Lamb, called for radical action in support of Boston. [26] The conservatives brushed the suggestion aside. Instead, they adopted a resolution stating that, while New York sympathized with the Bay City, she would act only in concert with other colonies. McDougall could only tell Paul Revere, who was waiting to carry New York's reply to Boston, that it would be wise if New York's Committee of Correspondence called immediately for a

Continental Congress. Since the conservatives who dominated the Committee of Fifty-One had said they would act if the other colonies moved, this call would put an end to their stalling tactics.[27]

The suggestion made sense to the Bostonians, and together the Liberty Boys and Sam Adams agreed on a date in early September. The idea was incorporated into the call for a Continental Congress by the Massachusetts House of Representatives on June 17. Three days later, a Philadelphia mass meeting approved the idea of a congress and recommended that a method be devised for the selection of delegates.[28]

Thus, it is clear that the idea of a Continental Congress originated with the leaders of the New York Sons of Liberty—Sears, Lamb, and McDougall—and was acted upon by the Liberty Boys of Boston. There is simply no support for Carl Becker's view that the idea came from the conservatives.[29] In fact, the call for the Congress and its endorsement in Philadelphia caught the New York conservatives completely by surprise. The Sons of Liberty did not give them a chance to recover. They forced the Committee of Fifty-One to go on record for a Continental Congress and to agree to send delegates from New York "at the time and place which shall be agreed upon by the other colonies." Colden informed the Earl of Dartmouth on July 6 that the "measure was so strenuously pushed" by the Sons of Liberty "that it was carried in the Committee of 51."[30]

When it came to the nomination of delegates to attend the first Continental Congress, the conservatives made sure to have only their own men chosen. The Committee of Mechanics complained that "the committee of merchants did refuse the mechanics a representation on their body, or to consult with their committee, or offer the names of the persons nominated to them for their concurrence."[31]

The Committee of Mechanics did more than complain; they called a public meeting for July 16, 1774. There, with full popular support, they nominated their own mechanics' ticket for delegates to the Continental Congress and obtained similar support for the platform on which the mechanics would run. The heart of the mechanics' program was contained in the following resolutions:

That it is the opinion of this meeting, that if the principal colonies on the continent shall come into a joint resolution to stop all importations from, and exportation to Great Britain, till the Act of Parliament for the blocking up of the harbour of Boston be repealed, the same will prove the salvation of North America and her liberties; and that, on the other hand, if they continue their exports and imports, there is great reason to fear that fraud, power, and the most odious oppression, will rise triumphant over right, justice, social happiness and freedom: Therefore,

Resolved, . . . That the deputies who shall represent this colony in the Congress of American deputies, to be held at Philadelphia, the first of September next, are hereby instructed, empowered, and directed to engage with a majority of the principal colonies, to agree for this city upon a non-importation from Great Britain, of all goods, wares and merchandises, until the Act for blocking the harbour of Boston be repealed, and American grievances be redressed; and also to agree to all such other measures as the Congress shall in their wisdom judge advancive of the great objects, and general security of the rights and privileges of America.

Resolved, . . . That the meeting will abide by, obey, and observe all such resolutions, determinations and measures, which the Congress aforesaid shall come into, and direct or recommend to be done, for obtaining and securing the important ends mentioned in the foregoing resolutions. And that an engagement to this effect be immediately entered into and sent to the Congress, to evince to them our readiness and determination to cooperate with our sister colonies for the relief of our distressed brethren at Boston, as well as for the security of our common rights and privileges.[32]

The enthusiastic popular support for the mechanics' ticket and platform caused the merchants to stop and reflect. Meetings were held between representatives of the Committee of Fifty-One and the Committee of Mechanics, and a plan was worked out under which the Committee of Mechanics would withdraw its own list of candidates in return for a pledge from the merchants' nominees to support the mechanics' program and press for non-intercourse at the forthcoming Congress.[33]

The withdrawal of the Committee of Mechanics' ticket is not surprising. The mechanics, after all, wanted to get their program adopted as that of New York City, and its endorsement by the Committee of Fifty-One was a great victory. It also signified that the rise of the mechanics was indeed a reality which the conservatives might ridicule but could not ignore. Again, it must be remembered that if the mechanics found it difficult to attend public meetings for any length of time because of the need to continue at their work, they certainly could not afford to take the time to serve as delegates at a congress in Philadelphia since the representatives were not paid for their time and expense.

After the slate of the Committee of Fifty-One was elected, the Committee of Mechanics wrote to the Boston Committee of Correspondence. It described the election as a victory for the Sons of Liberty, since New York's delegation to the Continental Congress was pledged to agree to any action adopted at Philadelphia. They added: "We now seem to be convinced of the honest intentions of each other's hearts; our divisions have subsided, and we are cemented in one firm body, and expect that the province of New York will be second to none, in this noble, generous and manly struggle for American liberty."[34]

This euphoria, however, did not blind the Sons of Liberty to the continual need for vigilance. When General Gage asked for supplies for the troops in Boston, the merchants were all too ready to do business with him. Sears, Lamb, and McDougall immediately demanded that no help be given the occupying army, and they emphasized their point with a threat that any merchant who leased his ship to the military deserved "the contempt and indignation of every generous mind."[35] Under the sponsorship of the Committee of Mechanics, mass meetings were held to protest the exportation of supplies for the use of the British garrison at Boston. The conservatives fumed at the mechanics' arrogance in trying to tell the merchants with whom they could do business, but in the end, as we have seen, Gage had to go to Nova Scotia to get supplies for the troops.[36]

When the Boston Committee of Correspondence sent Paul Revere to Philadelphia to ask for that city's support in opposing

"Parliamentary tyranny," conservative merchants dominated the meeting hastily called at the City Tavern to hear Boston's plea. As in 1765 and 1768, the merchants recommended nothing radical; rather, they argued, attempts should be made at reconciliation with England, through petitions drawn up at an intercolonial congress, and nonintercourse should be undertaken only as a very last resort. They insisted that acting alone before all the colonies had agreed would force the Philadelphia merchants to "risk their whole property, while the others were totally exempted from any risk."[37] In response the mechanics, who favored immediate adoption of nonintercourse, circulated a broadside on June 8, 1774, calling for a meeting of the artisan community the following day at the State House.[38]

The twelve hundred mechanics who met on June 9 listened to the reading of a letter from New York's mechanics, urging them to resist the blockade of Boston by halting all trade with the mother country. The meeting then appointed executive and corresponding committees, and instructed them to cooperate with the "patriotic merchants" in "measures that will effectually tend to unite us in the common cause of our country."[39] The "patriotic merchants" were the "wet goods" or lesser merchants, who had favored nonimportation in the earlier resistance movements and had agreed to ally themselves with the mechanics against the "do-nothing" policies of the conservative merchants. What the mechanics soon learned in 1774 was that the "patriotic merchants" were in favor of a moderate course, holding off nonintercourse until an intercolonial congress endorsed it.

The meeting of the mechanics frightened the conservative merchants, who now realized that they could not afford to sit on the sidelines and let events take their course. They therefore proposed a meeting for June 18 of all Philadelphia's inhabitants. They even sent delegates to the mechanics, indicating that at the meeting "resolves big with uncommon wisdom and spirit" would be proposed, and promising the appointment of "one grand joint committee to represent the whole inhabitants of this city and country."[40] At the same time, they entered into an alliance with the moderate merchants to prevent the meeting from endorsing the mechanics' program for immediate nonintercourse and to keep the mechanics from having any voice in the committee to implement whatever resolutions were adopted. Nevertheless, as Charles S. Olton observes, the fact that merchants "found it necessary to court mechanics" is convincing testimony that the city's artisan community "was achieving its most important political goal in the early Revolution—inclusion in the governing councils of the Province." In short, just as in Boston, Charleston, and New York, the mechanics of Philadelphia were "becoming a political power." [41]

Against a conservative-moderate merchant alliance, however, the "political power" of the mechanics was able to accomplish little. The merchants' coalition at the June 18 meeting produced a watered-down resolution which expressed sympathy for Boston and opposition to the Port Bill, but left the nonintercourse question to the discretion of an intercolonial congress. While the mechanics were not able to alter the policies agreed upon in advance, they did force an alteration in the plan to appoint a standing committee that would exclude mechanics. Fearing that this alteration would only goad the mechanics into forming their own separate committee, the conservative-moderate coalition agreed to add the names of seven mechanics to the slate, after having removed the names of the two most offensive to them. This concession meant only a partial victory for the mechanics, for they had been led to believe that the entire committee appointed at their June 9 meeting would serve on the standing committee. In the end, only half of this group was appointed, and they were outvoted in the standing committee by four to one. [42]

Nevertheless, the mechanics on the standing committee did put up a fight for a radical policy. They complained that the committee's letter to the people of Boston was "too cold" and that the committee had hesitated concerning an immediate nonimportation and nonexportation agreement. The merchants ignored these complaints. [43]

On July 11, the frustrated mechanics met for a second time in a renewed effort to put Philadelphia on the side of nonintercourse. They warned their fellow citizens that if a large commercial metropolis like Philadelphia held out, the plan would be defeated, for other cities would soon abandon it. They urged Philadelphians to "come to some agreement themselves or *expressly* leave it to be framed for them by Congress." They therefore called for another general meeting of inhabitants to instruct the Pennsylvania delegates to the Continental Congress to favor nonintercourse. They specified, however, that they did not wish to "enter into any controversy" with the existing standing committee. They pointed out that nothing this committee had done since its creation gave any cause for confidence that they would instruct their delegates to stand firm for nonintercourse: "Let us not send our deputies to the congress with their hands tied behind their backs, or with their fingers in their mouths."[44]

Throughout the summer of 1774, Philadelphia's mechanics pressed repeatedly for a new public meeting. They pointed out that the second and third Intolerable Acts presented a new situation that had not existed when the June 18 meeting was held and that it was likely that greater sentiment for nonintercourse would make itself felt at a new meeting. Still there was no action. Then, in late August, it was reported that a large quantity of English merchandise was on its way to Philadelphia, shipped by English manufacturers who hoped to sell their goods before the Continental Congress adopted any nonintercourse policy. When the June 18 standing committee hesitated to take a stand on the issue over the objections of the mechanics members, "An Artisan" published a letter in the *Pennsylvania Gazette* citing this hesitation as proof of the need for a new public meeting which would appoint "a new committee to watch over the public welfare, and to advise what ought to be done in every emergency which may happen."[45]

The rumored importation never materialized, nor was a new public meeting called before the Continental Congress convened.[46] Nonetheless, the mechanics continued their agitation for a more radical program right up to the very eve of the Congress, and even during the sessions themselves. With singleminded determination, they insisted on "the absolute necessity of withholding our trade from England, till our grievances are redressed."[47]

Soon after news of the Port Bill reached Charleston, the Sons of Liberty of that Southern city were ready with resolutions calling for nonintercourse with Britain. Christopher Gadsden informed the Boston Committee of Correspondence that, in view of the caution of both merchants and planters, it was decided to wait a few weeks before submitting the program to the public for approval. The fact, too, that Charleston had been left "holding the bag" on nonimportation in 1770 as one after another of the Northern cities abandoned the Association, made it more difficult to put over a radical program at this stage.[48]

A meeting was arranged for July 6, 1774, "to consider . . . such steps as are necessary to be pursued, in union with all the inhabitants of our sister colonies, on this continent . . . in order to avert the dangers impending . . . [because of] the late hostile acts of Parliament against Boston." The existing Committee of Correspondence, composed of thirteen mechanics, thirteen merchants, and thirteen planters supposedly representing the rural areas, sent notices of the meeting to every region of the province. The meeting, attended by 104 delegates, was marked by a heated debate between spokesmen for the merchants and the mechanics. The merchant group opposed immediate adoption of commercial nonintercourse, insisting that no action should be taken until all the other colonies agreed to a similar stand. Although the mechanics called these nothing but delaying tactics and urged the immediate adoption of nonintercourse, they were defeated by the planter-merchant coalition.

The mechanics thereupon fought for the sending of delegates to a colonial congress, and on this point, since they were joined by the planters, they were victorious. Then the mechanics advocated granting the delegates discretionary power to vote for an immediate plan of nonintercourse against Britain. Again they won with the support of the planters, a victory which they felt "was gaining a grand point."[49]

There still remained the selection of the delegation. Three tickets were put in the field—one each by the merchants, planters, and mechanics. Christopher Gadsden and Thomas Lynch, leaders of Charleston's Sons of Liberty, headed the mechanics' slate. The mechanics' platform called for immediate nonintercourse and the requirement that delegates make this demand in Philadelphia. The planters' platform was for nonintercourse to be instituted after it was agreed upon at Philadelphia and for the delegates then to support it. The merchants' platform urged a policy of petitions to Parliament and instructed its delegates to vote against nonintercourse at the Continental Congress.

While the merchants marched with their clerks in a body to the polls, the mechanics ran through the town mobilizing their supporters. The result of the election was a victory for the mechanics in Charleston, while the planters won in the country. Although the planters held a majority of the seats on the delegation, Christopher Gadsden, who was elected on the mechanics' ticket, was to play an important role in Philadelphia in advancing the Charleston mechanics' radical program. Silas Deane, representative to the Continental Congress from Connecticut, wrote:

> Mr. Gadsden leaves all New England Sons of Liberty far behind. He is for taking up his firelock and marching direct to Boston; nay, he affirmed this morning, that were his wife and all his children in Boston, and they were to perish by the sword, it would not alter his sentiment or proceeding for American liberty.[50]

There was considerable debate in the Continental Congress as conservatives like James Duane of New York and Joseph Galloway of Pennsylvania resisted the radical program of men like Sam Adams, Christopher Gadsden, and Patrick Henry, who favored complete nonintercourse, a denial of parliamentary authority, and the basing of colonial rights on the "law of nature." Reports reaching the Congress at Philadelphia, indicating that the British had every intention of relying on the military to put the Intolerable Acts into effect, helped move vacillating delegates over to the radical side.

On September 16, 1774, Paul Revere rode into the Quaker City with the Suffolk Resolves, which the Congress immediately adopted. These affirmed the unconstitutionality of Parliament's acts, the colonists' right to ignore them, and the necessity of nonimportation and nonexportation. On October 20, the Congress approved a nonimportation agreement and adopted the "Association." According to the agreement, after December 1, 1774, goods from Great Britain and the West Indies and East India tea would be excluded. If this economic pressure did not bring about a redress of grievances by September 10, 1775, the colonies would impose export penalties as well.

To insure that the provisions were carried out, the agreement called for committees in every town and county, to be elected by all qualified voters, "whose business it shall be attentively to observe the conduct of all persons touching the Association." Anyone found guilty of breaking the agreement would be condemned as an enemy of the people with whom no one should do business. It was left up to the respective committees and conventions to determine whether further punitive action would be necessary.

Having adopted the Association, Congress then drew up two lengthy memorials—one to the people of Great Britain, and the other to the people of America—explaining the reasons for their action. A few days later, they adopted similar addresses to the people of Quebec and to the king. Their work completed, the Congress adjourned with the recommendation that a second Congress assemble the following May if their grievances had not been redressed by then.[51]

The Association was not all that the mechanics had hoped for, since there was to be a delay of one year until nonintercourse went fully into effect. But the substance of their program had been realized, and nonimportation would start shortly. Moreover, unlike the case with the nonimportation agreements of 1756 and 1769, the implementation of this one would not be left to the merchants. It was now the work of the Congress, which imposed it on the merchants regardless of their wishes. Previously, the committees of resistance had been almost exclusively in the control of the merchants. The mechanics, laborers, and seamen had had to prod them into action and often had taken the implementation into their own hands when the established organizations either failed or refused to function. In Boston, during the resistance to the Townshend program, the mechanics had simply taken over the merchants' committee to maintain nonimportation. Now, however, the merchants would not automatically dominate the established implementing bodies. In fact, in several cities, the mechanics would have a prominent voice in enforcing the authority of the Continental Congress. This may not have been new in Boston and Charleston, but it had not happened before in either New York or Philadelphia.

An important result of the Continental Congress in New York was that the Committee of Fifty-One was dissolved by an agreement between itself and the Committee of Mechanics, and a new

Committee of Inspection was created to carry out the Association's policy. The Committee of Fifty-One's decision to dissolve itself was made, according to Colden, "with a view to protect the city from the ravages of the mob. . . . That if they did not, the most dangerous men among us would take the lead; and under the pretence of executing the dictates of the Congress would immediately draw the city into the most perilous situation."[52] In any case, sixty members of the Committee of Inspection were chosen from the two lists of one hundred names each separately proposed by the Committee of Fifty-One and the Committee of Mechanics.

At the election held on November 22, 1774, the ticket jointly nominated by the "Fifty-One" and the Mechanics was elected without a dissenting vote. On this new Committee of Sixty, the mechanics had an important, if not dominant, representation. There were twenty-nine holdovers from the old committee, and most of those removed eventually became Loyalists. For the first time, mechanics had an important voice in the extralegal machinery of the resistance movement in New York. Sears, Lamb, and McDougall had achieved a large measure of the program they had set out for the people when the news of the Tea Act reached the city.[53]

In Philadelphia, too, the mechanics emerged as a new force in the extralegal machinery of the resistance movement. Here, too, a new committee, vested with the authority to enforce the policy of the Continental Congress, was elected. The successful ticket for city committeemen in the November 1774 elections contained twelve mechanics, some of whom had been Sons of Liberty since 1765 and others who had joined later. The Committee of Observation and Inspection had a substantial, if not dominant, representation of mechanics.[54] As R. A. Ryerson points out in his excellent study of the resistance movement in Philadelphia:

In 1765 and 1769 middle-aged, wealthy, generally moderate merchants dominated both establishment politics and the committee-led resistance movement. . . . But [Charles] Thomson's coalition of radical young merchants and newly mobilized artisans carefully fostered by every radical strategist, finally broke the wealthy merchants' domination of the city's political life. In June, 1774, three-fourths of the Committee men were merchants, while only one-tenth were mechanics. After November, the merchants held two-thirds of the places and the mechanics over one-fourth. [55]

Thus, while there had been practically no mechanics on the various extralegal committees established in the 1760s to police the nonimportation agreements, in 1774 they made up 33 percent of the membership. [56]

In June, 1774, a radical commentator wrote from Boston:

Those worthy members of society, the tradesmen, we depend on, under God, to form the resolution of the other ranks of citizens, in Philadelphia and New York. They are certainly carrying all before them here. . . . This will insure a non-importation in this province, whether messieurs les marchands, will be graciously pleased to come into it or not. [57]

Events had proven him correct. Now, as the Association got under way, the rise of the mechanics to an important participatory role in the official enforcement machinery guaranteed that nonimportation and resistance to British measures would not be dropped as they had been in 1770.

The mechanics' increased political influence was certainly linked to their hatred of the British measures and their keen interest in nonimportation as a means of fostering the development of home industry; patriotism and economic self-interest coincided. As time went on, however, the mechanics more and more came to resent the wealthy merchants' control of the economic and political life of their towns. By the early 1770s, they were denouncing the pretensions of men of wealth who "have the impudence to assert that mechanics are men of no consequence," and who "make no scruples to say that the mechanics . . . have no right to speak or to think for themselves." They now publicly expressed their resentment against the previous political arrangements whereby "a certain company of leading men" chose a slate of candidates before each election, "without ever permitting the affirmative or negative voice of a mechanic to interfere." They took great pride in "the growing interest and importance of the worthy mechanics" and insisted that they be given a share in the city's elected offices. They identified themselves with the "noble struggle" in which the citizens of London—chiefly mechanics— were engaged during the Wilkes affair.[58]

It will be remembered that Gouverneur Morris blamed the politicization of the mechanics on the aristocrats for having talked so loudly about constitutional principles and the rights of man. What the young conservative did not mention was that this talk also had its effect on another group of workers who were present in large numbers in the colonies, although they played no part in the extralegal machinery of the resistance movement. These were the black slaves. "The Colonists are by the law of nature free born, as indeed all men are, white or black," James Otis had declared in his celebrated pamphlet of 1764 against the "writs of assistance." When John Adams heard these words, he, like Gouverneur Morris, "shuddered at the doctrine he taught" and "the consequences that may be drawn from such premises." John Adams' remarkable wife, Abigail, did not share her husband's fears. On the contrary, she saw more danger in an increase in slave insurrections than in emancipating the blacks. She shared the view of many Americans that there was a fundamental contradiction between the colonists' demand for liberty from British oppression and the existence of slavery. In her famous letter to her husband on September 22, 1774, she wrote: "I wish most sincerely there was not a slave in the province; it always appeared a most iniquitous scheme to me to fight ourselves for what we are daily robbing and plundering from those who have as good a right to freedom as we have."[59]

In the year of the Boston Tea Party, a group of Massachusetts slaves petitioned the General Court for their freedom, making use of the same issue of consistency which Abigail Adams had mentioned in her letter. They pointed to the conflict between the colonies and Great Britain in supporting their request: "We expect great things from men who have made such a noble stand against the designs of their *fellow-men* to enslave them." The petitioners expressed the hope that the legislators would remember their own struggle for liberty when they considered the appeal of the slaves.

In May 1774, while Boston was organizing resistance to the Intolerable Acts, the slaves sent another petition to the Massachusetts legislature, asking for their freedom. This time the tone was much bolder and definitely reflected the Revolutionary ideology of natural rights. The petitioners described themselves as a "great number of blacks of this province who are held in a state of slavery within the bowels of a free and Christian country." Their petition opened dramatically: "That your petitioners apprehend we have in common with all other men a natural right to our freedom without being depriv'd of them by our fellow men as we are a freeborn people and have never forfeited this blessing by any compact or agreement whatever." They pointed out that even if they were enslaved by law, there never was a law "to enslave our children for life when born in a free country." The petition concluded with a plea for gradual emancipation, with the slaves then in bondage to be freed at the age of twenty-one.

Six weeks later, in a followup appeal, the slaves asked not only for their freedom, but also for "some part of the unimproved land, belonging to the province for a settlement, that each of us may sit down quietly under his own fig tree."

Even though the slave petitioners enlisted the support of Sam Adams, their pleas failed to move the legislature. The final vote was to let the matter "now subside."[60]

The February 10, 1774, issue of the *Massachusetts Spy* published the plea of "A Son of Africa." The anonymous black man rejoiced to see "that there is in this and the neighboring provinces such a spirit of liberty," but he noted that "there is a cloud, and has been for many years" that was obscuring the rays of liberty:

> You are taxed without your consent, (I grant that a grievance), and have petitioned for relief, and cannot get any. . . . Are not your hearts also hard, when you hold men in slavery who are entitled to liberty by the law of nature, equal as yourselves? If it be so, pray, sir, pull the beam out of thine own eyes, that you may see clearly to pull the mote out of thy brother's eye; and when the eyes of your understanding are opened, then will you see clearly between your case and Great Britain, and that of the Africans. We all come from

one common Father, and He, by the law of nature, gave everything that was made, equally alike to every man richly to enjoy. If so, is it lawful for one nation to enslave another? The law of nature gives no such toleration.

The questions raised by "A Son of Africa" would still demand an answer as Americans moved toward independence.

8 _The Road to Independence

☐ Through the decisions of the Continental Congress, the American colonies had, for the first time, agreed upon a common plan of action. Its first test lay in the support it would receive from the people. As for the conservatives, they were both disheartened and angered by the decisions reached at Philadelphia not to import certain British goods after December 1, 1774; not to consume tea after March 1, 1775; and not to export to England after September 10, 1775. Their displeasure increased after the elections showed that the mechanics and workingmen were to have a prominent voice in the local committees of enforcement in the key cities. From Massachusetts to Georgia, a chorus of conservative wails arose. The governor of Georgia lamented the fact that in Savannah the "parochial committee are a parcel of the lowest people, chiefly carpenters, shoemakers, blacksmiths, etc." *Rivington's Gazeteer*, the voice of the most conservative elements in New York, warned the people to be careful that they did not exchange what was loosely called British "tyranny and oppression" for a real tyranny and oppression— "subjected to a domination the most abject and slavish, viz., that of the idle, the vicious and profane. . . . These are the men who excite seditions and commotions, nay, would even blow the trumpet of rebellion through the land, so they might in the confusion of the times but divide and share in your property."[1]

A Boston conservative bitterly complained that at public meetings, "the lowest mechanics discuss upon the most important points of government, with the utmost freedom." In Connecticut, Jonathan Trumbull resorted to verse to express his concern:

> Each leather-aproned dunce, grown wise,
> Presents his forward face t'advise,
> And tattered legislators meet,
> From every workshop through the street.
>
> From dunghills deep of blackest hue,
> Your dirt-bred patriots spring to view,
> To wealth and power and honors rise,
> Like new-winged maggots changed to flies.[2]

Anglican clergymen flooded the public with bitter, unrelenting criticism of the Continental Congress. A minister in Charleston told his congregation that the Congress had committed a blasphemy in providing that the people could select their local committees, for it was the law of God "that mechanics and country *clowns* had no right to dispute about politics, or what Kings, Lords, and Commons had done, or might do."[3] Samuel Seabury, a New York Anglican minister, writing under the pseudonym "A West Chester Farmer," urged the people not to obey the Congress, to disregard the local committees elected "by foolish and turbulent men," and to risk any form of reprisals from "mobs of ignorant men" that might result from putting his advice into effect: "No, if I must be enslaved, let it be by a King at least, and not by a parcel of upstart, lawless committeemen. If I must be devoured, let me be devoured by the jaws of a lion, and not gnawed to death by rats and vermin."[4]

The Sons of Liberty struck back. On the day Seabury's pamphlet appeared, it was called "one of the most treacherous, malicious and wicked productions that has yet appeared," and copies were publicly burned.[5] The Charleston minister who attacked "*mechanics* and country *clowns*" was dismissed by his congregation, and he and "all *such* divines" were told "that mechanics and country clowns (infamously so-called), are the real, and absolute masters of Kings, Lords, Commons and Priests."[6]

The Sons of Liberty had more to do, however, than answer conservative attacks. Its main task was to see that the nonimportation agreement was not destroyed by sabotage or violations. One danger was that the merchants who had been elected to the committees of enforcement by the merchants-mechanics coalition — the so-called "moderates" — would play a double game: on the one hand, proclaiming their support for the Association, and on the other, doing everything possible to prevent it from operating. The day after the Committee of Sixty was elected in New York, Son of Liberty Hugh Hughes wrote to John Lamb that he was "apprehensive that they [the merchants] will, thro' the medium of their creatures anticipate their best intentions." As this was their "last game," he warned, the Sons of Liberty could take it for granted that they would play it to the hilt, and extreme vigilance was required to frustrate their game.[7]

At the very first meeting of the committee, James Duane tried to wreck enforcement by proposing that a key feature of the Association be ignored. It proved that goods imported between December 1, 1774, and February 1, 1775, be either reshipped or sold, with the profits used for the benefit of Boston. Duane wanted the goods either destroyed or sold in such a way as to eliminate any profits for the stricken city. McDougall was immediately alarmed, convinced that the New York merchant leader was out "to destroy" the Association. Under his leadership, the mechanics on the committee put up a stiff fight against Duane's proposal and were able to defeat it.[8] The incident demonstrated that the coalition of merchants and mechanics was a fragile one.

On January 30, 1775, the Committee of Sixty formally decreed that all goods imported from Britain were to be returned to their place of shipment. The Sons of Liberty took steps to see that the decree was enforced. A Glasgow vessell was forced out of the harbor to prevent its landing, and the Sons of Liberty stationed a sloop, with armed Liberty Boys aboard, alongside the ship to prevent a secret landing.[9]

On February 16, the *Beulah* arrived, and the harbor pilots were ordered not to touch her. Isaac Sears and an armed crew of twenty, consisting of mechanic members of the Committee of Sixty and sailors, immediately set up guard on a nearby sloop. At that point, Robert and John Murray, two of the wealthiest merchants of the day, [10] came forward as the men to whom the cargo was assigned and petitioned the Committee of Sixty to permit them to land the merchandise. The committee informed the Murrays that they would be penalized if they brought their goods into the city.

To the New York merchants who hated the Association—and these were the majority—the *Beulah* offered an opportunity to break the whole movement. They urged the Murrays to ignore the Committee of Sixty. Alerted, the armed Liberty Boys, under Sears' leadership, had a sloop watching the *Beulah* as it lay off Sandy Hook, when a storm drove them to seek shelter in a cove. The Murrays now had the chance they had been waiting for. Another ship came alongside the *Beulah*, took off a considerable quantity of goods, and concealed it in a warehouse on Staten Island. The next day, the *Beulah* sailed for England, ostensibly with the goods consigned to the Murrays still on board.

Sears, suspicious that the goods had been landed while the Liberty Boys were forced from the scene, made inquiries of seamen in the area and discovered the whereabouts of the merchandise. Faced with the discovery, the Murrays confessed their guilt. The popular outcry was so great that not even their abject apologies and promises of future good behavior could deter the committee's mechanic members from their demand that the Murrays be banished. Nor could their wealth and prominence (their name was given to the present Murray Hill district at Forty-second Street) save them. In desperation, Mrs. Murray wrote a public letter to Sears and McDougall imploring them to intercede on behalf of her husband and brother-in-law. This plea brought the desired results. [11]

The outcome of the *Beulah* affair was a great victory for the Sons of Liberty and the Association in New York. McDougall was confident that "the punishment they [the Murrays] now, and will endure is sufficient to deter any man, however base, from another breach." [12] And so it was. The contemporary press does not reveal any further violations of the Association in New York.

In Charleston, too, the mechanics had to remain vigilant to prevent the Association from being destroyed. When their mercantile and planter counterparts on the Committee of Enforcement voted to allow a Carolina merchant returning from England to land horses intended for his personal use, the mechanics objected. Overruled, they went to the people. The Charleston mechanics threatened to kill the animals if they were landed. An armed guard was then brought in to protect the cargo while it was being landed, but a majority of the men, being Liberty Boys, threw down their arms and refused to obey orders. [13]

A petition from the artisan community to the committee pointed out that the mechanics, "who have the liberty of America much at heart," viewed the original vote as "an infringement of the Association entered into by the General Congress." To avoid further conflict in the community, the petitioners prayed "that there may be a reconsideration of the said matter." It was reconsidered, and this time the mechanics came to the meeting *en masse* to guarantee that the vote went for "the liberty of America." They cheered their spokesman, Christopher Gadsden, the Liberty Boys leader who had been elected to the committee on the mechanics' ticket, when he called for reversal of the original vote. They greeted those who spoke for landing the horses with "opprobrious terms and contempt," and when Edward Rutledge, who had been the chief advocate on the committee for the landing, condemned them as "an unruly mob," he "was received with a clamour." By the narrow vote of 35 to 34, the committee decided not to land the freight. "A general satisfaction was expressed upon this occasion, and the quiet of the community seems perfectly restored," commented the *South Carolina Gazette* on the following day. [14]

The reversal of the decision on the landing of the horses was as decisive for the future of the Association in Charleston as the outcome of the *Beulah* incident in New York. Richard Walsh writes:

> The Association was saved. Had the mechanics lost the issue, trivial as it seems, the consequences would have been disastrous. Lieutenant-Governor Bull noted that "if this question had been carried in the affirmative" the merchants "would have considered it as a recession of the nonimportation article" and immediately sent to England for goods as usual. This example would probably have been followed by New York and the other colonies. [15]

Bull gloomily recorded that a significant feature of the whole episode was the fact that even the more moderate leaders of the Sons of Liberty had to go along with the radical views of the mechanics. The mechanics "have discovered their own strength and importance," he intoned, and would not now be "so easily governed by their former leaders."[16] The truth of this observation was to be soon realized by none other than the idol of the Charleston mechanics, Christopher Gadsden, when he became increasingly more moderate.

In nearby Savannah, the committee to enforce the Association was so effective that it practically assumed control of the government. A conservative merchant wrote dolefully to a friend in England on December 26, 1775: "The Governor here, as well as in other Provinces, is a mere cipher; everything is transacted by the committee composed of barbers, tailors, cordwainers, etc., whose insolence and pertness would raise any Englishman's indignation."[17] It was a perceptive observation, for in Boston, New York, Philadelphia, and Charleston, as well as Savannah, the local committees to enforce the prohibition of all commerce with Britain and the West Indies rapidly replaced the official city government as the real power in local affairs.

Among other provisions of the Articles of Association, it was agreed "that all manufactures of this country be sold at reasonable prices," and that "vendors of goods or merchandise will not take advantage of the scarcity of goods that may be occasioned by this Association, but will sell the same at rates we have been respectfully accustomed to do, for twelve months last past." The local enforcement committees, with their leadership under constant pressure from the mechanics, carried out this provision. They watched "mercenary individuals" who intended "to take advantage of the public distress" by buying up large quantities of goods legally imported or manufactured in the colonies and holding them for a price rise. They published notices warning "such engrossers" to desist from "their mercenary schemes" and to "demand no more than the usual advance upon such goods and merchandise as they have by them." There were few further reports of monopolistic price gouging.[18]

"In the fall of '74 and the winter of '75," Paul Revere later recalled, "I was one of upwards of thirty, chiefly mechanics, who formed ourselves into a committee for the purpose of watching the movements of the British soldiers and gaining every intelligence of the movement of the Tories." [19] Holding regular meetings at the Green Dragon Tavern, this group was able to secure valuable information on the military plans of the British high command in New England. In December 1774, when Gage planned to move some military stores from Portsmouth, news of his intentions leaked out. Revere was sent posthaste to tell the Portsmouth Liberty Boys of the British plan. Forewarned, and with the aid of associates from Newcastle and Rye, they seized the supplies before the British could take them away. In like fashion, Gage's intention to arrest Sam Adams and John Hancock was uncovered by the mechanics' intelligence service. The information was passed on to Warren, who dispatched Revere to Lexington on April 16, 1775, to warn the two men of the impending danger. [20]

In March 1775, the Continental Congress designated units of the Massachusetts militia as "Minutemen" and instructed them to go into action if the British troops in Boston, under General Gage, took the offensive. Among the Minutemen militia of Massachusetts were such blacks as Peter Salem of Framingham, who had been granted his freedom by his master to join the town's company, and Lemuel Haynes, a native of West Hartford, Connecticut, who later served as pastor of white churches in Connecticut and Vermont.

On April 15, 1775, General Gage sent a detachment to Concord to destroy the military supplies gathered by the Sons of Liberty in that village. As seven hundred Red Coats moved toward Lexington on April 18, the famous warning was flashed by Paul Revere. The Minutemen and other militiamen turned out with their weapons and soon were firing the shots "heard 'round the world." Among those at Lexington and Concord on April 19, 1775, were blacks who were previously Minutemen and others who responded to the call for volunteers. They included Peter Salem, Samuel Craft of Newton, Cato Boardman of Cambridge, Cuff Whittemore and Cato Wood of Arlington, Prince Estabrook of West Lexington, and Pomp Blackman of "points unspecified."

Seventy-three British soldiers died and nearly two hundred

were wounded. The Americans suffered forty-nine killed and thirty-nine wounded. "Prince, a Negro" is listed in the Journals of the Provincial Congress of Massachusetts as one of the casualties of the battle.[21]

When the British army again took the offensive, the patriots gathered at Bunker Hill in Boston to forestall the Red Coats. On June 17, 1775, the Battle of Bunker Hill was fought. Here, too, blacks fought with the patriot forces: Barzillai Lew of Chelmsford, a cooper turned fifer, Cuff Whittemore, Pomp Fisk, Titus Colburn, Caesar Dickerson, Cato Tufts, Caesar Weatherbee, Seymour Burr, Grant Cooper, Charleston Ead, Sampson Talbert, Caesar Basom, Salem Poor, and Peter Salem. During the action, Salem Poor of Colonel Frye's regiment won honors for his bravery. On December 5, 1775, fourteen Massachusetts officers called the legislature's attention to Poor's conspicuous courage. Under fire, they pointed out, Poor had "behaved like an experienced officer, as well as an excellent soldier." To set forth particulars of his conduct, they wrote, would be tedious. "We would only beg leave to say in the person of this said Negro centers a brave and gallant soldier." The officers commended him to the Continental Congress, but there is no record of any reward being given to him.

Peter Salem had fought in both the battle of Lexington and Concord and that at Bunker Hill. He served in the War for Independence for seven years and was buried in 1816 in an unmarked grave in Framingham. On April 10, 1882, the town of Framingham voted to place a memorial stone over his grave. The granite memorial bore the inscription: "Peter Salem, a soldier of the revolution. Died Aug. 16, 1816. Concord, Bunker Hill, Saratoga. Erected by the town, 1882." Peter Salem's musket is in the Bunker Hill Monument.[22]

When news of Lexington and Concord reached New York City, Isaac Sears and John Lamb, followed by several scores of Liberty Boys, paraded through the town with "drums beating and colors flying" and called on the people to arm themselves in defense of the "injured rights and liberties of America." That same afternoon, two ships with provisions for General Gage at Boston were seized and unloaded. In the evening, Sears and Lamb led an assault upon the City Hall and seized five hundred muskets and quantities of powder. Back in December 1775, the Sons of Liberty had received a shipment of muskets, powder, and shot, but before they could be distributed, the arms were seized by the authorities. Now they were distributed to "the most active of the citizens who formed themselves into a voluntary corps and assumed the government of the city." They drilled every day, and on April 28, the armed citizenry, led by Sears and Lamb, took over all customs houses and public stores. Under the direction of the two leaders, all vessels in the harbor were detained. The purpose was twofold: to prevent supplies from being shipped to Boston for the British army, and at the same time to convince merchants that they had better not try to supply Gage by secret arrangements. When the merchants refused to heed this public warning, the Sons of Liberty seized a supply ship and forbade its crew to proceed on its voyage. Sears was arrested as the ringleader, but he was rescued by the mechanics and laborers and carried in triumph through the town.[23]

During the months of May and June, groups of armed Liberty Boys clashed with British regulars. On one occasion, under the leadership of Marinus Willett, they were successful in preventing the movement of British troops to Boston.[24]

It will be noted that the name of Alexander McDougall is conspicuously absent from the record of events during the exciting weeks following Lexington and Concord. McDougall tried to prevent the Sons of Liberty from arming. He was promptly pushed aside by the mechanics, and from this point on, the triumvirate leading the New York Sons of Liberty was made up of Isaac Sears, John Lamb, and Marinus Willett, all three unmitigated radicals and all fully responsive to the mechanics' wishes.[25]

The Committee of Sixty dissolved, and a new Committee of One Hundred was elected on May 1, 1775. Although the merchants constituted the largest group in the new committee, there was an increase in mechanic representation. Daniel Dunscomb, chairman of the Committee of Mechanics, Lamb, Sears, McDougall, and Hercules Mulligan, a laborer, were among the "One Hundred." For the first time, laborers as well as mechanics were represented on the extralegal revolutionary bodies.[26]

With the royal government "entirely prostrated" in New York, the "One Hundred" directed the province until the meet-

THE ROAD TO INDEPENDENCE

ing of the Revolutionary Provincial Congress. They kept order in the city, strictly enforced the Continental Association, and encouraged men to begin training for war. From the end of May 1775, New York was actually governed by four successive provincial congresses, or their committees of safety authorized to act in their place when they were not in session. These congresses operated as the effective government, and their committees watched the harbors and disposed of confiscated cargoes. Isolating opponents of the Association as enemies, they imprisoned anyone "hostile to American liberties."[27] The officers of the committees were merchants, but now these were from the more radical elements of the mercantile community. There were sufficient mechanic representatives so that their influence could always be felt. To assure that the leadership was prodded in a radical direction, the Committee of Mechanics remained in existence.[28]

Occurrences similar to those in New York took place throughout the colonies as the Americans moved from passive resistance to open rebellion. Everywhere, the accounts of Lexington and Concord produced the same reaction—the conviction that the policy of peaceful coercion to gain concessions from the mother country was at an end and that full-scale military conflict was imminent. Then began a race against time to secure, arms, powder, and ammunition, and to organize a body of trained men. In Charleston, the mechanics, long organized in the Sons of Liberty, joined with others in the formation of a Committee of Intelligence, whose major function was to obtain war supplies. This was followed by raids on royal magazines, with mechanics heading the raiding parties. Other mechanics made arms, ammunition, and cannon balls. The committee hired gunsmiths, saddlers, tailors, and other artisans to supply the militia. When the British evacuated the forts of Charleston and boarded their warship lying just outside the harbor, the mechanics prepared the forts for defensive use by the patriots. "The mechanics (almost to a man) were hearty in the cause and went cheerfully to work whenever they were called upon," a leading member of the committee reported.[29]

In the aftermath of Lexington and Concord, Pennsylvania took steps to create a stable military force, and the provincial Assembly began raising money to fight a war. However, men with means were permitted to escape military service by paying a modest fine or providing a substitute.[30] As a result, the Philadelphia militia drew most heavily on the poorer artisans and laborers, and included "a great many apprentices" and indentured servants as well. Blacks were excluded by law from participation in the militia, but some may have served illegally, for "David Owen, a person suspected of enlisting negroes," was "committed to the workhouse" late in 1775 by the city's Council of Safety.[31]

The militiamen described themselves as "composed of tradesmen and others who earn their living by their industry." They also emphasized that they were among the poorest workers— "persons who by a short neglect of the business of their employer would deprive themselves of their daily bread,"—who had left behind families "destitute of every means of acquiring an honest living," and who deserved, they maintained, public assistance, preference in employment, or even "public works." An analysis of the militia company commanded by Stephen Simpson, a shoemaker, reveals that these descriptions fitted most of its members. They were, in the main, journeymen rather than masters, with very modest amounts, if any, of property, and, in most cases, men who could not meet the property qualifications for voting.[32]

The role of the Philadelphia militia in the months following Lexington and Concord went beyond that of a military force in the conflict shaping up between the colonies and Britain. Through the militia, the journeymen, apprentices, and servants—the lower class of workers—moved into the political arena for the first time. In September 1775, the Committee of Privates was organized. Each neighborhood's military association sent three associators from among its privates as delegates to a meeting which established an association of these workers. Then a Committee of Correspondence was formed which wrote to privates elsewhere in the province, encouraging the formation of similar committees. Thus, a network of Revolutionary lower class workers was formed.

The chairman of the Philadelphia Committee of Privates was the above-named Stephen Simpson, a shoemaker. The Committee of Correspondence included Frederick Hagener, tailor, James Ryves, paper hanger, and Robert Bell, engraver. These men helped build an organization which was to exert a powerful influence both on the struggle against Britain and on that for greater democracy in Pennsylvania. None of them had been active in the artisan movements of the early 1770s.[33] Now they are bringing into the anti-British movement the views of the propertyless workers, those who worked for the most meager wages, and even, as in the case of servants and apprentices, for no wages at all. One scholar compares the Committee of Privates to the "New Model Army of the English War," noting that like the earlier army, the militia became "a school of political democracy."[34]

The demands of the militia privates, as they emerged in late 1775 and early 1776, revealed that they were learning quickly in this "school." First, they insisted on the right to elect their officers and even suggested that they be selected annually by secret ballot, in the same manner as assemblymen and local officials, "for annual election is so essentially necessary to the liberty of freemen." Second, they demanded the right of every associator to vote, regardless of whether he met the age or property qualifications. Thus, apprentices and servants could no longer be excluded from political life. Third, they insisted that militia service be made truly universal, or at least that men of wealth be required to make significant financial sacrifices if they did not serve. Fourth, they called for narrowing the gap between the top and bottom of Philadelphia society and for putting a halt to the increasing stratification of wealth. Non-Associators, they pointed out, included "some of the most considerable estates in the Province," and fines should be levied on them "proportioned to each man's property," with the proceeds used to support the families of Associators, "whose maintenance depends on their labour." Fifth, there was a need to overhaul the traditional means of assisting the poor in Philadelphia, since "no man, who is able, by his industry, to support his wife and children, could even consent to have them treated, by the Overseers of the Poor, as the law directs."[35]

The petitions drafted by the militia's Committee of Privates reveal that the lesser artisans, apprentices, and servants—the poor in general—were concerned not merely with the struggle against British tyranny, but also with the domination of Philadelphia's economic and political life by the wealthy and with the widening gap between the rich and the poor. Their "school of political democracy" enabled them to give articulate expression to their resentment over the situation. Another reflection of their political education was the card inserted by a militia company in the May 4, 1776, issue of the *Pennsylvania Evening Post*. The printer was urged to publish the resolution adopted by the militia-workers in order to "convince the public that *Common Sense* is not altogether destitute of proselytes in Pennsylvania." The resolution read:

> Resolved unanimously, That the independent principles of Common Sense are what we wish to be established, as soon as the wisdom of the Honorable Continental Congress shall think proper, as we look upon it to be the only alternative now left us to secure our liberties, and screen us from the disgraceful epithet of rebels in the eyes of the world.

The resolution referred to the call for the independence of the American colonies from Britain in the pamphlet written by Thomas Paine, a man who had begun life as an artisan, and whose writings, one historian has written recently, contain the voice of the "intelligent artisan come into his own at last." [36]

Thomas Paine was born on January 29, 1737, at Thetford in Norfolk, England, and spent the first thirty-seven years of his life in that country. He was the son of a poor corsetmaker who could barely afford to send him to a free school, where he was taught just enough to master reading, writing, and arithmetic. At thirteen, young Paine began to work with his father as a staymaker; three years later, he ran away from home, went to sea, and served as a sailor on a privateer in the Seven Years' War. He returned to London after two eventful voyages and lived by finding such occupations as he could. He worked for a while as a staymaker; then he became a government worker, holding a minor job in the collection of the excise. From his pitiful earnings as a staymaker and exciseman, he supplemented his meager education with books and scientific apparatus.

In the England of his youth and manhood, Paine saw the vicious effects of the enclosure system, which hurled thousands of small, independent farmers into the cities and transformed them from an independent yeomanry to landless urban workers and agricultural laborers. All about him, he saw thousands struggling in misery and degradation to eke out an existence, and he daily passed "ragged and hungry children, and persons of seventy and eighty years of age, begging in the streets." He knew, too, from his own intolerably inadequate salary how difficult it was to secure even a subsistence living standard when commodity prices were soaring and wages remained practically stationary. He also observed the vicious operation of the Poor Laws, which practically reduced workers to serfs. He witnessed the brutality of the criminal code and noted that it was directed chiefly against the lower classes.

These experiences left their mark on Paine. A workingman himself, he used his pen as a weapon to improve the status of the laboring classes. Indeed, his earliest known prose composition and his first important pamphlet, *The Case of the Officers of the Excise*, was written to achieve this purpose. In 1772, he was chosen by the excisemen to address Parliament in their behalf, requesting higher wages. After the pamphlet was written, Paine spent the winter of 1772-1773 trying to influence members of Parliament to grant the underpaid excisemen an increase in wages. Regarded as a troublemaker by the authorities for attempting to organize his fellow excisemen, he was dismissed from the service.

Paine lost his government job on April 8, 1774. A week later, he was forced to sell his shop and possessions to escape imprisonment for debt. He decided to begin a new life in the New World. He left England in October 1774 and on November 30, he landed in America bearing a letter of introduction from Benjamin Franklin, whom he had approached in London. Franklin's letter to his son-in-law, Richard Bache, recommended Paine as "an ingenious worthy young man," who might make good in Philadelphia as "a clerk, or assistant tutor in a school, or assistant surveyor."[37]

Paine arrived in Philadelphia with its varied artisan community at a time when the Whig leaders of the city—Thomson, Dickinson, and Reed—whose base was in the artisan community, dominated the resistance movement against Britain, and

when the mechanics themselves were exercising an important influence on the politics of resistance. He came, however, with the
nonrevolutionary aim of setting up an academy for the education
of young women. As a result of Franklin's letter of recommendation, he instead obtained a job as editor of the *Pennsylvania
Magazine*, a periodical launched by the publisher and bookseller,
Robert Aitken. From February to September 1775, Paine
worked as a day-to-day editor of the publication, contributing
poems and essays of his own. Among his essays were one of the
earliest pleas for the emancipation of women and the article,
"African Slavery in America," which ranks among the best of
the early attacks upon slavery in this country. Signing himself
"Justice and Humanity," Paine equated the enslavement of the
Negro people with "murder, robbery, lewdness, and barbarity,"
and he called upon Americans immediately to "discontinue and
renounce it, with grief and abhorrence." He asked Americans:
"With what consistence, or decency they complain so loudly of
attempts to enslave them, while they hold so many hundred
thousands in slavery; and annually enslave many thousands
more, without any pretence of authority, or claim upon them?"[38]

Paine's essay was published on March 8, 1775. A few weeks
later, he was among a group of Philadelphians who formed the
first abolitionist society in the world, the Society for the Relief of
Free Negroes Unlawfully Held in Bondage. The society aimed to
assist a number of free blacks unjustly enslaved to regain their
freedom, and it raised as its ultimate goal freedom for all the
slaves.

After the battles of Lexington and Concord, Paine's articles
contained more and more attacks on British policies. On September 16, 1775, he published a poem in the *Pennsylvania Evening
Post* entitled "The Liberty Tree," the last stanza of which attacked both the king and Parliament, and issued a call:

> From the East to the West blow the trumpet to arms,
>   Thro' the land let the sound of it flee:
> Let the far and the near all unite with a cheer,'
>   In defense of our Liberty Tree.

Paine was determined to change "the sentiments of the people from dependence to Independence, and from the monarchial to the republican form of government." The time was ripe for such a change. War between British troops and Americans had broken out in several colonies; the Second Continental Congress had gathered in Philadelphia, bringing to that city not only Sam Adams, Christopher Gadsden, and other spokesmen for the mechanics, but also such well-known as George Washington, Thomas Jefferson, Richard Henry Lee, and Patrick Henry. Through the summer of 1775, as the colonies actively enlisted troops, a debate raged in Congress between the advocates of vigorous opposition to the mother country and the proponents of reconciliation. In November, Britain virtually declared war on the American colonies, announcing both a naval blockade and its intention of sending German mercenaries to fight beside its own soldiers.

All these developments strengthened the position of Sam and John Adams, Christopher Gadsden, and other advocates of independence. But as yet, few voices were calling publicly for such a step. It was Paine's *Common Sense*, published in January 1776, that changed the terms of the political debate from the older controversy over colonial rights within the British empire to the new issues of the future. "With the publication of *Common Sense* in January 1776," writes John C. Miller, "Tom Paine broke the ice that was slowly congealing the revolutionary movement."[39]

So revolutionary was its approach that at first no typographer would agree to set the pamphlet in print. Finally, the "republican printer" Robert Bell agreed. On January 10, 1776, there came off the press the fifty-page work that has been called "the most brilliant pamphlet written during the American Revolution, and one of the most brilliant pamphlets ever written in the English language."[40]

Written in simple, direct language, easily read and understood by all, *Common Sense* became a best seller overnight. At a time when the most widely circulated colonial newspapers averaged sales of barely two thousand a week, and when the average pamphlet was printed in one or two editions, *Common Sense* went through twenty-five editions, and shortly after its publication, almost 150,000 copies were sold. (Comparable sales today would mean at least ten million.) Furthermore, many of the most significant paragraphs were reprinted in newspapers throughout the country. Soon the common people were quoting sections from the booklet which demanded separation, held hereditary monarchy up to comtempt, called the king of England "the Royal Brute of Great Britain," denounced the British ruling classes for exploiting the lower classes in America and England, and urged the colonies to declare themselves free and independent states so that they might establish in America a haven for refuge for the oppressed peoples of Europe.

> O! ye that love mankind! Ye that dare oppose not only tyranny but the tyrant, stand forth! Every spot of the old world is overrun with oppression. Freedom hath been hunted round the globe. Asia and Africa have long expelled her. Europe regards her as a stranger, and England hath given her warning to depart. O! receive the fugitive, and prepare in time an asylum for mankind.

"We have it in our power to begin the world over again," he wrote. "The birthday of a new world is at hand." That new world should be based on the principle that, while representative government is necessary in large societies, it should approximate as closely as possible a direct democracy in which every citizen participates; that representatives should be apportioned equally and rotated by frequent elections; that governments should be limited by written constitutions, providing for the security of persons and property and, "above all things, the free exercise of religion." These aspects of the New World that was to come into being with independence appealed, of course, to the mechanics and laborers, who were eager to play an influential role in its politics. Appealing, too, was Paine's emphasis on the possibilities for American economic development and for the growth of manufacturing, once the restrictions imposed by the British on American economic life were removed.[41]

Despite his poverty, Paine donated all proceeds from the sale of *Common Sense*, including the sum of $2,500 voted him by the Pennsylvania legislature, to the Revolutionary movement.

Although Paine's American friends included the radical artisans of Philadelphia (as well as Benjamin Rush, George Washington, and Thomas Jefferson), he did not aim *Common Sense* exclusively at the artisans, tradesmen, and laboring poor. More- over, at no point did he criticize existing rights of property; he attributed economic distinctions and inequalities of wealth to individual differences in talent, industry, and frugality rather than to any oppression by the rich. ("The distinctions of rich and poor." he wrote, "may in a great measure be accounted for, and that without recourse to the harsh ill-sounding names of oppres- sion and avarice. Oppression is often the *consequence*, but sel- dom or never the means of riches.") Nevertheless, to many con- servatives, the fact that Paine had begun life as an artisan, whom Gouverneur Morris called "a mere adventurer . . . without for- tune, without family or connexions," and that his writings had such a powerful appeal for the mechanics and laborers, was enough to condemn *Common Sense* in their minds, even aside from its call for immediate independence from Britain. [42]

The pamphlet did indeed have a powerful appeal for the me- chanics and laborers. The journeymen, apprentices, and servants in the militia spoke for their class when they identified them- selves as "proselytes" of *Common Sense*. The mechanics' rever- ence for the pamphlet was made clear by an episode that took place in New York City. On March 18, 1776, the printer Sam Loudon advertised for sale a pamphlet criticizing *Common Sense*. Loudon was at once summoned before the Committee of Mechanics by its charman, Christopher Duyckinck. Loudon asked that the matter be referred to the Committee of Safety of the Provincial Congress. The mechanics agreed, but only after locking up the printed sheets of Loudon's pamphlets. Loudon appeared before the Committee of Safety on March 19 and agreed to stop printing the offending pamphlets; but at ten that night, Duyckinck, with a "large company" of "unauthorized men," broke into Loudon's home, took the printed sheets, and burned them on the Common. [43]

Between January and July 1776, scarcely a week went by with- out a lengthy article in the urban press attacking or defending Paine's ideas. Among them, a number were by mechanics, who, like Paine, sought to move America toward independence. Most shared Paine's political philosophy. The mechanics discussed at length the need for both independence and for a different kind of government, which would include universal adult suffrage, annual elections, rotation of office, equal apportionment, the secret ballot, and popular election of all local offices. They identified the opponents of independence as the colonial wealthy classes who feared that a break with Britain would loosen their tight grip on colonial society. One denounced the men of wealth of Pennsylvania as "petty tyrants" who opposed independence because they dreamed of creating "millions of acres of tenanted soil." Another cautioned that "an aristocratical junto" was "straining every nerve to frustrate our virtuous endeavours and to make the common and middle class of people their beasts of burden." Still another, while admitting that the "Barons of America" did not hold hereditary prerogatives like their English counterparts, warned that they had "a prodigious itch for such patents," and that "men of some rank" desired to establish in America "the system of lord and vassal, or principal and dependent," common in Europe. [44]

Other mechanics envisaged a government under independence which would eliminate some of the defects of the existing political institutions and introduce a number of equalitarian features. As for the defects:

A poor man has rarely the honor of speaking to a gentleman on any terms, and never with familiarity but for a few weeks before the election. How many poor men, common men, and mechanics have been made happy within this fortnight by a shake of the hand, a pleasing smile and a little familiar chat with gentlemen; who have not for these seven years past condescended to look at them. Blessed state which brings all so nearly on a level! What a clever man is Mr. — says my neighbour, how agreeable and familiar! He has no pride at all! He talked as freely to me for half an hour as if he were neighbour—there! I wish it were election time always! Thursday next he will lose all knowledge of — —, and pass me in the streets as if he never knew me.

How kind and clever is the man who proposes to be Sheriff, for two months before the election; he knows everybody, smiles upon and salutes everybody, until the election is

over; but then to the end of the year, he has no time to speak
to you, he is so engaged in seizing your property by writ of
venditioni exponas, and selling your goods at vendue.

Thus the right of annual elections will ever oblige gentlemen to speak to you once a year, who would despise you for-
ever were it not that you can bestow something upon
them. . . .

In a word, electioneering and aristocratic pride are incom-
patible, and if we would have gentlemen ever to come down
to our level, we must guard our right of election effectually. . . . Be freemen then, and you will be companions for
gentlemen annually.[45]

A mechanic in New York visualized the future government,
under independence, first and foremost, as "a free popular government." While it should contain a legislature, an executive,
and a judiciary, the major emphasis must be placed on the political power of the people. The people should elect all officials from
legislature to local judges, sheriffs, and county attorneys, and
should have a means of compelling them to abide by the will of
the people. The traditional idea that the right to vote should depend on property ownership must be abandoned, along with the
concept that "riches" gave a man a right to office. As for the
argument that "the populace was too ignorant to manage public
affairs," this was simply a canard of the wealthy, and, indeed, if
the "rich and aspiring" were deprived of the power to corrupt,
bribe, and lead the people toward despotism, there would be no
problem on this score.[46]

The whole argument was summed up by a Philadelphia
"leather apron" wearer who wrote in the *Pennsylvania Evening
Post* of March, 14, 1776:

Do not mechanics and farmers constitute ninety-nine out of
a hundred of the people of America? If these, by their occupations, are to be excluded from having any share in the
choice of their rulers, or forms of government, would it not
be best to acknowledge at once the jurisdiction of the

British Parliament, which is composed entirely of
GENTLEMEN?

The Revolutionary mechanics, lesser artisans, laborers, and
even servants tried to achieve the dual goal of independence and
a more equalitarian and democratic society. They were among
the first and most active advocates of independence, and it was
they who envisioned an independent America in which a truly
republican government, with opportunity for all to "come in for
their fair share of the wealth" would make that independence
worth fighting for.

9 _____ The Coming of Independence

During the spring and summer of 1776, workingmen mobilized to achieve their twin goals: national independence and a more democratic order. In the first objective, they were part of a wider movement that ended in success; in the second, they were almost alone, and, in the main, unsuccessful. The reasons are not difficult to understand. In the decade before armed conflict, apart from Virginia, the resistance movement had been centered in the cities, especially Boston, New York, Philadelphia, and Charleston. Hence, the workingmen, operating through the Sons of Liberty, were able to affect events decisively, even though the leadership remained in the hands of the wealthy merchants and landed aristocrats. This was especially true after 1770, when workingmen began to function in increasing numbers as an independent force on the extralegal committees.

With the outbreak of armed insurrection, the theatre of action shifted to areas where the embattled farmers became a military force of great importance and where workingmen and their organizations were sparse. At the same time, the upper classes split, with some moving into the Tory camp and most remaining Whig. Once it was clear that independence was on the agenda, the substantial merchants, lawyers, and planters who were Whigs moved swiftly to prevent state power from slipping from their grasp by default. Nearly everywhere, a coalition of urban and rural wealthy classes—mercantile, legal, and landed aristocrats—succeeded in gaining control of the state governments established under the new nation.

Milton M. Klein argues that in New York at least, conservative lawyers were the key force preventing the Revolution from advancing rapidly in the directions envisaged by the mechanics. It was the lawyer-led delegation to the First Continental Congress "which delayed the province's approval of the decision for independence," and it was the conservative lawyers who "strove to insure that the new state government would keep power in the same men of rank and property" who had held them previously. While the lawyers also split into Whigs and Tories, the more perceptive ones among them saw the necessity, throughout this period, "to swim with the tide in order to control its course." However, Klein also argues, in order to achieve this goal, these lawyers had to move in a more radical direction than they had originally intended.[1]

All but two state governments differed only slightly from their royal predecessors. The lower houses were popularly elected, but strong governors and upper houses kept them in check. Property qualifications for voting and even higher ones for holding office succeeded in maintaining the conservative elite in power. In Rhode Island, moreover, independence made the state's constitutional system even more rigid than it had been during the colonial era. The Charter of 1663 had no amendment procedure; it could only be changed by petitioning the imperial authorities in London. After 1776, such appeals meant nothing, so that unless the established authorities in Rhode Island were willing to grant reforms, there was simply no regular way to bring about constitutional change. "Ironically then," writes Marvin Gettleman, "the American Revolution rendered Rhode Island in some sense less free."[2]

Still, in one colony—New York—the conservatives were not entirely able to triumph, and in another—Pennsylvania—they suffered a stunning defeat.

On November 10, 1774, Thomas Young wrote to John Lamb from Boston: "I understand by all hands that you have an over-proportion of tories with you to any place in the continent. I heartily pity you if anything like the above is true."[3] It was true, and those who were not Tories were so moderate that they were aghast at the very thought of independence. The New York Provincial Assembly refused to acknowledge the authority of the Continental Congress or to break off relations with the royal governor, William Tryon.

It was the Committee of Mechanics in New York City which forced the issue of independence to the fore. On May 29, 1776, the mechanics requested that the Provincial Congress instruct New York's delegates to the Continental Congress to "cause these united colonies to become independent of Great Britain." The request was carried to the Congress by Lewis Thibon, chairman of the Committee of Mechanics. The chair first cleared the house of all spectators before Congress would determine whether it was "proper" to receive the memorial. Having "inspected" the document, the congressmen opened the doors and invited Thibon to read it to the house. When he had finished, the Congress replied coldly: "We consider the mechanics in union as a voluntary association. We flatter ourselves that neither the association, nor their committee, will claim any authority whatsoever in the public transactions of the present time." It was up to the Continental Congress "alone" to decide "upon those measures which are necessary for the general welfare." Until independence was brought up in Philadelphia, New York would not "presume" to instruct its delegates on the subject.

By publishing its letter, the Committee of Mechanics brought the issue of independence squarely before the public. It was generally acknowledged that, while conservatives and moderates stalled on the issue, "the mechanics of the city have voted independence."[4]

Ten days after their rebuff, the mechanics sent a letter to the Provincial Congress, asserting their right to speak out on political issues whenever they saw fit.[5] They then proceeded to raise the issue of "who should rule at home." The Provincial Congress had called for a new (fourth) Congress to be elected to draft a framework for a government. The merchants of New York City were quite satisfied with the arrangement. But the Committee of Mechanics immediately sent a memorial to the Congress, noting the failure of their proposal to mention the submission of the new constitution to the people for ratification—an "inalienable right" and "the birthright of every man," the renunciation of which would cast the people into "absolute slavery." The people's free assent, it wrote, constituted the "only characteristic of the true lawfulness and legality that can be given to human institutions." Was it the intention of the Congress to force the people into "a renunciation of our inalienable right to ratify your laws?" It was up to the Congress to "prove that you have fully restored to us the exercise of our right finally to determine on the laws by which this colony is to be governed: a right of which, by the injustice of the British Government, we have till now been deprived."

As a result of Britain's deprivation of the colonists' right to determine their own laws, the mechanics considered that existing laws "have but a relative legality, and that not one of them is lawfully binding upon us." Any similar procedure by the Provincial Congress would produce laws with the same lack of binding power. In short, neither a "foreign or domestic oligarchy" could do as it wished with the fundamental rights of the people.

The mechanics' memorial went on to insist that the people must have the power to amend their Constitution easily: "This power necessarily involves that every district, occasionally to renew their deputies to committees and congresses, when the majority of such district shall think fit, and therefore, without the intervention of the executive or any other power, foreign to the body of the respective electors." In conclusion, the mechanics' committee warned that unless the Constitution was submitted to the people for ratification, it would be assumed that the new government was illegal, tyrannical, and the offspring of "the selfish principles of corrupt oligarchy."[6]

"By implication the Committee of Mechanics raised the question of class power and condemned rule by an elite," writes Bernard Mason.[7] The Provincial Congress reached the same conclusion, although the congressmen, mostly conservatives from the rural areas, did not think it was only "by implication." Indeed, they were so furious that they refused to enter the mechanics' memorial into the journal.[8]

Fortunately for the conservatives, the military situation in New York City in June 1776 served to hinder the forces they feared. When the Committee of Mechanics failed to obtain any response from the Congress, it sent letters to the newspapers calling for independence and popular ratification of the new form of government for New York. Most of the people, fearing a British occupation, left the city, and the rapid exodus hampered any large-scale effort by the mechanics to mobilize pressure on the Provincial Congress.

On July 2, Sir William Howe and a British army of ten thousand troops landed on Staten Island, and ten days later, Lord Admiral Richard Howe arrived with 150 transports. In the weeks that followed, George Washington and the Continental Army were slowly forced to give way, and on September 15, the British entered New York City in triumph.

One of the mechanics' goals was realized: the Fourth Provincial Congress that convened on July 9, 1776, did endorse the Declaration of Independence, and New York became the thirteenth state to do so. Their second goal remained unfulfilled. However, the conservatives had a narrow escape; as Roger Champagne points out, "only the timely invasion of Long Island by the British saved the aristocrats from a political crisis of an explosive character."[9] With this development, New York City, the center of radical activity for over a decade, came under the control of the British. After September 1776, all political activity was concentrated in the rural areas where the people were generally scattered and where there were no effective organizations as existed in New York City. Thus, the Revolutionary government of New York, seated in Albany, did not have to concern itself with the memorial of the Committee of Mechanics, and the Constitution was never submitted to the people for ratification.

Still, the aristocracy of landed and mercantile wealth did not get its way completely. Even before the committee on the Constitution was organized, mechanics were calling for a complete transformation of government. "So far as private property will allow," they declared, "we must form our government in each province, just as if we had never had any form of government before." The new political system must be "a free popular government," for the "populace" was quite able to manage its affairs, provided it was not corrupted by the "rich and aspiring" who would lead it into despotism. The Constitution of 1777, when finally completed, reflected some of this view, even though the mechanics themselves had not been represented in the Constitutional Convention. The Constitution, as Alfred Young points out, "made several democratic departures from provincial precedent." Assembly elections were to be made annually, and the offices of the governor and the senate, unlike the royal council, were to be elective. There was neither a Bill of Rights nor taxpayer suffrage, as the mechanics had insisted upon, but trial by jury, due process of law, and religious liberty were guaranteed.[10]

So the New York mechanics achieved one of their goals and part of the second. Isaac Sears, John Lamb, and Alexander McDougall were then in military service and were not on hand to witness the end of the colonial era. Even so, they could take comfort from the knowledge that their leadership, and the activities of the mechanics, laborers, and seamen who had followed them in the decades before, were as responsible as any other factors for the existence of a state of New York instead of a colony of New York.

It was only in Philadelphia, as a result of a unique combination of circumstances, that the dual goal of the urban workingmen was realized. In almost every other colony, the established leadership joined the movement for independence or split into Tory and Whig factions. In Pennsylvania, however, the old elite stubbornly opposed any talk of independence, and the Assembly united with the Proprietary group to fight a prolonged delaying action against separation from Britain. In addition, the leaders of the resistance movement of the early 1770s—men like Charles Thomson, Joseph Reed, and John Dickinson—were either drawn off into national affairs, serving in the army or in the Congress, or else they lapsed into political silence as the movement for independence accelerated.

Into this vacuum of political leadership stepped a new radical group of Philadelphians. This group based its political power on the mechanics and on the extralegal committees and militia, made up of lesser artisans, journeymen, and apprentices. They provided the ideological leadership and much of the day-to-day political direction for the popular upsurge that committed Pennsylvania to independence, overthrew the provincial government, and established in its place the most democratic state constitution of the Revolutionary period.[11]

The Philadelphia radicals included Thomas Paine, Timothy Matlock, Christopher Marshall, James Cannon, David Rittenhouse, Owen Biddle, and Charles Willson Peale. As a group, they were men of modest wealth. Matlock, son of a Quaker brewer, had fallen into debt as a hardware storekeeper and had close links with the lower classes of Philadelphia because of his fistfighting prowess and his prize bantams, which won several cockfighting matches. Marshall, Cannon, and Matlock associated with the United Company for Promoting American Manufactures, an enterprise close to the hearts of the city artisans. Cannon, a guiding light of the militia's Committee of Privates, worked closely with its chairman, Stephen Simpson. Rittenhouse, Biddle, and Peale were artisans of great skill. Rittenhouse had a wide following among Philadelphia mechanics, who chose him in 1774 as a member of the eleven-man committee to represent the artisans' political interests. Peale, who had risen from poverty to become, in due course, a silversmith, clockmaker, and America's leading painter, had been a republican since the Stamp Act—a man who "would never pull off his hat as the King passed by." He was also an early advocate of independence and home manufacturing. Thomas Paine, the former artisan, was already revered by the mechanics, lesser artisans, and laborers for his pioneer effort in behalf of independence and his advocacy of republican doctrines. [12]

In 1776, the radical mechanics gained permanent ascendancy in the Philadelphia City Committee. The members of the new Committee of Observation and Inspection, elected in February, were almost entirely artisans. In March, the new radical committee called on the Assembly to adopt resolutions favoring independence. When this proposal was rejected, a coalition of three working-class groups began a movement to bypass the Assembly and place Pennsylvania on record for independence, thereby creating a new frame of government. The coalition was made up of the Philadelphia Committee of Observation and Inspection, now an organization of radical mechanics; the Patriotic Society, which was composed entirely of mechanics; and the Committee of Privates, made up of lesser artisans, journeymen, apprentices, and servants. The new radical leaders gave voice to the aspirations of the workingmen's coalition. [13]

In the elections of delegates to a Constitutional Convention, a provision, adopted by the radicals, stated that anyone voting would have to take an oath renouncing allegiance to George III. This provision caused many Pennsylvanians of the elite class, who opposed independence, to boycott the election. Nevertheless, to insure that the delegates elected would be of a radical persuasion, broadsides were circulated by the network of the Committee of Privates urging citizens "to choose no rich men, and [as] few learned men as possible to represent them in the [Constitutional] Convention." Again: "Let no men represent you. . . .who would be disposed to form any rank above that of freemen."[14]

The Pennsylvania radicals won a complete victory. The instrument of government which the Constitutional Convention created was practically all that was desired by the mechanics, the lesser artisans, and the laborers. It declared the state legally separated from Britain and guaranteed freedom of religious worship, free elections, security of property, freedom of speech and press, the right to bear arms, and the freedom of assembly and petition. It stated the people's rights to regulate the internal police, to make their governmental officials accountable, to recall their public officers, and to be free from peacetime standing armies.

The outstanding feature of this new frame of government was the role played by the people. At every point, the people were given protection against arbitrary government. Even the legislature, which most closely approximated the people's voice in the government, was placed under the electors' control. The legislators' tenure of office was limited to one term of seven years, and the one thing they were forbidden to do was to alter the Constitution. Every seven years, the people were to elect a "Council of Censors" to review the proceedings of the government "to enquire whether the Constitution has been preserved inviolate in every part; and whether the legislative and executive branches of government have performed their duty as guardians of the people, or assumed to themselves, or exercised other or greater powers than they are entitled to by the Constitution."

The Constitution even attempted to institutionalize a form of direct democracy by providing that all laws must be published for public debate before being acted upon. It also dispensed entirely with property qualifications for officeholding and granted the suffrage to all men over twenty-one who paid taxes. It contained other advanced provisions: that debtors not guilty of fraud should not be imprisoned after their property had been surrendered to creditors; and that schools should be established with low fees in every county in the state. It was to be years before such provisions were incorporated in other constitutions of the new nation.

On one question the Pennsylvania Constitution did not go as far as the Philadelphia radicals wanted. It rejected a clause which read: "That an enormous proportion of property vested in a few individuals is dangerous to the rights, and destructive of the common happiness of mankind; and therefore every free state hath a right by its laws to discourage the possession of such property."[15] Nevertheless, most workingmen could be well satisfied with the Constitution. Insofar as Pennsylvania was concerned, they had seen their dual goal—independence and a more democratic order—achieved almost completely. The Constitution, wrote one contemporary commentator, represented a new departure for America:

Although it be granted, on all hands, that all power originates from the people; yet it is plain, that in those colonies where the government has, from the beginning, been in the hands of a very few rich men, the ideas of government both in the minds of those rich men, and of the common people, are rather aristocratical than popular. The rich, having been used to govern, seem to think it is their right; and the poorer commonality, having hitherto had little or no hand in government, seem to think it does not belong to them to have any.[16]

But the radicals had put an end to this doctrine. Bewailing this new development, John Adams placed the blame for it on Matlock, Cannon, Young, and Paine. The Pennsylvania Constitution, he wrote in his *Diary*, was their work.[17] He might have added that it was also the work of the coalition of Philadelphia workingmen—the Committee of Observation and Inspection, the Patriotic Society, and the Committee of Privates.

Radical though it was, the Pennsylvania Constitution of 1776 still excluded the unfree—slaves, indentured servants, and apprentices—as well as those free citizens so poor that they were excused from the payment of taxes, and hence could not vote. Moreover, the convention's Council of Safety, with David Rittenhouse as chairman and Cannon, Matlock, and Biddle as members, adopted a resolution calling for the discharge from the militia of all apprentices and indentured servants, on application of their masters, and forbidding their enlistment in the future without the master's consent. [18]

The exclusion of slaves from the protections of the Constitution followed a national trend. Despite the contributions of blacks at the battles of Lexington, Concord, and Bunker Hill, Revolutionary leaders began to have second thoughts about using them in the armed forces. An important reason was their fear that armed slaves might join forces with their fellow bondsmen in an uprising. When the militia marched to Lexington in 1775, the slaves were reported to be mobilizing to massacre those left behind. So seriously did the citizens of Framingham take these reports that they armed themselves with axes, clubs, and pitchforks, and locked themselves inside their homes until the militia returned. Why then, they asked, put guns into the hands of potential allies of their slaves?

On May 29, 1775, the Massachusetts Committee of Safety prohibited the enlistment of slaves in the armies of that colony. As the committee put it, "the admission of any persons as soldiers into the army now raising, but only such as are freemen, will be inconsistent with the principles which are to be supported, and reflect dishonor on this colony." Instead of solving this dilemma by advocating the emancipation of the slaves, the committee decreed "that no slaves be admitted into this army upon any consideration whatsoever."

The action in Massachusetts foreshadowed the national policy on black soldiers. When the Continental Congress took over the patriot army around Boston on June 15 and appointed George Washington as Commander-in-Chief, the question of enlisting blacks arose. Since he was a substantial slaveholder who believed in the inferiority of all Negroes, Washington's answer to this question was what might be expected. On July 9, five days after he assumed command at Cambridge, he issued an order to

all recruiting officers instructing them not to enroll "any desert-
er from the Ministerial army, nor any stroller, negro or vaga-
bond."

On October 8, Washington asked his generals "Whether it will
be advisable to enlist any negroes in the new army? or whether
there be a distinction between such as are slaves and thos that
are free?" It was unanimously agreed to reject all slaves, and, by
a large majority, to bar all blacks, even those who were free. Ten
days later, the Continental Congress voted agreement with the
chief officers of the army, and on November 12, an order was
issued stating that "neither Negroes, boys unable to bear arms,
nor old men unfit to endure the fatigue of the campaign" were to
be enlisted.

Behind this decision lay the assumption that blacks were by
nature too cowardly and servile to make good soldiers, coupled
with the fear of slave insurrections. Others who shared neither
these prejudices nor fears simply believed that it was inconsistent with the principles of the Revolution to have slaves fighting
in the armies that sought to win freedom from tyranny.

The British were more practical than the Americans and were
able to stifle their disdain for the use of blacks as soldiers. As
early as June 12, 1775, General Gage wrote to Lord Barrington,
the secretary-at-war, that "things are now come to that crisis,
that we must avail ourselves of every resource, even to raise the
Negroes in our cause." The first Britisher to put this idea into
action was John Murray, Earl of Dunmore, who was royal governor of Virginia. On November 7, 1775, he issued a call summon-
ing black and white bondsmen to the British cause with the promise of freedom.

By December 1775, the British had nearly three hundred
slaves in military uniform, with the inscription "Liberty to
Slaves" sewn on the breast of their coats. The governor officially
designated them "Lord Dunmore's Ethiopian Regiment" and
informed London that, were it not for a devastating fever that
carried off many in his "Ethiopian corps," he "could have had
two thousand blacks, with whom I should have no doubt of pene-
trating into the heart of this colony."

Even the presence of three hundred slaves in uniform was
enough to panic the slaveowners. John Adams noted in his diary
in the fall of 1775 that he had heard from Southerners that they

were convinced that should one thousand regular British troops
land in Georgia, and should the commander "proclaim freedom
to all the negroes who should join his camp, twenty thousand
negroes would join it from the two provinces (South Carolina and
Georgia) in a fortnight. The negroes have a wonderful art of com-
municating intelligence among themselves; it will run several
hundred miles in a week or fortnight." Leaving nothing to
chance, the South Carolina legislature passed an act preventing
sedition or insurrection among the slaves and fixing the death
penalty for blacks found guilty of inducing others to leave for the
enemy lines or of fleeing themselves to the British.

The feeling of panic was not confined to the South. A rumor
spread through Philadelphia that a Negro had jostled whites on
the streets and had told them to wait until "Lord Dunmore and
his black regiment came, and then we will see who is to take the
wall."

Dunmore's black troops had an electrifying effect on the
course of events. On December 26, 1775, Washington wrote in
alarm to Colonel Henry Lee: "If that man, Dunmore, is not
crushed before the spring, he will become the most dangerous
man in America. His strength will increase like a snowball running down hill. Success will depend on which side can arm the Negroes the faster." Four days later, a chastened Washington instructed his officers to reenlist free Negroes who had already
served in the army, since, if they were rejected, "they may seek
employment in the Ministerial army." On January 16, 1776, Congress, on the general's recommendation, agreed to the reenlist-
ment of free blacks "who have served faithfully in the army at
Cambridge . . . but no others." Many free Negroes and all slaves
had been excluded, but necessity—the problem of raising sufficient troops to wage the war—would soon bring about a change.

Lord Dunmore's call to the Negro slaves' was also chiefly responsible for moving uncommitted Southern planters into the
camp of rebellion. Even those planters who were reluctant to join
the patriot cause now saw in its army a force to suppress internal
rebellion as well as to fight for independence. In issuing its call
for independence, the Virginia convention denounced Lord Dunmore for "carrying on a piratical and savage war against us,
tempting our slaves by every artifice to resort to him, and train-

ing and employing them against their masters." To crush a slave rebellion of major proportions, it was now necessary to rebel against the mother country. [19]

*   *   *

On June 7, 1876, Richard Henry Lee of Virginia proposed a resolution in the Continental Congress in favor of separation from England. On June 28, a committee of five was appointed to draft a Declaration of Independence. On July 2, Lee's motion was adopted by the Congress. The manifesto, drawn up by Thomas Jefferson and presented on behalf of the committee of five, was then debated. Though himself a slaveowner—in 1774, he owned 187 black men, women, and children—Jefferson had no sympathy for the institution of slavery. The draft of the Declaration of Independence he presented to the Continental Congress contained a sharp indictment of the slave trade. George III, he wrote "has waged cruel war against human nature itself, violating its most sacred rights of life and liberty in the persons of a distant people who never offended him, captivating and carrying them into slavery into another hemisphere, or to incur miserable death in their transportation thither."

That portion of the document, however, was deleted because of the hostility of South Carolina and Georgia. On July 4, the Declaration of Independence was adopted, with its celebrated self-evident truth "that all men are created equal, that they are endowed by their Creator with inherent and inalienable rights, that among these are life, liberty and the pursuit of happiness." [20]

Thus, the new nation, under a republican form of government, came into being, proclaiming liberty for all while keeping half a million men, women, and children—one out of every six Americans—enslaved because the color of their skin was black.

The birth of the American nation marked the culmination of one phase of the struggle waged by colonial workingmen over the previous decade. The other—the establishment of a more democratic order—lay in the future. The Revolutionary decade had altered the politics of the country. The politicization of the urban working classes had created trends that would accelerate in the coming decades.

10 _____ The Winning of Independence

□ Much of the population in the cities occupied by the British fled during the War for Independence. (About half of New York City's population of twenty to twenty-five thousand left the city in the summer and fall of 1776.) Among those who remained and worked for the British were artisans, mechanics, and laborers, as well as merchants.[1] American seamen were impressed into the British navy, and some of the thirty thousand captured American seamen defected to the British when they were given the choice of fighting against their country or remaining in prison. However, as Jesse Lemisch has noted, "to an extraordinary degree, captured American seamen remained Americans. . . .Out of every one hundred men who arrived in the [prison] ship [Jersey at New York], only eight chose to defect."[2]

The vast majority of free workers served the American cause. While the army under General Washington's command was composed mainly of farmers, workers did make their contribution. A number of officers for the American forces came from a Boston artillery company headed by Captain Paddock and composed entirely of mechanics. Of fifty-seven men in two companies of the Pennsylvania Regiment whose trades have been listed, only seven were farmers; the rest were workers of all trades and common laborers.

At first, the artisans fought in their working clothes. To give the army some semblance of order, Washington recommended that the men wear hunting shirts, but many did not have such a garment. A description of one unit went: "Some had one boot, hoseless with their feet peering out of their shoes, others in breeches that put decency to blush, some in short jackets, others in long coats—all however with dragoon caps."[3] As this description reveals, the army suffered from the lack of supplies, a condition that persisted throughout the war. In 1776, an army of twelve thousand men in the Ticonderoga area had only nine hundred pairs of shoes. As late as 1782, General Greene declared that the American soldiers were almost naked for want of overalls and shirts and that the greater part of the army went barefoot.

Workers supplied the labor force of the Revolutionary Army—teamsters, blacksmiths, gunsmiths, and artisans of a dozen crafts. Following a colonial practice, Congress recommended exemption from military service for workers in powder mills and munitions factories. Generally, the states also exempted a portion of the craftsmen employed in flour and grist mills, shipyards, foundries, ropewalks, and on ferries. However, they were on notice that "when occasion requires," they were "to act the part of soldiers in either attack or defence as well as artificers."[4]

Throughout the war, the Continental Congress was short of troops. In December 1776, Washington's army barely numbered three thousand, only fourteen hundred of whom were effective. Moreover, the short-term enlistments—generally for three months—and the reluctance of the patriots to fight any distance from their homes, brought even this small force to the brink of dissolution. On September 16, 1776, Congress ordered the raising of eighty-eight battalions, allotting them to the various states on the basis of their population. Virginia and Massachusetts, the most populous states, were asked to contribute fifteen battalions each; Pennsylvania, twelve; Rhode Island, two, and Delaware, one.

The response was so meager that in January 1777 Congress had to resort to the draft. All the states were requested "forthwith to fill up by drafts from their militia or in any other way . . . their respective battalions of continental troops." Although Congress could request, it lacked the power to enforce, and most states continued to do little to supply men for Washington's depleted army.

In this desperate situation, it was inevitable that Congress would turn to the unfree workers. It began offering indentured servants freedom from their contracts if they would enlist, an offer that evoked mixed reactions from masters throughout the colonies. Many employers refused to contribute the services of their servants. In May 1777, a Cumberland (Pennsylvania) County Committee opposed the enlistment of servants without the consent of their masters because "all apprentices and servants are the property of their masters and mistresses, and every mode of depriving such masters and mistresses of their property is a violation of the rights of mankind, contrary to the . . . Continental Congress, and an offence against the peace of the good people of this state." Actually, Pennsylvania found it necessary to compensate masters because many of their servants ran away and enlisted.[5]

In his instructions issued to recruiting officers on January 2, 1777, Washington had retreated from his previous position excluding all blacks from the Continental Army and had permitted the enlistment of "freemen," regardless of color. But there still existed an unwillingness to encroach upon the property rights of slaveowners and a fear that arming slaves might invite revolts. Hence, the national and state governments continued to exclude slaves from the American forces. So desperate was the need for troops, however, that even this attitude had to change. There were obvious advantages to the "unthinkable" idea of recruiting slaves. Once promised their freedom if they enlisted, slaves were bound to join up in large numbers, and if the condition of gaining freedom was that they sign up for long enlistments, the evil of short-term enlistments could be partially overcome. Since they had fewer reasons to cling to the regions from which they had left for service, the slaves were less likely to desert and return home.

Thus, slaves were finally allowed to serve. Their numbers grew after Congress began to impose quotas on the states in 1777 and after masters, who preferred not to serve, sent their slaves as substitutes. Already by October 23, 1777, a Hessian officer was writing in his journal: "The negro can take the field instead of his master; and therefore no regiment is to be seen in which there are not negroes, in abundance, and among them are able-bodied, strong and brave fellows."[6]

Most blacks who enlisted served in mixed regiments and fought side by side with whites. Rhode Island had a black battalion of 226 officers and enlisted men, commanded by Colonel Christopher Greene: the battalion fought until the end of the war in 1783, acquitting itself with courage and skill at the battles of Rhode Island, Red Bank, Yorktown, and Fort Oswego. However, except for Maryland, slaves were enlisted only in the North. Virginia would not tolerate the idea, and South Carolina and Georgia rejected appeals from the Continental Congress for the "immediate . . . raising" of three thousand "able-bodied negroes" and their formation into separate battalions commanded by white officers. Congress proposed to compensate the owners up to $1,000 for each Negro man of "standard size" not over thirty-five years of age who enlisted for the duration of the war and passed muster. The black soldiers were to receive neither pay nor bounty, but were to be clothed and sustained at the expense of the United States; "every negro who shall well and faithfully serve as a soldier to the end of the present war, and shall then return his arms" was to "be emancipated, and receive the sum of fifty dollars."[7]

Determined to protect slavery—the foundation on which the economic and social structure of white society rested—and fearing that arming slaves was "a most unpleasant way to commit suicide," South Carolina and Georgia rejected the congressional plan.[8] Christopher Gadsden summed up the general feeling in the two states when he wrote from Charleston: "We are much disgusted here at the Congress recommending us to arm our slaves, it was received with great resentment, as a very dangerous and impolitic step."[9]

Rather than arm the slaves, South Carolina preferred to use them to spur white enlistments. The legislature substituted for the Congressional plan one that promised a slave as a bounty to each white enlistee. General Thomas Sumter also used this method in his scheme, known as "Sumter's law." Under his plan, he enlisted regulars for ten months' service, to be paid in slaves plundered from the Tories; the pay scale ranged from three and one-half slaves per annum for a colonel to a full-grown slave for a private for each month's enlistment.

Neither the patriot slaveowners nor the Southern Sons of Liberty seemed to be bothered that the British would take advantage of the Americans' reluctance to use slaves. And take advantage they did. About sixty-five thousand blacks fought with or worked for the enemy in return for the promise of freedom. On the other hand, only five to eight thousand blacks served in the Continental Army. Other blacks, however, made valuable contributions to the patriot cause as military laborers. They were employed in manufacturing the supplies of war and in working with the army as drivers and guides, as well as in repairing roads and building redoubts and outworks. As Benjamin Quarles has pointed out, the black was often the man "behind the man behind the gun." [10]

While rejecting the idea of enlisting slaves as soldiers and instead using them only sparingly in the army, the Virginia legislature, late in 1779, voted to employ a thousand blacks in the navy. Their rationale, no doubt, was that at sea, far removed from the plantations, fighting blacks posed no threat to the institution of slavery. Hence, the Continental Navy, such as it was, the state navies, the privateers, and vessels sailing under letters of marque, all carried blacks on their rosters. In the state navies, Negroes held rank as seamen of different classes. Some served as pilots, and in South Carolina, where black pilots served in significant numbers, black artisans were employed to erect naval fortifications. [11]

Black women, usually slaves, served with the American army as nurses and cooks. General William Smallwood wrote to the president of the Maryland Council: "I shall be glad that the sale of two Negro women . . . might be suspended. Their services will not only be valuable to me, but will promote the good of the service as they will supply the place of soldiers—who other ways must be necessarily employed in my kitchen." [12]

On the homefront, women, black and white, nursed the wounded, folded bandages, and sent food to the soldiers. The Daughters of Liberty spun cloth and made shirts for the soldiers. Women managed the farms during the absence of their husbands and sons, took care of their husbands' business, and continued to handle all the chores of the home. [13]

Three women fought on the patriot side during the war. Margaret (Molly) Corbin, a farm laborer who followed her husband into the Continental Army, went into action beside him during the battle of Fort Washington on November 15, 1776, firing a two-gun battery. When he fell mortally wounded, she kept serving his gun until she herself was severely wounded, one arm nearly severed and part of her breast mangled by three bursts of grapeshot. Partially recovering after a jolting wagon journey to Philadelphia, she was released to the American army's Invalided Corps. The Continental Congress voted "Captain Molly" a pension on July 6, 1779, decreeing that she receive "during her natural life or the continuance of said disability the one half of the monthly pay drawn by a soldier in the service of these States . . . and one complete suit of clothes or the value therein in money." For the rest of her life, she drew medical and commissary supplies from West Point.

Margaret (Molly) Hayes, another farm laborer, also followed her husband to war. During the Battle of Monmouth in New Jersey on June 28, 1778, with the temperature soaring close to 100 degrees, she brought pitcher after pitcher of cool water to the troops from a nearby spring, thereby acquiring the name "Molly Pitcher." On one of her trips, she saw her husband wounded. Grasping the rammer staff from his hand, she fired the cannon until the end of the battle. General Washington issued her a warrant as a noncommissioned officer. Although she received state honors, "Molly Pitcher" was never awarded the army pension to which she was entitled.

The third woman to serve was Deborah Sampson Gannett, an enlisted soldier in the Continental Army. Left fatherless at five, she was bound out as an indentured servant at the age of ten. When her indenture ended, she determined to serve her country. Disguised in a man's clothing, she made her way to the town of Uxbridge, Massachusetts, where, using the alias "Robert Shurtleff," she enlisted in April 1781. She served with the 4th Massachusetts Regiment through months of hard fighting at White Plains, Tarrytown, and Yorktown. Noted in the forefront of every action, she suffered both sword and bullet wounds, but fearing that her sex would be discovered, she made light of her injuries. On the march north after the Battle of Yorktown, she succumbed to a fever in Philadelphia. She was carried, unconscious, to the hospital, where her secret was discovered, but it was kept by the doctor until she was discharged.

For her services to the nation, Deborah Sampson Gannett received pensions from both the federal government and the state of Massachusetts. After her death, her husband became the first American to be granted a pension as a soldier's widower. At the time of the award, the Congressional Committee on Revolutionary Pensions paid the following tribute to the female indentured servant who became the only woman to enter the ranks of the Continental Army as a common soldier: "The Committee believes they are warranted in saying that the whole history of the American Revolution furnishes no other similar example of female heroism, fidelity and courage."[14]

*   *   *

In April 1779, General Washington complained that "a wagon load of money will scarcely purchase a wagon load of provisions." By this time, prices had risen so enormously that they soared over 45 percent in a single month. At the close of 1779, prices were more than seven times their level at the beginning of the year.[15]

The inflationary trend had started with the outbreak of the war as the value of Continental currency dropped and merchants took advantage of the wartime scarcity of goods to raise prices to exorbitant levels. Workers reacted to this attack on their living standards by demanding higher wages. To counteract the inflation, the Continental Congress, interstate conventions, states, and towns tried to institute price and wage controls. These efforts came to nothing, however, and a few continued to get rich while many, including the soldiers fighting the war, went hungry.[16] "Four months' pay of a private will not procure his wretched wife and children a single bushel of wheat," one soldier complained. Another echoed: "Few of us have private fortunes: many have families who already are suffering everything that can be received from an ungrateful country. Are we then to submit to all the inconveniences, fatigue and dangers of a camp life, while our wives and children are perishing for want of common necessaries at home?"

Joshua Huntington, who had left Yale just before graduation to join the army, graphically described the tribulations of soldiers with whom he came into contact. Criticizing the Connecticut legislature for failing to pay the soldiers, or even provide for their families if no money was given to them, he wrote:

> not a day passes my head, but some soldier with tears in his eyes, hands me a letter to read from his wife painting forth the distresses of his family in such strains as these "I am without bread, and cannot get any, the Committee will not supply me, my children will starve, or if they do not, they must freeze, we have no wood, neither can we get any—pray come home."[17]

In the absence of legal controls, which were little more than paper regulations, it was easy for employers to keep wages at legal levels while violating the price provisions. Workers found themselves victimized by "an insatiable thirst for riches." A writer signing himself "Mobility" warned in the *Pennsylvania Packet* of December 10, 1778:

> This country has been reduced to the brink of ruin by the infamous practises of Monopolizers and Forestallers. Not satisfied with monopolizing European and West-Indian goods, they have lately monopolized the *STAFF OF LIFE*. It has been found in Britain and in France, that the people have always done themselves justice when the scarcity of bread has arisen from the avarice of forestallers. They have broken open magazines—appropriated stores to their own use without paying for them—and in some instances have hung up the culprits, who have cheated their distress, without judge or jury. Hear this and tremble, ye enemies to the freedom and happiness of your country. We can live without sugar, coffee, molasses and rum—but we cannot live without bread—Hunger will break through stone walls, and the resentment executed by it may end in your destruction.

Shortly after this notice was published, sailors struck for higher wages in Philadelphia. Approximately 150 sailors marched through the southeastern part of the city, boarded some ships, unrigged them, and dragged away some soldiers who would not join them in the demand for higher wages. The strike was put down by Continental troops, and the strikers were brought before the Justices of the Peace. Fifteen leaders were arrested and fined. [17]

Discontent grew, and some workers began to feel that they were shedding blood "merely in order to exchange the rule of one oligarchy for that of another no less oppressive and self-seeking." However, this was not the general mood. The lower classes decided to enforce price controls in their own way. In Albany, New York, "monopolizers" were forced to stand on a scaffold in the marketplace and swear to observe regulations. In New England, Major General Horatio Gates blamed British agents for price increases and ordered the apprehension of "extortioners," so that they "may be dealt with as the case may require." Workers went from shop to shop and put Gates' order into operation by compelling the merchants to sell their goods at legal prices. [18]

In Boston, a mechanic calling himself "Joyce Jr.," a name he took from the original Joyce who had arrested King Charles I, advertised for other patriots "to carry into execution the act of this state to prevent monopoly and oppression." Abigail Adams, writing to her husband John, described how a band of five hundred followed Joyce Jr., "who was mounted on horseback, with a red coat, a white wig, and a drawn sword, with drum and fife following." This band "carted" five terrified "Tory villains" outside the town limits of Boston, overturned the cart, and warned them not to return to the city. Joyce Jr. advertised his thankfulness that his warning to the shopkeepers had reminded at least some of them of their duty to sell at fixed prices. Abigail Adams also described how a group of Boston women treated a merchant who hoarded coffee:

> A number of females, some say a hundred, some say more, assembled with a cart and trunks, marched down to the warehouse and demanded the keys, which he refused to deliver. Upon which one of them seized him by his neck and tossed him into the cart. Upon his finding no quarter, he delivered the keys when they tipped up the cart and discharged him; then opened the warehouse, hoisted out the coffee themselves, put it into the trunks and drove off. [19]

Another method used to enforce price controls was the "publication" of monopolizers and price gougers as "enemies of the country." Watertown, Massachusetts, ordered that persons selling goods at excessive prices be labeled "enemies of their country and cried as such by the town clerk" for six months after every public town meeting. Patriotic newspapers mounted a campaign against "dirty little hawkers and forestallers" who undermined the cause of independence and oppressed the poor by adding to the "exorbitant price" of necessities and "increasing the price of labour." In a letter to the *Boston Gazette*, a mechanic addressed himself to "monopolizers": "You are a vermin among people. . . . You are worse enemies to the country than Burgoyne [the British general]." Another correspondent called price violators robbers and thieves. [20] In 1779, the Committee of Thirteen, appointed by the town of Boston, published the names of offenders "as enemies of their country, that the public may abstain from all trade and conversation with them, and the people at large inflict upon them that punishment which such wretches deserve." [21]

The most serious popular uprising occurred that same year— 1779—in Philadelphia. Pennsylvania had passed a price-fixing law in October 1778, but it had not been enforced. In January 1779, the Supreme Council of Pennsylvania renewed its efforts to keep the price of "bread and other necessaries of life" at reasonable levels. Monopolizers, whose "most heinously universal" actions had been "ruinous to the industrious poor," were to be searched out and persecuted. Then when food prices, especially of bread, continued to rise as a result of manipulation by "monopolizers," tough penalties were prescribed for such offenses by the General Assembly. Without enforcement, however, laws were of no use, and prices continued to rise. [22]

On May 12, 1779, the 1st Company of the Philadelphia Militia Artillery, composed of "the poor and laboring part of the city," [23] sent a long memorial to the Supreme Executive Council. It began by reminding the council that the militia had "again been called out in defence of the state," and again were "willing to exert" themselves "in behalf of the United States" and in support of "the virtuous cause of freedom and independency." Nevertheless, they also noted certain "circumstances and grievances" that they and others of their "worthy fellow countrymen" were forced to endure. The militia had been called out many times for service in the war, and each time they had had to leave their families "at every risk of distress and hardship." Each time they returned to Philadelphia from a campaign, they found that many had taken advantage of their absence and had "enormously advanced the prices on every necessary and convenience of life." After one battle in which several militiamen had been killed, those who had "return'd (as we thought) happily to the city" found to their dismay that "every article of life or convenience was rais'd upon us, eight, ten, or twelve fold at least; and many of us are at a loss to this day what course a station of life to adopt to support ourselves and families."

While the militia thus suffered, the rich were escaping military service. Fines for not serving in the armed forces had been "artfully evaded" by many, and even when the fines were increased, they had little effect, "for men in these exorbitant times can acquire more by monopolizing, or by and under trade, in one day, than will defray all their expence of fines or penalties in a whole year." Thus, the poor were still bearing the burdens and found themselves "fighting the battles of those who are avariciously intent on amassing wealth by the destruction of the more virtuous part of the community."

In short, it was a poor man's war, and because of the monopolizers, the poor were getting poorer. Such a state of affairs could no longer be tolerated. Describing the abuses they had endured during 1777, the militia observed: "We had arms in our hands, and knew the use of them; but instead of avenging ourselves or retaliating on our innate and worst of enemies, we patiently waited the interference of the legislative authority." But there was a limit to patience, and an equitable solution *had* to be found immediately.

The militia called on the council to use its influence to get the Assembly to remedy the existing evils. They wanted prices controlled, the power of the monopolizers broken, and a law passed which would fine each person who did not serve "in proportion to his estate." Or else the Assembly could drop all fines and leave it to the militia to compel "every able bodied man to join them." [24]

Ten days after the militiamen presented their memorial, notices appeared in Philadelphia for a public meeting to deal with

the question of regulating prices. When a man, generally believed to be "a great speculator," tried to pull one of the posters
down, "the militia," noted Sarah Bache, a contemporary,
"seized him, and after taking him about on a horse, bareheaded,
lodged him in the old Gaol. They took up several others and put
them in the same place." [25] During the day, "men with clubs"
went to several stores and "obliged people to lower their prices."
When a person laughed as these regulators passed by, they put
him in jail. [26]

That night, the Germantown militia stood guard at the public meeting. Daniel Roberdaux, a mechanic, who opened the proceedings, denounced those who were "getting richer by sucking
the blood of this country." The only way to overcome exploita-
tion of the people "by monopolizers," he said, was to reduce the
price of "goods and provisions." Since "combinations have been
formed for raising the prices of goods and provisions . . . the community, in their own defence, have a natural right to counteract
such combinations, and to set limits which affect themselves."
Pointing out that "it is a surprising thing that the more goods we
have brought into this city, the dearer they have been," he called
for a week-by-week reduction in prices.

The resolutions adopted by the mass meeting provided for the
appointment of a committee to examine the dealings of the al-
legedly patriotic financier, Robert Morris. Another committee
was to gather information on charges or complaints leveled
against persons in the public service. They resolved that anyone
"who by sufficient testimoney can be proved inimical to the interest and independence of the United States" should not be allowed "to remain among us." The various investigating committees were directed to "take measures" to execute this resolve.

The meeting pointed out that prices charged by the merchants
for rum, sugar, coffee, flour, and tea had "greatly arisen within
this week past, without any real or apparent cause." It insisted
that the people would not allow themselves to be "eaten up by
monopolizers and forestallers," and it demanded "that the prices
of those articles be immediately reduced to what they were" on
May 1. A committee was appointed to ascertain and publish
what the May 1 prices were and to receive in writing any complaints against dealers who refused to accept or who obstructed

"this necessary regulation." These prices were to remain in effect until July 1, when the prices would revert to their April 1
level. On August 1, the prices would become what they had been
on March 1, and so on, until prices would not be more than they
had been on January 1, 1779. The committee was also to prepare
a plan for effecting such price reductions throughout the United
States.

The meeting pledged to carry out its resolves "at the hazard of
our lives," if need be.[27] The militia, many of whom were at the
meeting, must have been pleased. But Sarah Bache was worried,
even though she hoped "the regulation will have a good effect,"
as people believed guilty of crimes against the populace were
being clapped into jail. Conservative Philadelphians, who had
warned that separation from the mother country might unleash
the "mob," were now able to say, "We told you so."[28]

In an attempt to stop the committees from going about their
work, Joseph Reed, the president of Pennsylvania, and 599 other
leaders presented a memorial to the Continental Congress, requesting action to improve the economic situation. That body,
"by unanimous consent," issued an address "To the inhabitants
of the United States of America" on May 26, 1779. It was immediately printed in the newspapers and issued in the form of a
handbill. Those who had signed the memorial were disappointed,
however. Congress appeared to justify the people's actions to
put a stop to "the artifices of men who have hastened to enrich
themselves by monopolizing the necessaries of life," and conceded that the state governments had not used "as much dili-
gence . . . in detecting and reforming [such] abuses" as they had
"in complaining of them." Thus, Congress admitted that more
action was needed, and the address concluded by declaring that
it was essential for victory to "prevent the produce of the country from being monopolized."[29]

With the blessing of the Congress of the United States, the
committees appointed by the Philadelphia public meeting went
into action. Tom Paine and a Committee of Inspection visited
Robert Morris and seized a cargo of flour, ignoring the wealthy
Philadelphian's complaint that it was "inconsistent with the
principles of liberty to prevent a man from the disposal of his
property on such terms and for such considerations as he may

think fit." Alarmed, other monopolizers fell into line, and prices began to drop.[30]

On June 26, the General Committee set up by the public meeting issued a lengthy address to all citizens of the United States. It told of the good work of the Philadelphia committee and urged every state and county to establish similar committees to fight high prices. It asserted boldly that, even though "there are offences against society which are not in all cases offences against law, and for which no written laws can be timely constructed or sufficiently applied," this did not mean that the people could not act to uphold their interests. For the people "maintain the right, as well as the necessity, of holding every man accountable to the community for such parts of his conduct by which the public welfare appears to be injured or dishonored, and for which no legal redress can be obtained."[31]

The news of what was happening in Philadelphia spread far and wide. In Boston, handbills appeared, reading:

> Sons of Boston! Sleep no longer!
> You are requested to meet on the floor of the Old-South Meeting House tomorrow . . .
> Rouse and catch the Philadelphia spirit: rid the community of those Monopolizers and Extortioners, who, like cancer-worms, are gnawing upon your vitals. They are reducing the currency to waste-paper, by refusing to take it for many articles. The infection is dangerous. . . .Public examples, at this time, would be public benefits![32]

VENGEANCE.

The committee, which was composed of mechanics, did more than theorize about the people's right to act. A contemporary Philadelphian wrote on June 26:

> Ye bellman went about ye City at near ten this night, desiring ye people to arm themselves with guns or clubs, and make a search for such as had sent any flour, gunpowder, etc. out of town [against the Committee's order], with great threats to the Tories — said it was by order of a Committee.[33]

Two days after the mechanics of Philadelphia had acted through the committee appointed by the town meeting, the same militia company of laboring poor that had memorialized the council in May issued a public statement in support of the committee's action. The body was pessimistic about the value of resolutions in solving the serious problems facing the poor, and it proclaimed: "We have arms in our hands and know the use of them, — and are ready and willing to support your Honorable Board in fully executing the righteous and equitable measures for which you were appointed; nor will we lay them down till this is accomplished. We wish not to have the preeminence; but we will no longer be trampled upon." They went on to pledge: "We will see the virtuous, innocent and suffering part of the community redressed, and endeavour to divest this city of the disaffected, inimical, and preyers on the vitals of the inhabitants, be their rank and station what they may."

The militia closed their "unanimous" statement with the warning that "if by reason of the obstinancy and perverseness of individuals, your Committee find themselves inadequate to the task, *our drum shall beat to arms.*" [34]

Early in August 1779, the position of the public meeting was endorsed by a popular vote. Two separate slates were submitted to the electorate: one favored enforcing price control by committee action, while the other was lukewarm. The result was an overwhelming victory for the slate that had come out vigorously for committee action — 2,115 to 281. On August 18, a group of eighty merchants sent a long memorial to the Committee of Enforcement, defying the popular vote and refusing to accept price control by committee. The committee angrily threatened to stop price gouging, but the merchants, for the most part, ignored its blasts. By the end of September, it was clear that the efforts to control the monopolizers were a failure; the merchants were as "impolitic" as ever, and prices as oppressive as ever. With another denunciation of the monopolists, the committee went out of existence. [35]

On October 2, 1779, the Committee of Privates published a newspaper notice "earnestly" requesting that all militiamen attend a mass meeting of the militia to be held two days later. The meeting resolved to take action against the chief monopolizers, and groups of militiamen went around the city and took the four leading ones under guard to the Commons. Once they had arrived there, the prisoners were led through the streets "with the drum after them, beating ye Rogue's March," to Fort Wilson. Meanwhile, a number of men, fearful that they were to be the next targets of the crowd, armed themselves and gathered at the home of James Wilson, a defender of Tories and a leading critic of price regulation. As the crowd passed Wilson's house, at Third and Walnut streets, shots rang out. Several people were killed, and many were "dangerously wounded."

While a number of historians have charged that the "Fort Wilson Riot" was the result of a vicious "mob" of militiamen who went about senselessly shooting innocent citizens, John A. Alexander, in his excellent study of the affair, demonstrates that "the exchange of fire between the militia and the Fort Wilsoners began after most of the militia had marched past the house [of James Wilson]. This would indicate that there was, in fact, no plan to attack the house." Even more, Alexander sees the incident as a significant illustration of the views of such historians as George Rudé, Edward P. Thompson, Eric Hobsbawm, and their followers. They contend that the popular uprisings that occurred in preindustrial France, England, and America were consciously directed by the rioters, aimed at particular prevailing combinations of the economic, political, and social grievances, needs, and aspirations of the participating crowds. Among Alexander's conclusions are: (1) that the grievances of the militia — psychological, political, and economic — were legitimate as well as varied; (2) that the militia, as well as the town meetings, believed in the Revolutionary principle that citizens had a right to directly redress those grievances that a government either would not or could not correct; (3) that the militia, lacking effective economic and political power, was compelled to use physical coercion to achieve its ends; and (4) that the militia, only after other means had been exhausted, and with adequate organization and planning, went into the streets as a purposeful body, keeping its explosive elements in check and limiting its violent and destructive tendencies. [36] When one also considers the fact (which Alexander does not mention) that the militia was made up of lesser artisans, journeymen, and laborers, we can see that they were acting to redress, not only their own specific grievances, but those of most of the Philadelphia working class as well.

A troop of cavalry was called in to restore law and order, and it arrested and imprisoned twenty-seven militiamen. However, conservative Philadelphians were convinced that the events of October 4 were only the beginning of an uprising of the poverty-stricken. "God help us—terrible times," one cried out. "The poor starving here and rise for redress. Many fly the city for fear of vengeance."[37]

Nothing of the kind happened. One reason was that no legal action was taken against anyone involved in the incident. For another, an agreement was worked out between Pennsylvania officials and the militiamen under which the militia would choose a captain and two privates from each battalion to "lay their grievances before the Assembly." The council and the Assembly then acted swiftly to prevent further uprisings of the poor. Acknowledging that there was "great distress among poor housekeepers in this city, from the high price of flour," the council asked the Assembly to authorize the distribution of one hundred barrels of flour. In the distribution, a "preference" was to be given "to such families as have performed militia duty."[38]

On October 11, after consulting with delegates from the militia, the Assembly enacted a law that dealt with one of its chief grievances. It dropped the flat fine of one hundred pounds for failure to serve in the militia and provided that thereafter fines would be levied with "a due regard to the value of such delinquent's estate and circumstances." An individual could be fined up to one thousand pounds, and no fine was to be less than one hundred pounds, "except in cases of inability of body and estate."[39]

The council and the Assembly also issued a strongly worded warning to the merchants and traders of Philadelphia, urging them to learn from the Fort Wilson incident and to prevent any future uprisings by avoiding price gouging.[40] This warning brought a halt to monopolistic practices—but only temporarily. In February 1780, a multistate convention met in Philadelphia, but nothing was done about methods to "prevent monopoly and oppression." The merchants throughout the states, including, of course, those in Philadelphia, were quick to take their cue. As price controls passed from the scene, price gouging resumed at an increased rate, leaving the workers at the mercy of both their employers and the monopolistic merchants and traders. [41]

Despite the misery of the working class during most of the war, the British and their Tory allies were never able to persuade them to turn against the Revolution. They distributed literature assuring the workers that desertion of the American cause "would bring lasting honor and immediate rewards instead of the uncertainty and poverty they had otherwise to face." Some workers did capitulate, but a more typical reaction was that of the Baltimore Whig Club, consisting of sailors, watchmakers, tailors, and shoemakers. In 1777, they ordered a Tory printer, William Goddard, "to leave town by morning and the country in three days," or else he would be "subject to the resentment of a *Legion*." Goddard sneered at the humble occupations of the members of the club and asked scornfully how a man who was only fit to "patch a shoe" had the temerity to patch a state. After a personal call by a committee of the club, he found it wise to leave Baltimore. [42]

In another incident, the British commander, Sir Henry Clinton, heard that the Pennsylvania 11th Regiment, many of whose members were Philadelphia workers, were threatening mutiny because they "had not seen a paper dollar in the way of pay for nearly twelve months," and their families were starving. Clinton sent them enticing messages and dispatched representatives to negotiate with them. The emissaries fared badly. A few of them were captured by the soldiers and hanged. Their bodies were left to swing in the wind for five days as a lesson to those who questioned the workingmen's loyalty to the Revolution. [43]

Among the grievances of the workingmen in the 1st Company of the Philadelphia Militia Artillery was that wealthy opponents of America were at large in Philadelphia. At the militia's insistence, the Assembly enacted a law depriving such people of the opportunity "to spread disaffection" or "enjoy the same freedom which the good citizens of this commonwealth, who have given proofs of their attachment to the common cause, enjoy." A person judged "an enemy to the American cause" could be held without bail until the Assembly considered the case, or at the discretion of the officials he could be sent out of the state. [44] With the home front more secure, the workers of the militia fought for the American cause until they were mustered out in 1783.

In the second of his *Crisis* essays, written to lift the morale of soldiers and civilians alike, Thomas Paine revealed an uncanny grasp of the advantages of the Revolutionary Army, despite its continual setbacks. Writing in January 1777, he predicted that the British army would find it impossible to conquer the colonies:

> Like a game of drafts, we can move out of *one* square to let you come in, in order that we may afterwards take two or three for one. . . . In all the wars which you have formerly been concerned in you had only armies to contend with; in this case you have both an army and a country to combat.

The British, he insisted could capture American cities, but they could never truly subdue the countryside. [45]

With Cornwallis's surrender at Yorktown in 1781, the British were finally convinced that even a fortune in lives and money were not sufficient to conquer the Americans. In February 1782, the House of Commons voted to end the war, and the Treaty of Paris in 1783 formally recognized American independence. Thus, in 1783, the American republic, born of revolution, took its place among the nations of the world—an independent nation, free from imperial regulation, free to plan, to organize, to expand, and to build without being subjected to foreign authority.

American labor could take pride in the final outcome. The mechanics, lesser artisans, seamen, and laborers had been the driving force, exerting pressure from below for militant resistance to British policies, and were among the first to call for independence. While some workers had cooperated with the British, the majority, despite hardships and impoverishment, had given effective aid to the patriot cause, either in the armed forces or as civilian producers. Throughout the Revolution and war, labor had been in the forefront of the struggles both for home rule and over who should rule at home.

What did this dual struggle bring labor? The answer remains a matter of controversy among historians. Some have made a strong case that colonial merchants, property owners, and planters emerged from the Revolution with greater economic and political power than before, and labor with less; that in cities like New York, Philadelphia, and Charleston, many prominent merchants, although Loyalist or at least "neutralist," were able to return to power after the war, while the city artisans and laborers who supported the Revolutionary cause remained relatively powerless; that the subjection of women was buttressed by their exclusion from the Declaration of Independence; that the Revolution accelerated the trend toward a consolidation of wealth and a deterioration of the conditions of the lower classes; and that the lower classes as a whole, profited very little.

In 1827, this very point was stressed by a worker who called himself "Unlettered Mechanic" in an address delivered before the Mechanics and Working Classes of the city and county of Philadelphia. The speaker, believed to be William Heighton, a 27-year-old shoemaker who worked in Philadelphia, insisted that, even though the Revolutionary artisans, mechanics, and laborers had given their blood and lives to maintain the "inalienable rights" of "life, liberty, and the pursuit of happiness," the descendants of these workers living in the Jacksonian era had not benefited from their sacrifices: "Every candid and reflecting mind must admit that the working class of our country do not enjoy the rights of liberty and equality." The "Unlettered Mechanic" gave the following reason for this state of affairs:

If the wealth producing class (the working classes) had claimed their rights at the birth of our national liberty, and maintained them unimpaired to this day, we should not have been in our present degraded condition. But for the want of information relative to their rights and power, they were controlled by those possessing superior skill, who assumed the power of forming laws which have ever since chained the working class down to poverty. For the want of knowledge among our predecessors, they were led to surrender their rights to the nonproductive and accumulating class, and thereby subjected themselves to degradation and oppression, which has been handed down to us, and will continue to grow deeper and more severe until we shall obtain the requisite information to claim and possess these rights. [46]

Other historians have insisted that the politicization of the
urban workers during the Revolutionary era initiated a trend
that could never be reversed; that the war immediately contributed to the extension of democratic rights and that labor gained
both short-and long-term benefits; that the American war swept
away most of the remaining vestiges of feudalism, and freed
American capitalism from mercantilist control; and that independence provided the basis for the extension of American democracy and the conditions for economic expansion, thus serving the long-range interests of both black and white workers. [47]

Many workers did gain immediate benefits from the Revolution, while others benefited over a longer period of time. Thousands of indentured servants obtained their freedom through enlistment in the army, and the traffic in them ceased during the
war years. A meeting of New York citizens on January 24, 1784,
called for the abolition of the "traffic in white people, heretofore
countenanced in this state, while under the arbitrary control of
the British government," because such traffic was contrary "to
the idea of liberty this country has so happily established." Despite this plea, the importation of servants was renewed vigorously after the war, the number imported from Germany and Ireland rivaling that of the prewar years. In the long run, however,
and partly as a result of the Revolution, indentured servitude
disappeared. [48]

While it took a bloody Civil War almost a century later to abolish chattel slavery completely, the War for Independence did
result in some concrete gains for blacks as well. Many who served
in the American or British forces did secure their freedom. Others were liberated as a result of the increasing number of manu-
missions granted by masters influenced by the ideology of the
Revolution. Finally, largely as a result of this ideology (although
the hostility of white workers toward the competition of black
slaves also played a part), by 1804, all the Northern states and
the Northwest Territory had abolished slavery. This was accomplished either by immediate emancipation, as in Vermont, New
Hampshire, and Massachusetts, or by gradual emancipation in
the other states. The terms of emancipation were that children
born of slave mothers were freed after an apprenticeship lasting
from eighteen to twenty-eight years, during which the slaveowners were entitled to the unpaid services of the blacks. [49]

The American Revolution created a change in the relations between employer and employed. Jonathan Boucher, A Tory minister, noticed this change in 1773:

> Both employers and the employed, much to their mutual
> shame and inconvenience, no longer live together with any-
> thing like attachment and cordiality on either side; and the
> laboring classes, instead of regarding the rich as their
> guardians, patrons, and benefactors, now look on them as
> so many overgrown collossuses, whom it is no demerit in
> them to wrong.[50]

The War for Independence widened the gap between employer
and worker. The demands of the military establishment put less
of a premium on quality and more on quantity, with the result
that the small shop, presided over and often solely occupied by
the individual entrepreneur, began to give way to the early factory. Newspaper advertisements referred to a "brass gun factory," or a "Continental factory." Reports in the same papers
mentioned that where little skill was required, the managers of
these factories employed women (especially in the textile plants),
military prisoners, the poor, and other types of unskilled labor.[51]
As Richard B. Morris points out:

> The rise of the factory, the transition from custom work to
> wholesale order work, and the concentration of workers in
> certain expanding industries served to bring about more
> distinct class stratifications. This period was marked by a
> decline in the apprenticeship system; inexpert workmen
> now came into direct competition with skilled journeymen,
> as middlemen now pitted master against master giving
> their orders to the lowest cost producer.[52]

While some workers were better off after the Revolution and
others were not, all emerged from it with a greater class consciousness and a greater ability to voice their grievances. For
thousands in the working classes, the experience of ten years of
political participation and seven years of war carried over into
the American labor movement. The American labor movement

was itself a product of both the freeing of American economic life from the restrictions of British mercantile policy and the widening gap between employer and worker during the war years.

American labor gained precious experience from the Revolution. Through the Sons of Liberty, it learned the value of collective action and militancy, and through its Committees of Correspondence it learned the importance of close contacts with workers of other cities and countries. From its activities in extra-legal bodies, it learned how to organize together with allies to achieve common objectives, and, when necessary, to act as an independent political force. Finally, it learned to reject the upper-class view that workers must defer to their so-called betters, and to assert its right to have a leading voice in its country's affairs.

In short, the Revolution would fundamentally alter the future of American labor. In the continuing struggle of American workers for a better social order, the American Revolution stands as a momentous landmark.

The American Revolution also exerted a powerful influence over succeeding generations of American workers. "Your fathers of the Revolution," declared the *Workingman's Advocate* of October 31, 1829, in urging the formation of a labor party, "secured to you a form of government which guarantees to you, almost universally, the elective franchise. . . . If you possess the rights of freemen, you have exercised them as the privileges of slaves. . . . Awake, then, from your slumbers; and insult not the memories of the heroes of '76, by exhibiting to the world, that what they risked their lives, their fortunes, and their sacred honour to obtain, you do not think worth preserving."

In June 1836, the Journeymen Cordwainers' Union of Philadelphia responded as follows to the warning of employers that they would not hire any shoemakers who belonged to a labor organization:

It is our prerogative to say that institutions we will be members of, that being bequeathed to us by our fore-fathers — the toilworn veterans of '76 who nobly moistened the soil with their blood in defense of equal rights and equal privileges, that we, their descendants, might enjoy the blood-bought legacy free and unmolested. [53]

In 1835, the Philadelphia workers went out on the first general strike in American history (a strike for the ten-hour day, which they won) after they read a circular containing the sentence: "We claim BY THE BLOOD OF OUR FATHERS, shed on our battle fields in the war of the Revolution, the rights of American citizens, and no earthly power shall resist our righteous claim with impunity."[54] In 1846, New England textile workers planned (without success) a general strike for the ten-hour day to start on the Fourth of July, calling it "a second Independence Day."[55] "What has the ten hour system to do with this day?" asked a New England labor spokesman. "Why, it is part of the Declaration of Independence, 'the pursuit of happiness.' The all day system does not allow the pursuit of happiness and hence there is propriety in connecting with the Fourth, labor's effort to reduce the hours of labor from an indefinite number to ten."[56]

Ira Steward, the champion of the eight-hour day, launched one of the struggles to achieve that goal at the 1878 Fourth of July celebration in Chicago, declaring that "no two words shall be spoken together so often as Fourth of July and eight hours." The meeting resolved "that while the Fourth of July was heralded a hundred years ago in the name of liberty, we now herald this day in behalf of the great economic measure of Eight Hours, or shorter day's work for wageworkers everywhere."[57]

The great 1860 shoemakers' strike in Lynn, Massachusetts, started on George Washington's birthday, and strikers called that celebration "sacred to the memory of one of the greatest men the world has ever produced."[58] During the momentous railroad strike of 1877, a radical Massachusetts clergyman called the strikers "the lineal descendants of Samuel Adams, John Hancock, and the Massachusetts yeomen who began so great a disturbance a hundred years ago . . . only now the kings are money kings and then they were political kings."[59]

Mother Jones began her famous "March of Mill Children" on July 4, 1903, in Philadelphia's Independence Square, in the shadow of the Liberty Bell. The striking band of maimed and crippled nine- to eleven-year-olds from the Kensington mills marched through towns in New Jersey and New York, led by three children dressed as Revolutionary soldiers representing the "Spirit of '76." The group marched on President Roosevelt's summer home at Oyster Bay, Long Island, and although the President was "not at home," the march succeeded in making labor's fight against child labor front page news. [60]

For many generations, almost until the twentieth century, the Fourth of July was celebrated by American labor as *its* day. The practice began in the 1790s, when the first trade unions of shoemakers, printers, coopers, carpenters, and other crafts joined officially with the Democratic-Republican Society in the community and drank toasts to "The Fourth of July, may it ever prove a memento to the oppressed to rise and assert their rights." [61]

At its Fourth of July dinner in 1794, the General Society of Mechanics and Tradesmen toasted "the republican societies of the City of New York." The following year, it accepted the invitation of the Democratic Society for a joint celebration of Independence Day with them, the Tammany Society (another Republican club), and the Coopers Society, a trade union of barrelmakers. A committee worked out the details of an observance that was repeated every year threafter. It began with a parade to a church, where militia officers were seated in front of the pulpit, the mechanics to the right of the center aisle, the Democrats to the left, and Tammany and the Coopers off to either side of the aisle. The ceremony consisted of the reading of the Declaration of Independence, followed by a patriotic oration by a Republican leader. In the evening, the groups dined separately, toasted each other, and exchanged deputations. [62]

Other cities followed the pattern established in New York, and the trade unions and Democratic-Republican Societies turned Independence Day into a Republican festival. The day was "more universally celebrated," a contemporary reported, "than it had been for years." [63]

By the 1820s and 1830s, the Fourth of July had become fixed as the working-class day of celebration. It was a day of parades, banquets, and festivals—a day for renewing the Spirit of '76, for dramatizing the demands of the working class, for rewriting the Declaration of Independence to restore the rights employers "have robbed us of," [64] and a day for toasts like "The Working Men—the legitimate children of '76; their sires left them the legacy of freedom and equality. They are now of age, and are laboring to guarantee the principles of the Revolution." [65]

The great Revolutionary expression—life, liberty, and the pursuit of happiness—underlay labor's desire for higher wages, shorter hours, and better working conditions. The sacrifices their Revolutionary fathers had made stimulated the workers of the nineteenth century in their demands for a greater share of the wealth produced by their labor.

In a "Workingmen's Centennial Song," subtitled "Our Country Born 100 Years Ago," published in 1876, Frank Loring wrote:

And shall *Freedom's* pledge be broken now?
Shall the rich for greed and gain,
Deny the workingmen their rights,
And thus end Freedom's reign?
No! rather let all Freemen rise
To strike those *tyrants* low,
Who dare *undo* what *Freedom* did
One hundred years ago. [66]

Notes

Preface

1. *An Oration Delivered before the Mechanic Apprentices' Library Association, July 4, 1835* (Boston 1835), p. 11.
2. Frederick Saunders, editor, *Our National Jubilee. Orations, Addresses, and Poems Delivered on the Fourth of July 1876, in the Several States of the Union* (New York, 1877), p. 264.
3. Published as Herbert M. Morais, "Artisan Democracy and the American Revolution," *Science and Society* 6 (Summer 1942): 228.
4. See, for example, Richard Walsh, *Charleston's Sons of Liberty: A Study of the Artisans, 1763-1789* (Columbia, S.C., 1959); Roger J. Champagne, "The Sons of Liberty and Aristocracy in New York Politics," Ph. D. dissertation, University of Wisconsin, 1960; Staughton Lynd, "The Revolution and the Common Man: Farm Tenants and Artisans in New York Politics, 1777-1788," Ph.D. dissertation, Columbia University, 1962; Jesse Lemisch, "Jack Tar vs. John Bull: The Role of New York's Seamen in Precipitating the Revolution," Ph.D. dissertation, Yale University, 1962; Charles S. Olton, "Philadelphia Artisans and the American Revolution," Ph.D. dissertation, University of California, Berkeley, 1967; Richard A. Ryerson, "Leadership in Crisis, The Radical Committees of Philadelphia and the Coming of the Revolution in Pennsylvania, 1765-1776: A Study in the Revolutionary Process," Ph.D. dissertation, Johns Hopkins University, 1972; Dirk Hoerder, "People and Mobs: Crowd Action in Massachusetts During the American Revolution, 1765-1780," Inaugural Dissertation, Doctor of Philosophy, Free University, Berlin, 1971; Steven J. Rosswurm, "'That They Were Grown Unruly': The Crowd and Lower-Classes in Philadelphia, 1765-1780," M.A. thesis, Northern Illinois University, 1974.

A number of these same authors have summarized aspects of their doctoral dissertations in articles in scholarly journals. See Staughton Lynd, "The Mechanics in New York Politics, 1774-1788," *Labor History* 5 (Fall 1964): 224-246; Jesse Lemisch, "Jack Tar in the Streets: Merchant Seamen in the Politics of Revolutionary America," *William and Mary Quarterly*, 3d Series, 25 (July 1968): 371-407; Charles S. Olton, "Philadelphia's Mechanics in the First Decade of Revolution, 1765-1775," *Journal of American History* 59 (September 1972): 311-326; and R. A. Ryerson, "Political Mobilization and the American Revolution: The Resistance Movement in Philadelphia, 1765-1776," *William and Mary Quarterly*, 3d Series, 31 (October 1974): 565-588. The anthology *Towards a New Past: Dissenting Essays in American History* (New York, 1968), edited by Barton J. Bernstein, includes Jesse Lemisch's important article, "The American Revolution Seen from the Bottom Up," pp. 3-45. Important sections of Roger Champagne's doctoral dissertation are published in his "The Military Association of the Sons of Liberty," *New York Historical Society Quarterly* 51 (July 1957): 344-360; "New Radicals and the Coming of Independence," *Journal of American History* 2 (June 1964): 21-42, and "Liberty Boys and Mechanics in New York City, 1764-1774," *Labor History* 8 (Spring 1967): 123-135. There is, however, no reference to labor, workingmen, artisans, mechanics, craftsmen in the two-volume, 1,900-page *A History of the American Revolution* by Page Smith (New York, 1976). *See also* Israel Shenker, "Historians Still Debating the Meaning of the American Revolution — If It Was a Revolution," *New York Times*, July 6, 1976, p. 13.

For evidence that none of the enormous output challenging the consensus historical interpretation of colonial society and the role of mechanics and artisans in the American Revolution has had any real impact on one consensus historian, see Robert E. Brown's review of Charles S. Olton, *Artisans for Independence: Philadelphia Mechanics and the American Revolution* (Syracuse, New york, 1975) in *Pennsylvania Magazine of History and Biography* 100 (April 1976): 263-265.

5. Daniel J. Boorstin, *The Genius of American Politics* (Chicago, 1953); Bernard Bailyn, *The Ideological Origins of the American Revolution* (Cambridge, Mass., 1967); Bernard Bailyn, editor, *Pamphlets of the American Revolution, 1750-1776* (Cambridge, Mass., 1955); *The Revolution in Massachusetts, 1691-1780* (Cambridge, Mass., 1955); Robert E. Brown, *Middle-Class Democracy and the Revolution in Massachusetts, 1691-1780* (Ithaca, N.Y., 1955); Robert E. Brown, *Virginia 1705-1786; Democracy or Aristocracy?* (Cambridge, Mass., 1964).

Chapter 1

1. Carl Bridenbaugh, *Cities in Revolt: Urban Life in America, 1743-1776* (New York, 1955), p. 283; Benjamin W. Labaree, *Patriots and Partisans: The Merchants of Newburyport, 1764-1815* (Cambridge, Mass., 1962), pp. 4-5.

2. Milton M. Klein, "Democracy and Politics in Colonial New York," *New York History* 40 (1959): 221-223; Olton, "Philadelphia Mechanics in the First Decade of the Revolution, 1765-1775," p. 316.

3. Alfred Young and Staughton Lynd, "After Carl Becker: The Mechanics and New York City Politics, 1774-1801," *Labor History* 5 (Summer 1964): 217-218; Carl Bridenbaugh, *The Colonial Craftsman* (New York, 1955), p. 155; Carl

Bridenbaugh, *Cities in Revolt*, pp. 283-286; Mary Roys Baker, "Anglo-Massachusetts Trade Union Roots, 1730-1790," *Labor History* 14 (Summer 1973): 352.

4. Bridenbaugh, *Colonial Craftsman*, p. 155.

5. Young and Lynd, op. cit., p. 218.

6. Esther Forbes, *Paul Revere and the World He Lived In* (Boston, 1942), pp. 371-373, 396, 400, 458-459.

7. Richard Walsh, "The Charleston Mechanics: A Brief Study, 1760-1776," *South Carolina Historical Magazine* 60 (1959): 136.

8. Ibid., p. 123.

9. Champagne, "The Sons of Liberty and the Aristocracy in New York Politics," pp. 3-5.

10. "Account of the Grand Federal Procession in Philadelphia," *American Museum* 4 (July 1788): 57-75.

11. *New York Packet*, August 5, 1788.

12. James A. Henretta. *The Evolution of American Society, 1700-1815* (Lexington, Mass., 1973), pp. 105-106.

13. Richard B. Morris, *The American Revolution Reconsidered* (New York, 1967), p. 129. Olton (op. cit., p. 129) rejects this assertion, but offers little evidence to contradict it.

14. Victor S. Clark, *History of Manufacturing in the United States, 1607-1860* (Washington, D.C., 1916), p. 162.

15. Bridenbaugh, *Colonial Craftsman*, p. 129; Richard B. Morris, *Government and Labor in Early America* (New York, 1946), p. 42.

16. Morris, *Government and Labor in Early America*, p. 40; Oscar T. Barck, *New York City During the War for Independence: With Special Reference to the Period of British Occupation* (New York, 1931), p. 140.

17. Philip S. Foner, *History of the Labor Movement in the United States* (New York 1947), I, pp. 14-24.

18. Abbott Emerson Smith, *Colonists in Bondage: White Servitude and Convict Labor in America, 1607-1776* (Chapel Hill, N.C., 1947), p. 28.

19. Philip S. Foner, *History of Black Americans: From Africa to the Emergence of the Cotton Kingdom* (Westport, Conn., 1975), pp. 104-112, 118-210.

20. Philip S. Foner, *Organized Labor and the Black Worker: 1619-1973* (New York, 1974), pp. 3-4.

21. Foner, *History of the Labor Movement*, I, p. 20; Jesse Lemisch, "Jack Tar vs. John Bull: The Role of New York's Seamen in Precipitating the Revolution," pp. 2-3; Lawrence W. Towner, "A Good Master Well Served, A Social History of Servitude in Massachusetts, 1620-1750," Ph.D. dissertation, Northwestern University, 1955, pp. 64-68; Lawrence W. Towner, "The Indentures of Boston's Poor Apprentices: 1734-1805," *Publications of the Colonial Society of Massachusetts* 43 (1956-1963), pp. 417-434.

22. Jackson Turner Main, *The Social Structure of Revolutionary America* (Princeton, N.J., 1965), p. 69; Marcus W. Jernegan, *Laboring and Dependent Classes in Colonial America* (Chicago, 1931), p. 54; Foner, *History of Black Americans*, pp. 194-202.

23. Sam Bass Warner, Jr., *The Private City* (Philadelphia, 1968), p. 246.

24. Main, op. cit., p. 282; Bridenbaugh, *Colonial Craftsman*, pp. 129, 172; Harry D. Berg, "The Organization of Business in Colonial Philadelphia," *Pennsylvania History* 10 (July 1943): 159.

25. Main, op. cit., pp. 298-299; Bridenbaugh, *Colonial Craftsman*, pp. 174-175.

26. Philip S. Foner, editor, *The Complete Writings of Thomas Paine* (New York, 1945), I, p. 203; Benjamin Franklin, "The Internal State of America," edited by Verner W. Crane, *William and Mary Quarterly*, 3d Series, 15 (1958): 225; Morris, *Government and Labor in Early America*, pp. 44-45.

27. Main, op. cit., pp. 132-133; Steven J. Erlanger, "The Colonial Worker in Boston, 1775," U.S. Department of Labor, Bureau of Labor Statistics, New England Regional Office, *Regional Report 75-2*, 1975, pp. 7-8. Morris, *Government and Labor in Early America*, pp. 59, 65, 78-79, 81.

28. Morris, *Government and Labor in Early America*, pp. 47-48; U.S. Bureau of Labor Statistics, *Bulletin 49*, 1929, pp. 50-51; Talcott Williams, *Labor a Hundred Years Ago* (New York, 1887), p. 9; *The Arts and Crafts in New York, 1726-1776*, New York Historical Society Collections (New York, 1936), p. 235.

29. Lemisch, "Jack Tar vs. John Bull," p. 252; Samuel J. McKee, Jr., *Labor in Colonial New York, 1664-1776* (New York, 1935), pp. 11-12; Leonard Lundlin, *Cockpit of the Revolution* (Princeton, N.J., 1940), p. 27.

30. Joseph G. Rayback, *A History of American Labor* (New York, 1966), p. 21.

31. James A. Henretta, "Economic Development and Social Structure in Colonial Boston," *William and Mary Quarterly*, 3d Series, 22 (January 1965): 85-92; Allan Kulefoff, "The Progress of Inequality in Revolutionary Boston," *William and Mary Quarterly*, 3d Series, 28 (July 1971): 376; Dirk Hoerder, *People and Mobs: Crowd Action in Massachusetts During the American Revolution, 1765-1780* (Berlin, 1971), p. 54.

32. John A. Alexander, "Philadelphia's 'Other Half': Attitudes Toward Poverty and the Meaning of Poverty in Philadelphia, 1760-1800," Ph.D. dissertation, University of Chicago, 1973, pp. 33, 136-137, 153-165; Henretta, *Evolution of American Society*, pp. 105-106. For a picture of poverty in Philadelphia during an earlier period, see Peter J. Parker, "Rich and Poor in Philadelphia, 1709," *Pennsylvania Magazine of History and Biography* 99 (January 1975): 3-17; Gary B. Nash, "Poverty and Poor Relief in Pre-Revolutionary Philadelphia," *William and Mary Quarterly*, 3d Series, 33 (January 1976): 28.

33. Douglas Lamar Jones, "The Strolling Poor: Transiency in Eighteenth Century Massachusetts," *Journal of Social History* (Spring 1975): 41-42.

34. Foner, *Organized Labor and the Black Worker*, p. 4.

35. Bridenbaugh, *Colonial Craftsman*, p. 201. For examples of protests of Southern wage earners against the use of Negro slaves, see, Yates Snowden, *Notes on Labor Organization in South Carolina, 1742-1861* (Columbia, S.C., 1914), p. 7; Allen D. Chandler, editor, *The Colonial Records of Georgia* (Atlanta, 1908), V, pp. 378-379.

36. Walsh, op. cit., pp. 136-137; Richard B. Morris, "Labor and Mercantilism," in Richard B. Morris, editor, *The Era of the American Revolution* (New York, 1939), pp. 80-81; Baker, op. cit., p. 364.

37. Morris, *Government and Labor in Early America*, pp. 164-169; Miller, op cit., p. 275; *Pennsylvania Chronicle and Universal Advertiser*, March 27, 1769; U.S. Bureau of Labor Statistics, *Bulletin 499*, p. 10; Foner, *History of Labor* I, p. 25.

38. Jonathan Grossman, "Wage and Price Controls During the American Revolution," *Monthly Labor Review* 96 (September 1973): 3-9.

39. Norman J. Ware, *Labor in Modern Industrial Society* (New York, 1935), p. 8; Herbert Harris, *American Labor* (New Haven, Conn., 1938), p. 5n; Morris, *Government and Labor in Early America*, p. 142n.

40. McKee, op. cit., pp. 44-45.

41. Lemisch, "Jack Tar vs. John Bull," pp. 61-62.

42. Robert F. Seyboldt, "Trade Agreements in Colonial Boston," *New England Quarterly* 2 (April 1929): 309; *Boston Weekly Newsletter*, February 12, 1741.

43. John R. Commons and Associates, *History of Labor in the United States* (New York, 1918), I, p. 25; Richard B. Morris, "Criminal Conspiracy and Early Labor Combinations in New York," *Political Science Quarterly* 52 (March 1937): 77.

44. *New York Journal*, April 7, 1768.

45. Walsh, op. cit., p. 134.

46. "Anglo-Massachusetts Trade Union Roots, 1130-1790," *Labor History* 14 (Summer 1973): 352-396.

47. *Minutes of the Common Council of New York City*, V, p. 15; E. B. O'Callaghan, editor, *Documents Relating to the Colonial History of the State of New York* (Albany, N.Y., 1855), III, pp. 16, 309, 326, 328; Marianna G. Van Rensselaer, *History of New York in the Seventeenth Century* (New York, 1909), I, p. 68; II, p. 219.

48. *New York Mercury*, August 7, 1758.

49. *Georgia Colonial Records*, I, p. 495.

50. O'Callaghan, editor, op. cit., V, p. 322; Rev. A. G. Vermilye, *The Leisler Troubles of 1689* (New York, 1891), p. 25.

51. George W. Edwards, "New York Politics Before the American Revolution," *Political Science Quarterly* 36 (September 1921): 586-602; *New York Gazette*, May 27, October 14, 1734; *New York Weekly Journal*, October 14, 1734; Handbill signed by Timothy Wheelwright and John Chissel, dated September 8, 1734, and "A Song-1734," both in the New York Public Library, Rare Book Room.

52. Edwards, op. cit., pp. 587, 593; O'Callaghan, editor, op. cit., VI, pp. 7-8.

53. Albert B. Hart, editor, *American History Told by Contemporaries* (New York, 1898), II, p. 198.

54. Carl Becker, *The History of Political Parties in the Province of New York, 1760-1776* (Madison, Wis., 1909), pp. 5, 11, 22, 256, 275. See also A. E. McKinley, *The Suffrage Franchise in the English Colonies* (Philadelphia, 1905), p. 36; Arthur M. Schlesinger, *The Colonial Merchants and the American Revolution, 1763-1776* (New York, 1918); Charles H. Lincoln, *The Revolution Movement in Pennsylvania, 1769-1776* (Philadelphia, 1901); James Truslow Adams,

Revolutionary New England, 1691-1776 (Boston, 1923); Richard Hofstadter, *The Progressive Historians* (New York, 1968), p. 441.

55. Robert E. Brown, "Democracy in Colonial Massachusetts," *New England Quarterly* 25 (1952): 291-313; Robert E. Brown, *Middle-Class Democracy and the Revolution in Massachusetts, 1691-1780*, pp. 27-30, 401.

56. Henretta, *Evolution of American Society*, pp. 105-106.

57. Chilton Williamson, *American Suffrage from Property to Democracy, 1760-1860* (Princeton, N.J., 1960), p. 111. Champagne, op. cit., p. 8; Michael D'Innocenzo, "Voting in Colonial New York," M.A. thesis, Columbia University, 1950, Appendix A, p. 78.

58. John Cary, "Statistical Method and the Brown Thesis on Colonial Democracy," *William and Mary Quarterly*, 3d Series, 20 (April 1963): 257-258.

59. Henretta, "Economic Development and Social Structure in Colonial Boston," p. 85.

60. Young and Lynd, op. cit., p. 223.

61. Main, op. cit., pp. 156-165, 175, 193, 271, 287.

62. *Rebels and Democrats: The Struggle for Equal Rights and Majority During the American Revolution* (Chicago, 1965), pp. vii-ix.

63. Lemisch, "The American Revolution Seen from the Bottom Up," in Bernstein, editor, *Towards a New Past*, p. 8.

For a carping criticism, without much justification, of Lemisch's article and an effective response by Lemisch, see review of *Towards a New Past* by Aileen S. Kraditor, *American Historical Review* 74 (1968): 529, and Lemisch's letter in ibid. 74 (1969): 1766-1768.

64. Ibid.

65. There are several books and articles dealing with this development, but the best summary and analysis is Gary B. Nash, "The Transformation of Urban Politics, 1700-1765," *Journal of American History*, 60 (December 1973): 605-632.

66. Jackson Turner Main, "Government by the People: The American Revolution and the Democratization of the Legislatures," *William and Mary Quarterly*, 3d Series, 23 (July 1966): 397.

67. Recent studies have shown that the major cities had an even smaller percentage of rich who controlled the wealth. In Boston, for example, the richest 10 percent controlled 65 percent of the wealth in 1771. In 1775, the richest 10 percent of Philadelphia owned over half of the wealth of the city—more than three times the amount controlled by the 10 percent immediately below them. Main, *The Social Structure of Revolutionary America*, pp. 22, 38-39, 43, 60-61, 112-113; Henretta, *Evolution of American Society*, pp. 105-106; Henretta, "Economic Development and Social Structure in Colonial Boston," pp. 86-87.

68. Carl and Jessica Bridenbaugh, *Rebels and Gentlemen* (New York, 1942), p. 14; *Proceedings of the Massachusetts Historical Society* 49 (June 1916): 454.

69. *Pennsylvania Gazette*, September 27, 1770.

70. Ibid. A writer, signing himself "A Brother to the Brethren of the Chip," attempted to reply to "A Brother Chip," but his effort merely denounced the attempt "to persuade the good people of this province, to choose mechanics to

represent them at the ensuing election" (*Pennsylvania Chronicle*, October 1, 1770).

Chapter 2

1. Curtis P. Nettels, "The Menace of Colonial Manufacturing, 1690-1720," *New England Quarterly* 4 (April 1931): 240-266; Clarence V. Alvord, *The Mississippi Valley in British Politics* (Cleveland, 1917), I, pp. 88-99.

2. Curtis P. Nettels, "British Mercantilism and the Economic Development of the Thirteen Colonies," *Journal of Economic History* 12 (Spring 1952): 105-114.

3. John C. Miller, *Origins of the American Revolution* (Boston, 1943), p. 23.

4. Clarence Edwin Carter, editor, *The Correspondence of General Thomas Gage with the Secretaries of State, 1763-1775* (New Haven, Conn., 1931-1933), II, p. 615-616; Bridenbaugh, *Colonial Craftsman*, pp. 141-142. [Italics mine. P.S.F.]

5. Walsh, op. cit., pp. 137-138.

6. Marc Engal and Joseph A. Ernst, "An Economic Interpretation of the American Revolution," *William and Mary Quarterly*, 3d Series, 29 (January 1972): 15-20; Anne Bezanson, *Prices and Inflation During the American Revolution: Pennsylvania, 1770-1790* (Philadelphia, 1951), p. 12.

7. Engal and Ernst, op. cit., pp. 18-20; Lemisch, "Jack Tar vs. John Bull," p. 53; Charles H. Lincoln, op. cit., pp. 81-85.

8. Lemisch, "Jack Tar vs. John Bull," pp. 29, 38, 50; Joel A. Shufro, "Impressment and Economic Decline in Boston: Context for Conflict, 1740-1760," Unpublished paper delivered at the American Studies Association, October 1971, p. 17.

9. Curtis P. Nettels, *Roots of American Civilization* (New York, 1938), pp. 17-22; Shufro, op. cit., pp. 13-16.

10. Bailyn, editor, *Pamphlets of the American Revolution, 1750-1776*, I, pp. 60-85.

11. Douglas Adair and John A. Schutz, editors, *Peter Oliver's Origin & Progress of the American Rebellion: A Tory View* (San Marino, Calif., 1961), p. 65.

12. Pauline Maier, "Revolutionary Violence and the Relevance of History," *Journal of Interdisciplinary History* 2 (1971), p. 130.

13. See, for example, George Rudé, *The Crowd in History: A Study of Popular Disturbances in France and England, 1730-1848* (New York, 1964); Eric Hobsbawm, *Primitive Rebels: Studies in Archaic Forms of Social Movement in the 19th and 20th Centuries* (New York, 1959); and Eric Thompson, *The Making of the English Working Class* (New York, 1963).

14. Cf. Edward Countryman, "The Problem of the Early American Crowd," *Journal of American Studies* 7 (April 1973): 79-80; Gordon S. Wood, "A Note on Mobs in the American Revolution," *William and Mary Quarterly*, 3d Series, 23 (October 1966): 635-642; Pauline Maier, *From Resistance to Revolution: Colonial Radicals and the Development of American Opposition to Britain, 1765-1775* (New York, 1972), pp. 1-11, 24, 57-59; Arthur M. Schlesinger, "Political

Mobs and the American Revolution, 1765-1776," *Proceedings, American Philosophical Society* 99 (August 1955): 243-249; Richard M. Brown, "Violence and the American Revolution," in Stephen G. Hurtz and James H. Hutson, editors. *Essays on the American Revolution* (Chapel Hill, N.C., 1973), pp. 94-97, 117-120.

15. Allan and Katherine Day, "Another Look at the Boston Caucus," *Journal of American Studies* 5 (April 1971): 19-42; Merle Curti, *Growth of American Thought* (New York, 1943), p. 45; Foner, *History of Labor*, I, pp. 28-29; Richard Hofstadter and Michael Wallace, *American Violence: A Documentary History* (New York, 1970), pp. 109-110; Lloyd Rudolph, "The Eighteenth-Century Mob in America and Europe," *American Quarterly* 11 (1959): 447-459. An excellent study applying the Rudé thesis to the American Revolutionary scene is Dirk Hoerder, *People and Mobs: Crowd Action in Massachusetts During the American Revolution, 1765-1780*, originally a doctoral dissertation in a German University. Unfortunately, it is still mainly inaccessible in this country.

16. Lemisch, "Jack Tar vs. John Bull," pp. 38-47; Shufro, op. cit., pp. 17-20.

17. Lemisch, "Jack Tar vs. John Bull," p. 50.

18. Bailyn, op. cit., pp. 581-583. Bailyn, however, sees nothing "revolutionary" about "Revolutionary mobs" in America, and even questions their "meliorist aspirations" (ibid., p. 581). For a criticism of this view, see Jesse Lemisch, "The Radicalism of the Inarticulate: Merchant Seamen in the Politics of Revolutionary America," in Alfred F. Young, editor, *Dissent: Explorations in the History of American Radicalism* (DeKalb, Ill., 1968), pp. 56-58.

19. Peter Force, editor, *American Archives*, 4th Series, I, p. 432.

20. J. H. Trumbull, "Sons of Liberty in 1755," *The New Englander* 35 (1913), 308-311.

21. Morris, *Government and Labor in Early America*, p. 189.

22. Jared Ingersoll to Thomas Fitch, London, February 11, 1765, in F. B. Dexter, editor, "The Correspondence and Miscellaneous Papers of Jared Ingersoll," *New Haven Colony Historical Society Papers* (New Haven, 1918), IX, p. 311.

23. Herbert M. Morais, "Artisan Democracy and the American Revolution," *Science and Society* 3 (Spring 1952): 229-230; Edmund S. and Helen M. Morgan, *The Stamp Act Crisis: Prologue to Revolution* (Chapel Hill, N.C., 1953), pp. 231-240; Maier, *From Resistance to Revolution*, Appendix, pp. 297-312.

24. Samuel Adams has long been treated as the man who operated as puppeteer and who manipulated the common people into revolutionary action. John C. Miller, in his scholarly biography published in 1936, *Sam Adams: Pioneer in Propaganda* (Boston), described Adams as "transforming American discontent into revolutionary fervor," and as a man who "pulled the wires that set the Boston town meeting in motion against royal government" (Boston, 1936, pp. 144, 276, 342). However, William Appleman Williams points out that Adams could not alone control Boston's Sons of Liberty, and he rejects the view of Adams as "a rabble-rousing demagogue who stood on street corners in Boston directing the mob" ("Samuel Adams: Calvinist, Mercantilist, Revolutionary,"

Studies on the Left, I, 1960, pp. 50, 52). See also Stewart Beach, *Samuel Adams: The Faithful Years, 1764-1776* (New York, 1965), pp. 9, 78, and Pauline Maier, "Coming to Terms with Samuel Adams," *American Historical Review* 81 (February 1976): 16-18. While Professor Maier refutes the thesis that Adams manipulated the common people, she also deprives him of any stand in favor of independence.

25. Morais, op. cit., pp. 231-232; Philip Davidson, "Sons of Liberty and Stamp Men," *North Carolina Historical Review* 9 (January 1932): 50-54; Herbert M. Morais, "The Sons of Liberty in New York," in Richard B. Morris, editor, *The Era of the American Revolution* (New York, 1939), pp. 272-273; George P. Anderson, "Ebenezer Mackintosh: Stamp Act Rioter and Patriot," *Colonial Society of Massachusetts Publications* 26 (1924-1926): 15-64, 348-361; George P. Anderson, "Pascal Paoli: An Inspiration to the Sons of Liberty," ibid., pp. 180-210.

26. Allan and Katherine Day, "Another Look at the Boston Caucus," pp. 19-42.

27. Alfred P. Young, "Some Thoughts on Mechanic Participation in the American Revolution," Unpublished paper presented at Third Annual Conference on Early American History, Newberry Library, Chicago, November 1, 1974, p. 13.

28. Olton, "Philadelphia Mechanics in the First Decade of the Revolution, 1765-1775," p. 314*n*.

29. Charles Francis Adams, editor, *Familiar Letters of John Adams and His Wife, Abigail Adams, During the Revolution* (New York, 1876), pp. 149-150.

30. Foner, *History of Black Americans*, pp. 292-294.

31. Benson J. Lossing, *Pictorial Field-Book of the Revolution* (New York, 1860), I, p. 482; R. J. Burker, "The Daughters of Liberty," *American Historical Register* 1 (1894): 29-36; *Boston Chronicle*, September 28, 1769.

32. Miller, *Origins of the American Revolution*, p. 344; *Ms.*, letter datd Boston, April 4, 1776, Rhode Island Historical Society.

33. *Ms.*, Boston Committee of Correspondence, VI, pp. 472-473, New York Public Library, Manuscripts Division; William Cutter, *Life of Israel Putnam* (New York, 1861), p. 133; R. S. Longley, "Mob Activities in Revolutionary Massachusetts," *New England Quarterly* 6 (March 1933): 98-130; Elizabeth May Blacke, "Opposition to the Stamp Act in New York City," M.A. thesis, Syracuse University, 1936, p. 38.

34. H. L. Calkin, "Pamphlets and Public Opinion During the American Revolution," *Pennsylvania Magazine of History and Biography* 64 (January 1940): 30; *South Carolina Gazette*, September 22, 1768.

35. "A New Song—Address'd to the Sons of Liberty on the Continent of America," Broadside, in the Library of the Historical Society of Pennsylvania; *New York Gazette*, January 6, 1776; Philip S. Foner, *American Labor Songs of the Nineteenth Century* (Urbana, Ill., 1975), p. 22.

36. H. B. Dawson, *The Sons of Liberty in New York* (Poughkeepsie, N.Y., 1859), pp. 76-77.

37. R. W. Postgate, *That Devil Wilkes*, (New York, 1929), pp. 24-28.

38. Ibid., pp. 87-89, 98; George Rudé, *Wilkes and Liberty* (London, 1962), pp. 39-43.

39. Rudé, op. cit., pp. 49-56.

40. Ian R. Christie, *Wilkes, Wyvill and Reform* (London, 1962), pp. 33-34.

41. Rudé, op. cit., pp. 105-148, 176-184, 189-190.

42. Worthington C. Ford, editor, "John Wilkes and Boston," *Proceedings of the Massachusetts Historical Society* 47 (1913-1914): 190-191; D. M. Clark, *British Opinion and the American Revolution* (New Haven, Conn., 1930), p. 155; Philip Davidson, *Propaganda and the American Revolution* (Chapel Hill, N.C., 1941), pp. 186-187.

43. Ford, op. cit., pp. 192, 196; Bernard Bailyn, *The Ideological Origins of the American Revolution*, pp. 110-111.

44. Ibid., p. 197.

45. *South Carolina Gazette*, April 19, 1770. See also Richard J. Hooper, "The American Revolution Seen Through a Wine Glass," *William and Mary Quarterly*, 3rd Series, 11 (1954): 61.

46. Jack P. Greene, "'Bridge to Revolution', The Wilkes Fund Controversy in South Carolina, 1769-1775," *Journal of Southern History* 29 (February 1963): 21.

47. Michael Kraus, "America and the Irish Revolutionary Movement in the Eighteenth Century," in Richard B. Morris, editor, *The Era of the American Revolution*, pp. 337-339.

48. *The Magazine of History*, New York, Extra No. 65, XVI, 1918, p. 324.

49. *New York Journal*, June 8, 1775.

50. Margaret Wheeler Willard, editor, *Letters on the American Revolution, 1774-1776* (Boston, 1925), pp. 121, 216; *Newport Mercury*, March 12, 1775; Glenn C. Smith, "An Era of Non-Importation Associations," *William and Mary Quarterly*, 2d Series, 40 (June 1932): 94.

Chapter 3

1. Morgan, *The Stamp Act Crisis*, p. 28.

2. R. W. Gibbes, editor, *Documentary History of the American Revolution* (New York, 1855), I, pp. 1-12; Morgan, op. cit., pp. 88-95.

3. (Boston, 1764), p. 13.

4. Morgan, op. cit., pp. 102-105.

5. *Correspondence of Thomas Gage*, I, p. 81.

6. H. A. Cushing, editor, *The Writings of Sam Adams* (New York, 1904-1908), II, p. 201.

7. Ibid., I, p. 59; Thomas Hutchinson, *History of the Province of Massachusetts Bay* (London, 1828), pp. 120-125; *Boston Evening Post*, August 19, 1765; *Boston Gazette*, Supplement, September 16, 1765.

8. *Boston Evening Post*, August 19, September 2, 1765.

In "Thomas Hutchinson and the Stamp Act" *New England Quarterly* 21 (December 1948): 459-463), Edmund S. Morgan contends that Hutchinson was innocent of the charges that he helped foster the Stamp Act. But he ignores the fact that though he was given an opportunity to deny the accusations, he rejected it. Bernard Bailyn also ignores this fact in *The Ordeal of Thomas Hutchinson* (Cambridge, Mass., 1974).

9. *Boston Gazette*, August 26-27, 1765.

10. Miller, *Sam Adams, Pioneer in Propaganda*, p. 215.

11. *Boston Gazette*, November 11, 1765.

12. Ibid., December 23, 1765.

13. *Proceedings, Massachusetts Historical Society* 60 (1923): 282; Hutchinson, op. cit., p. 140.

14. Miller, *Sam Adams*, p. 137; Richard D. Brown, *Revolutionary Politics in Massachusetts: The Boston Committee of Correspondence and the Towns, 1772-1774* (Cambridge, Mass., 1970), pp. 23-24.

15. *Boston Gazette*, Supplement, August 11, 1766.

16. *Newport Mercury*, September 2, 1765.

17. Morgan, op. cit., p. 147; *Newport Mercury*, October 21, 1765.

18. Morgan, op. cit., p. 151.

19. *Records of the Colony of Rhode Island* VI, pp. 451-452.

20. J. McEvers to Barlow Trecothick, August 1765, quoted in Morgan, op. cit., p. 152.

21. Cadwallader Colden to Sir William Johnston, August 31, 1765, *Colden Letter Books, New York Historical Society Collections* (1918-1937), II, p. 27. For a study of Colden, see S. B. Rolland, "Cadwallader Colden: Colonial Politician and Imperial Statesman," Ph.D. dissertation, University of Wisconsin, 1952.

22. *New York Gazette and Weekly Post-Bcy*, November 7, 1765. Hereinafter cited as *New York Gazette*.

23. Ibid.

24. O'Callaghan, editor, op. cit., VII, p. 770.

25. Ibid., p. 774.

26. *New York Gazette*, November 7, 1765.

27. Ibid.

28. Champagne, "The Sons of Liberty and the Aristocracy in New York Politics," p. 85.

29. Lemisch, "Jack Tar vs. John Bull," pp. 106-107.

30. Ibid., pp. 91-92; *New York Gazette*, November 7, 1765.

31. Isaac Q. Leake, *Memoir of the Life and Times of General John Lamb* (Albany, N.Y., 1850), pp. 13-14n.

32. Lemisch, "Jack Tar vs. John Bull," pp. 95-100, gives a vivid description of the pressure on Colden to give up the stamps.

33. *New York Gazette*, December 9, 1765; O'Callaghan, editor, op. cit., VII, p. 761.

34. *New York Gazette*, December 26, 1765.

35. Ibid., January 9, 13, February 20, 1766.

36. Ibid., January 7, 1766.

37. Virginia D. Harrington, *The New York Merchants on the Eve of the Revolution* (New York, 1935), p. 330; John Lamb Papers, 1762-1773, Folder #21, New York Historical Society.

38. *New York Gazette*, November 28, 1765.

39. Champagne, "The Sons of Liberty and the Aristocracy in New York Politics," p. 92.

40. *New York Gazette*, November 28, 1765.

41. Ibid., December 27, 1765. A summary of the article appears in Lemisch, "Jack Tar vs. John Bull," pp. 112-114.

42. Morgan, op. cit., p. 162; Champagne, "The Sons of Liberty and the Aristocracy in New York Politics," p. 98; Lemisch, "Jack Tar vs. John Bull," pp. 120-126.

43. Morgan, op. cit., p. 120.

44. Champagne, "The Sons of Liberty and the Aristocracy in New York Politics," pp. 102-103; *New York Mercury*, January 2, 1766.

45. *New York Mercury*, February 24, 1766.

46. Irving Mark, *Agrarian Conflicts in Colonial New York, 1711-1775* (New York, 1940), Chapter V; Staughton Lynd, *Anti-Federalism in Dutchess County, New York* (Chicago, 1962), Chapter III; Patricia U. Bonomi, *A Factious People: Politics and Society in Colonial New York* (New York and London, 1971), Chapter VI.

47. Irving Mark and Oscar Handlin, "Land Cases in Colonial New York, 1765-1767: The King vs. William Prendergast," *New York University Quarterly Review* 9 (January 1942): 183.

48. *New York Gazette*, November 7, 1765.

49. See *Freedom in Arms, A Selection of Leveller Writings*, edited by A. L. Morton (New York, 1976).

50. Lynd, *Anti-Federalism in Dutchess County*, p. 50.

51. James and John Montressor, *The Montressor Journals, New York Historical Society Collections* 24(1882): 363.

52. Champagne, "The Sons of Liberty and the Aristocracy in New York Politics," p. 119.

53. Morais, "Sons of Liberty in New York," p. 276.

54. Robert H. Woody, "Christopher Gadsden and the Stamp Act," *Proceedings of the South Carolina Historical Association* (1939): 5-6; Richard Walsh, *Charleston's Sons of Liberty: A Study of the Artisans, 1763-1789* (Columbia, S.C., 1959), pp. 36-39.

55. *Boston Gazette*, Supplement, January 27, 1766.

56. Robert M. Weer, "'The Harmony We Were Famous For': An Interpretation of Pre-Revolutionary South Carolina Politics," *William and Mary Quarterly*, 3d Series, 26 (October 1969): 483.

57. Pauline Maier, "The Charleston Mob and the Evolution of Popular Politics in Revolutionary South Carolina, 1765-1784," in *Perspectives in American History*, IV (1970), p. 176.

58. Woody, op. cit., p. 9.

59. William S. Hanna, *Benjamin Franklin and Pennsylvania Politics* (Stanford, Calif., 1964), p. 206; Benjamin H. Newcomb, *Franklin and Galloway: A Political Partnership* (New Haven, Conn., 1972), pp. 18-26, 84; G. B. Warden, "The Proprietary Group in Pennsylvania, 1754-1764," *William and Mary Quarterly*, 3d Series, 26 (July 1964): 367-389.

60. Benjamin H. Newcomb, "Effects of the Stamp Act in Colonial Pennsylvania Politics," *William and Mary Quarterly*, 3d Series, 23 (April 1966): 257-

272; John J. Zimmerman, "Charles Thomson: 'The Sam Adams of Philadelphia,'" *Mississippi Valley Historical Review*, 45 (1958): 468; James Hutson, *Pennsylvania Politics, 1746-1770: The Movement for Royal Government and Its Consequences* (Princeton, N.J., 1972), pp. 112-116.

61. Morgan, op. cit., pp. 246-252; *Pennsylvania Journal*, October 10, 1965.

62. *The Letters and Papers of Cadwallader Colden*, New York State Historical Society *Collections for 1923* (New York, 1923), VII, 1765-1775, p. 95.

63. "The Lamentation of Pennsylvania, on Account of the Stamp Act" (Philadelphia, 1765), *Evans 10031*. See also Steven J. Rosswurm, "'That They Were Grown Unruly': The Crowd and Lower-Classes in Philadelphia, 1765-1780," p. 25; George Beib, "A History of Philadelphia, 1776-1780," Ph.D. dissertation, University of Wisconsin, 1969, pp. 23-24.

64. Benjamin Rush to Ebenezer Hazard, November 8, 1765, L. H. Butterfield, editor, *Letters of Benjamin Rush* (Princeton, N.J., 1951), I, p. 18. Morgan, op. cit., pp. 161-162.

65. Olton, "Philadelphia Artisans and the American Revolution," pp. 57-60.

66. Charles Thomson to Messrs. Wels, Wilkinson & Co., November 7, 1765, *New York State Historical Society Publications for 1878* (New York, 1878), p. 5.

67. Francis Von A. Cabeen, "The Society of the Sons of Saint Tammany of Philadelphia," *Pennsylvania Magazine of History and Biography* 35 (1901): 439.

68. Allicothe to (Lamb?), November 21, 1765, John Lamb Papers, Box 1; Alexander McDougall to John Smith in Philadelphia, November 12, 1765, Alexander McDougall Papers, both in New York Historical Society.

69. Davidson, *Propaganda and the American Revolution*, p. 178.

70. *Montressor Journals*, p. 242.

71. Conway to American governors, October 24, 1766, *Boston Gazette*, January 13, 1766; *Boston Evening Post*, February 3, 1766.

72. "Sons of Liberty: New London Agreement, December 25, 1765," in William Gordon, *The History of the Rise, Progress, and Establishment of the Independence of the United States of America* (London, 1788), I, pp. 195-198, and reprinted in Richard B. Morris, editor, *The American Revolution, 1763-1783: A Bicentennial Collection* (New York, 1970), pp. 114-115.

73. Champagne, "The Military Association of the Sons of Liberty," pp. 344-347.

74. Morgan, op. cit., p. 202.

75. Sons of Liberty of New York to Sons of Liberty in Boston and Providence, April 2, 1766, John Lamb Papers, Box 1, New York Historical Society.

76. Champagne, "The Military Association of the Sons of Liberty," pp. 348-350.

77. Joseph Allicock to John Lamb, November 21, 1765, John Lamb Papers, Box 1, New York Historical Society; Miller, *Sam Adams*, p. 77; Champagne, "The Military Association of the Sons of Liberty," p. 346.

78. Maier, *From Resistance to Revolution*, pp. 77-78.

79. Jonathan Sturges to Isaac Sears, March 26, 1766, John Lamb Papers,

Box 1, New York Historical Society.

    80. *Newport Mercury,* March 17, 1767.

Chapter 4

    1. Davidson, op. cit., p. 73.

    2. Morais, "Artisan Democracy," p. 234.

    3. *New York Gazette,* May 22, 1766; *Montressor Journals,* p. 368.

    4. *Montressor Journals,* p. 375.

    5. Ibid., pp. 363-384; *New York Gazette,* August 14, 21, 26, 1766; Carter, editor, *Gage Correspondence,* I, pp. 103-104; Governor Moore to the Duke of Richmond, August 23, 1766, O'Callaghan, editor, op. cit., pp. 867-868; Lemisch, "Jack Tar vs. John Bull," pp. 131-136; Champagne, "The Sons of Liberty and the Aristocracy in New York Politics," p. 124.

    6. *New York Gazette,* September 25, 1766.

    7. Sons of Liberty to Nicholas Ray, October 10, 1766; Leake, *Life of John Lamb,* pp. 36-37.

    8. Woody, op. cit., p. 11; Walsh, *Charleston's Sons of Liberty,* p. 40.

    9. *Boston Gazette,* Supplement, April 14, 1766.

    10. *South Carolina Gazette,* June 22, 1769.

    11. Ibid., March 23, 1769.

    12. Ibid., July 13, 1769.

    13. Walsh, *Charleston's Sons of Liberty,* p. 49.

    14. *South Carolina Gazette,* July 13, 1769.

    15. Davidson, op. cit., p. 81.

    16. *New York Journal,* March 23, 1769.

    17. Ibid.

    18. Broadside, Boston, 1770, Portfolio 37, No. 2A, Library of Congress, Rare Book Room.

    19. Miller, *Origins of the American Revolution,* p. 271.

    20. Davidson, op. citl, pp. 75-76.

    21. G. B. Warden, *Boston: 1689-1776* (Boston, 1970), pp. 241-242.

    22. Maier, *From Resistanct to Revolution,* pp. 126-129, 138.

    23. *South Carolina Gazette,* July 19, 21, 23, 25, 1769.

    24. The names of the members of the thirty-nine-member committee appear in the *South Carolina Gazette* of July 27, 1769, under the headings, "Esquires, Merchants, Mechanics."

    25. Walsh, *Charleston's Sons of Liberty,* p. 50.

    26. Ibid., p. 51; letters of Lieutenant Governor Bull, December 12, 1769, October 20, 1770, in Maier, "Charleston Mob and Evolution of Popular Politics in Revolutionary South Carolina," pp. 178-179.

    27. *New York Journal,* March 23, 1769; Champagne, "Sons of Liberty and Aristocracy in New York Politics," p. 241.

    28. Bonomi, *A Factious People,* pp. 234-235.

    29. For the details of the elections of 1768 and 1769, see Champagne, "Liberty Boys and Mechanics of New York City, 1764-1774," pp. 123-135.

30. *New York Journal*, March 23, 1769.
31. Harrington, *New York Merchants on the Eve of the Revolution*, p. 338.
32. "Resolutions of the United Sons of Liberty," July 7, 1769, original broadside in New York Public Library, Rare Book Room, and reprinted in Evans 11379.
33. Harrington, op. cit., p. 341; *New York Journal*, July 20, 27, 1769; Maier, *From Resistance to Revolution*, p. 154.
34. Miller, *Sam Adams*, p. 201; New York Sons of Liberty to Philadelphia Sons of Liberty, May 11, 1770, Lamb Papers, Box 1, New York Historical Society.
35. A Son of Liberty, "To the Betrayed Inhabitants of the City and Colony of New York," New York, December 16, 1769, copy in New York Historical Society.
36. O'Callaghan, editor, op. cit., III, 528-532.
37. *New York Journal*, December 28, 1769.
38. Ibid., February 15, 1770.
39. Ibid., March 14-15, 1770.
40. Maier, *From Resistance to Revolution*, p. 193; *New York Journal*, March 22, 29, 1770.
41. Champagne, "Sons of Liberty and Aristocracy in New York Politics," p. 235; William Smith to Philip Schuyler, April 29, 1770, Philip Schuyler Papers, Box 23, New York Public Library, Manuscripts Division.
42. Miller, *Origins of the American Revolution*, p. 366.

Chapter 5

1. Gage to Lieutenant Colonel William Dalrymple, January 8, 1770. Gage Manuscripts, American Series, Boston Public Library, Rare Book Room, p. 89.
2. Lemisch, "Jack Tar vs. John Bull," pp. 138-139.
3. This account of the events leading up to, and during, the Battle of Golden Hill is based on the following contemporary sources: *New York Gazette and Weekly Post-Boy*, February 5, 1770, which contains a very extensive account by "An Impartial Citizen," *New York Journal*, January 18, 22, March 1, 1770; Broadside, "To the Inhabitants of the City," January 22, 1770; Broadside, Brutus, "To the Public," January 18, 1770; Broadside, "The Times," February 1770; Broadside signed by the 16th Regiment of the Foot (January 19, 1770), all in the New York Historical Society. Historical accounts used in the discussion are Henry B. Dawson, *The Sons of Liberty in New York*, pp. 110-117; Roger Champagne, "Sons of Liberty and Aristocracy in New York Politics," pp. 225-229; Jesse Lemisch, "Jack Tar vs. John Bull," pp. 146-162; and Lee R. Boyer, "Lobster Backs, Liberty Boys, and Laborers in the Streets: New York's Golden Hill and Nassau Street riots," *New York Historical Society Quarterly* 57 (October 1973): 281-307.

While Lemisch and Boyer treat the subject fully, the Lemisch account is more sympathetic to the workers than is Boyer's. Though Boyer concedes that the grievance of competition from off-duty soldiers was a real one and though he dismisses the charge that the entire affair was a conspiracy of the New York Sons of Liberty, he tends to support the position of the military authorities and the Corporation. He does not mention that a sailor was killed in the battle, a statement based on Dawson and Lemisch.

4. *New York Journal*, February 8, 1770.

5. Dawson, op. cit., pp. 116-117.

6. Ibid., p. 115.

7. Champagne, "Sons of Liberty and Aristocracy in New York Politics," p. 229.

8. See also *Boston Gazette and Country Journal*, March 12, 1770.

9. Quoted in Hiller B. Zobel, *The Boston Massacre* (New York, 1970), p. 45.

10. Oliver M. Dickerson, *The Navigation Acts and the American Revolution* (Philadelphia, 1951), pp. 254-255.

11. Forbes, *Paul Revere*, p. 133.

12. Zobel, op. cit., pp. 4, 94, 96-102, 132.

13. Quoted in ibid., pp. 89-90.

14. Miller, *Sam Adams*, p. 176.

15. John W. Shy, *Toward Lexington: The Role of the British Army in the Coming of the American Revolution* (Cambridge, Mass., 1969), pp. 309-311.

16. See, for example, Zobel, op. cit., pp. 109-110, 247; Forbes, op. cit., pp. 135-140; Miller, *Sam Adams*, pp. 177-185.

17. Shy, op. cit., pp. 305-307.

18. Morris, *Government and Labor in Early America*, p. 190.

19. For the events leading up to and the Boston Massacre, see *Boston Evening Post, Boston Gazette and Country Journal*, March 12, 1770; and F. Kidder, *History of the Boston Massacre, March 5, 1770*, (Albany, N.Y., 1870). Since then, there have been many accounts of the Boston Massacre. The most complete, although a pro-British, Tory account, is that by Hiller B. Zobel, op. cit.

20. Zobel, op. cit., p. 303. The term *Tory account* is by Jesse Lemisch in his devastating review of Zobel's book in *Harvard Law Review* 84 (1970): 485-504.

21. See Morris, op. cit., pp. 191-192.

22. Foner, *History of Black Americans*, pp. 212-213.

23. *Boston Evening-Post*, March 12, 1770; Zobel, op. cit., pp. 202-204.

24. Oliver M. Dickerson, "The Commissioners of Customs and the 'Boston Massacre,'" *New England Quarterly* 27 (September 1954): 307-325. Dickerson also presents evidence that the customs commissioners or their employees probably fired on the crowd from a window in the customs house during the fight with the soldiers on the night of March 5, 1770.

25. *Massachusetts Archives* 26 (1895), 369-370, 380-382.

26. Brown, *Middle-Class Democracy and Revolution in Massachusetts, 1691-1780*, p. 264.

27. Charles Francis Adams, editor, *The Works of John Adams* (Boston, 1850-1856), X, pp. 252-253.

28. Morais, "Artisan Democracy," p. 236; Davidson, op. cit., pp. 182-183.

29. Gage to Hillsborough, April 10, 1770, in Carter, editor, *Gage Correspon-*

dence, I, p. 250; Colden to Hillsborough, Colden Letter Books, II, p. 217.
    30. *Boston Gazette*, March 9, 1772.

Chapter 6

    1. Zimmerman, "Charles Thomson, 'the Sam Adams of Philadelphia,'" p. 475.
    2. See "Tradesman" in *Pennsylvania Chronicle*, October 10, 1770; "A Spectator" in *Pennsylvania Gazette*, June 14, 1770; Isaac Sears in *New York Journal*, May 10, 1770.
    3. H. H. Edes, "Memoir of Thomas Young," in *Publications of the Colonial Society of Massachusetts, Transactions, 1906-1907* 11, p. 28; Miller, *Sam Adams*, p. 217.
    4. Champagne, "Sons of Liberty and the Aristocracy in New York Politics," p. 279.
    5. "For Erecting and Encouraging a New Manufactory," Evans 1555.
    6. *New York Journal*, June 7, 1770.
    7. Ibid.
    8. "Son of Liberty," in ibid., June 21, 1770.
    9. *New York Journal*, June 21, 1770.
    10. Ibid., July 12, 1770.
    11. Ibid., June 21, 1770.
    12. Ibid., June 21, July 6, 26, 1770.
    13. Champagne, "Sons of Liberty and the Aristocracy in New York Politics," p. 270.
    14. Evans 11785.
    15. O'Callaghan, editor, op. cit., VIII, pp. 218-220.
    16. *New York Mercury*, July 23, 1770.
    17. *New York Journal*, July 26, August 2, 1770; Alexander McDougall Papers, Box 1, New York Historical Society.
    18. Champagne, "Sons of Liberty and the Aristocracy in New York Politics," p. 275.
    19. *New York Journal*, July 19, 26, August 6, September 6, 1770.
    20. *To the Tradesmen, Farmers, and Other Inhabitants of the City and County of Philadelphia*, Philadelphia, September 24, 1770, Pamphlet, copy in Historical Society of Pennsylvania.
    21. Zimmerman, op. cit., pp. 476-477.
    22. *Pennsylvania Journal*, July 5, 1770; Rosswurm, op. cit., pp. 66-68.
    23. *Pennsylvania Gazette*, September 20, 27, 1770.
    24. Olton, "Philadelphia Mechanics in the First Decade of the Revolution 1765-1775," p. 322.
    25. Zimmerman, op. cit., p. 479.
    26. *Boston Gazette and Country Journal*, August 20, September 3, 1770. Richard Walsh, editor, *The Writings of Christopher Gadsden* (Columbia, S.C., 1966), pp. 94-95.

27. Brown, *Revolutionary Politics in Massachusetts*, pp. 122-148; Richard Frothingham, *History of the Siege of Boston* (Boston, 1873), p. 29; *Massachusetts Gazette and Boston News-Letter*, December 30, 1773; *Boston Gazette and Country Journal*, January 3, 1774; *Dictionary of American Biography* XV, p. 515.

28. *New York Gazette*, March 25, 1771; Brown op. cit., p. 68.

29. *Pennsylvania Gazette*, August 19, 1770.

30. Olton, op. cit., p. 322; Joseph Reed to the Earl of Dartmouth, December 27, 1773; William B. Reed, editor, *Life and Correspondence of Joseph Reed* (Philadelphia, 1847), I, p. 55; Rosswurm, op. cit., p. 75.

31. Benjamin W. Labaree, *The Boston Tea Party* (New York, 1964), pp. 66-77.

32. Massachusetts Committee of Correspondence Circular, Letter, October 21, 1773, in Cushing, editor, *The Writings of Samuel Adams*, III, pp. 62-68.

33. "A Mechanic," in *Pennsylvania Gazette*, December 3, 1773.

34. North End Caucus minutes, October 23, 1773, in Elbridge H. Goss, *The Life of Colonel Paul Revere* (Boston, 1891), II, pp. 641-642.

35. North End Caucus minutes, November 2, 1773, ibid., pp. 641-643.

36. *Boston Gazette and Country Journal*, November 8, 15, 1773.

37. Quoted in Forbes, *Paul Revere*, p. 182.

38. *Tea Leaves, etc., with introductory Notes, and Biographical Notices of the Boston Tea Party*, by Francis S. Drake (Boston, 1884), pp. xiix, lxvi-lxvii.

39. For contemporary newspaper accounts of the Boston Tea Party, see *Boston Gazette and Country Journal*, December 20, 1773; and *Massachusetts Gazette and Boston Weekly News-Letter*, December 1773. The best documentary account is *Tea Leaves, etc.* The best scholarly account is Labaree, *The Boston Tea Party*.

40. *Tea Leaves*, pp. cixiv-cixvi; Brown, *Revolutionary Politics in Massachusetts*, pp. 158-159.

41. Labaree, op. cit., pp. 164-167; Brown, op. cit., pp. 164-165; Morais, "Artisan Democracy," p. 237. There was a second Boston Tea Party on Sunday, March 6, 1774, that involved tea that did not come from the East India Company.

42. Forbes, op. cit., p. 82; Goss, op. cit., I, p. 128. Goss used the adjective *bold* before the name of Revere.

43. *Pennsylvania Gazette*, October 20, 1773.

44. *New York Journal*, December 2, 1773.

45. *Pennsylvania Gazette*, December 29, 1773.

46. See "Poplicola" in *Rivington's Gazetteer*, November 18, 1773; *New York Journal*, October 14, 21, November 25, 1773; Champagne, "Sons of Liberty and the Aristocracy in New York Politics," pp. 298-299.

47. *New York Journal*, December 2, 1773; Morais, "Sons of Liberty in New York," p. 285.

48. The full text of the articles is in Evans 12652; a summary may be found in "Brutus," Force, editor, *American Archives*, 4th Series, I, pp. 252-258.

49. Miller, *Origins of the American Revolution*, p. 351.

50. *New York Journal*, December 16, 1773.

51. Ibid., December 23, 1773.

52. Brown, op. cit., p. 152.

53. *New York Journal*, December 16, 1773.

54. Bernard Mason, *The Road to Independence: The Revolutionary Movement in New York, 1773-1777* (Lexington, Ky., 1966), p. 17.

55. New York Committee of Correspondence to Boston Committee, February 28, 1774, Boston Committee of Correspondence Minute Book, IX, pp. 742-746, New York Public Library, Manuscripts Division.

56. The indifference of the New York City Sons of Liberty to the grievances of rural elements, already demonstrated in the case of the antirent movement, was also reflected in their failure to condemn Governor Tryon for his role in suppressing the Regulators On the other hand, the Sons of Liberty in Boston supported the Regulators and denounced Tryon. One of them noted: "The occasion of these people's rising in opposition to the government was owing to exorbitant taxes laid upon them, from which they could get no redress. Therefore, they thought it justifiable in redressing themselves by force of arms. Their conduct was in general approved of—and the conduct of Governor Tryon condemned and though he may escape punishment in this world, he will no doubt hereafter be called to answer for this Bloody Massacre" (John Boyle, "Boyle's Journal of Occurrences in Boston, 1759-1778," *New England Historical and Genealogical Register* 84 (1930): 269-270. Boston Sons of Liberty were said to be "in heart Regulators" (*Boston Evening-Post*, June 10, 1771).

57. *New York Journal*, March 17, 1774.

58. Ibid., April 21, April 28, 1774; *Rivington's Gazetteer*, May 12, 1774.

59. In his new biography of Alexander J. McDougall, Roger J. Champagne writes that it was the "official" party of "Mohawks" who dumped tea into New York Harbor in April 1774. Actually, it was the unorganized populace which did the dumping. See *Alexander McDougall and the American Revolution in New York* (Schenectady, N.Y., 1975), p. 50.

60. Leake, *Life of John Lamb*, p. 81; Forbes, *Paul Revere*, p. 322.

61. *Rivington's Gazetteer*, April 28, 1774.

62. *New York Journal*, April 28, 1774.

63. *South Carolina Gazette*, January 17, 1774.

64. Walsh, *Charleston's Sons of Liberty*, pp. 59-60.

65. George C. Rogers, Jr., "The Charleston Tea Party: The Significance of December 3, 1773," *South Carolina Historical Magazine* 75 (July 1974): 164.

66. *South Carolina Gazette*, November 21, 1774.

67. Miller, *Origins of the American Revolution*, pp. 351-352.

68. Willard, editor, *Letters on the American Revolution*, p. 4.

69. Miller, *Origins of the American Revolution*, p. 352.

Chapter 7

1. Miller, *Origins of the American Revolution*, p. 370.

2. Charles Chauncey, *A Letter to a Friend, Giving a Concise but Just Rep-*

resentation of the Hardships and Sufferings of the Town of Boston (Boston, 1774), p. 6. "A Bostonian," quoted in Common Sense, People's Bicentennial Commission, IV, No. 1, 1976, p. 39.

3. A. H. Hoyt, "Donations to the People of Boston Suffering Under the Port Bill," New England Historical and Genealogical Register 30 (July 1876): 368-379.

4. Force, American Archives, 4th Series, I, pp. 312-313.

5. Morais, "Artisan Democracy," p. 239; Forbes, Paul Revere, p. 227.

6. Boston Gazette and Country Journal, September 26, 1774.

7. Carter, editor, Gage Correspondence, I, pp. 376-377; Richard Frothingham, The Siege of Boston (Boston, 1873), p. 364; Force, American Archives, 4th Series, I, pp. 991-992.

8. Evans 13668; New York Journal, September 29, 1774.

9. Morris, Government and Labor in Early America, p. 192. Force, American Archives, 4th Series, I, p. 974.

10. Governor Francis Legg to Secretary of State in England, Halifax, Nova Scotia, 29th May 1774, Letters from Governors of Nova Scotia to Secretaries of State in England, Public Archives, Nova Scotia, Record Group 1, vol. 44, Halifax, Nova Scotia.

11. Brown, Revolutionary Politics in Massachusetts, pp. 191-193.

12. Ibid., pp. 194-195.

13. Richard Frothingham, Life and Times of Joseph Warren (Boston, 1865), p. 137.

14. "Political memorandum relative to the Conduct of the Citizens on the Boston Port Bill," May 13, 1774, Alexander McDougall Papers, Box 1, New York Historical Society.

15. Ibid., May 14, 1774.

16. Ibid., May 15, 1774.

17. Champagne, "The Sons of Liberty and the Aristocracy in New York Politics," pp. 318-319.

18. Morais, "Sons of Liberty in New York," pp. 286-287.

19. "Political memorandum . . . ," May 19, 1774; Roger Champagne, "New York and the Intolerable Acts, 1774," New York Historical Society Proceedings, 45 (1961): 203-204.

20. Champagne, "The Sons of Liberty and the Aristocracy in New York Politics," pp. 321-322.

21. Colden to the Earl of Dartmouth, N. Y., June 1, 1774, Force, American Archives, 4th Series, I, pp. 373-374.

22. Gouverneur Morris to Mr. Penn, May 20, 1774, Force, American Archives, 4th Series, I, pp. 342-343.

23. W. C. Abbott, New York in the American Revolution (New York, 1929), p. 41; Morais, "Sons of Liberty in New York," pp. 287-288.

24. "Political memorandum . . . ," May 20, 1774; Evans 13670; Champagne, "Sons of Liberty and the Aristocracy in New York Politics," pp. 324-325.

25. Champagne, "New York and the Intolerable Acts, 1774," pp. 206-207.

26. "Political memorandum . . . ," May 23, 24, 1774, Boston Committee of

Correspondence Minute Book, New York Public Library, Manuscripts Division.

27. Sears and McDougall to Sam Adams, June 20, 1774, McDougall Papers, Box 1, New York Historical Society; Brown, *Revolutionary Politics in Massachusetts*, pp. 218-219.

28. *Pennsylvania Gazette*, June 20, 1774.

29. In his article, "New York and the Intolerable Acts" (pp. 199-200), Champagne states that it was the radicals who promoted the idea of a Congress, a position which Staughton Lynd endorses. See Champagne's article "The Mechanics in New York Politics, 1774-1788," p. 227. For Becker's view, see Carl Becker, *The History of Political Parties in the Province of New York, 1760-1776*, p. 118n.

30. O'Callaghan, editor, op. cit., VIII, pp. 469-470.

31. Broadside, July 6, 1774, quoted in Becker, op. cit., p. 123n.

32. Force, *American Archives*, 4th Series, I, pp. 312-313.

33. Becker, op. cit., pp. 119-136.

34. Champagne, "Sons of Liberty and the Aristocracy in New York Politics," p. 352.

35. Force, *American Archives*, 4th Series, I, pp. 782, 806-810.

36. Governor Francis Legge to Secretary of State in England, Halifax, Nova Scotia, Record Group 1, vol. 44, Halifax, Nova Scotia.

37. William Smith, "Notes and Papers on the Commencement of the American Revolution," William Smith Papers, 1765-1774, Historical Society of Pennsylvania; Olton, "Philadelphia Mechanics in the First Decade of the Revolution," p. 323.

38. *To the Manufactures and Mechanics of Philadelphia, the Northern Liberties, and District of Southwick*, Philadelphia, June 8, 1774, copy in Historical Society of Pennsylvania.

39. *Pennsylvania Gazette*, June 13, 1774.

40. Ibid., June 18, 1774.

41. Olton, op. cit., pp. 323-324.

42. Smith, "Notes and Papers . . ."

43. Olton, "Philadelphia Artisans and the American Revolution," p. 177.

44. *Pennsylvania Gazette*, July 20, 1774.

45. Ibid., August 31, 1774.

46. Olton, "Philadelphia Artisans and the American Revolution," pp. 183-184.

47. "A Card," in *Pennsylvania Gazette*, September 7, 1774.

48. Walsh, editor, *Writings of Christopher Gadsden*, pp. 100-103.

49. Walsh, *Charleston's Sons of Liberty*, pp. 100-101.

50. Ibid., pp. 102-103; Walsh, editor, *Writings of Christopher Gadsden*, p. xxi.

51. Worthington C. Ford, et al., editors, *Journals of the Continental Congress* (Washington, D.C., 1904-1937), I, pp. 13-26, 39, 75, 76-80, 81-101; Edmund Cody Burnett, *The Continental Congress* (New York, 1941), pp. 153-155.

52. O'Callaghan, editor, op. cit., VII, pp. 832-833.

53. Becker, op. cit., pp. 160-163; Champagne, "Sons of Liberty and the Aristocracy in New York Politics," p. 366.

54. *Pennsylvania Packet*, November 17, 1774.

55. Ryerson, "Political Mobilization and the American Revolution: The Resistance Movement in Philadelphia, 1765 to 1776," p. 577.

56. Robert F. Oaks, "Philadelphia Merchants and the First Continental Congress," *Pennsylvania History* 40 (April 1973): 158.

57. Thomas Young to John Lamb, June 19, 1774, Lamb Papers, New York Historical Society; also published in Leake, *Life of John Lamb*, p. 89.

58. See above, pp. 40-43, and "A Lover of Liberty and a Mechanic's Friend," *To the Free and Patriotic Inhabitants of the City of Philadelphia*, Broadside, May 31, 1770 (Evans No. 11882); "A Brother Chip," *Pennsylvania Gazette*, September 27, 1770; "A Mechanic," *Pennsylvania Chronicle*, September 27, 1773.

59. Foner, *History of Black Americans*, pp. 295-296.

60. Ibid., pp. 297-299.

Chapter 8

1. Letter of Governor James Wright to Lord Dartmouth, December 19, 1775, *Georgia Historical Society Collections*, III, 1873, p. 228. *Rivington's Gazetteer*, October 20, 1774. See also issues of December 8, 15, 1774, January 19, 1775.

2. Reprinted in *Common Sense*, People's Bicentennial Commission, IV, No. 1, 1976, p. 38.

3. *Newport Mercury*, September 26, 1774.

4. Clarence H. Vance, editor, *Letters of a West Chester Farmer* (White Plains, N.Y., 1930), pp. 43-61.

5. *New York Journal*, November 24, 1774. For Alexander Hamilton's reply to Seabury's attack on the Continental Congress, see Henry Cabot Lodge, editor, *The Works of Alexander Hamilton* (New York, 1904), I, pp. 5-12.

6. *Newport Mercury*, September 26, 1774; Walsh, *Charleston's Sons of Liberty*, p. 71.

7. Lamb Papers, Box 1, New York Historical Society.

8. Champagne, "Sons of Liberty and the Aristocracy in New York Politics," pp. 370-371.

9. Becker, op. cit., p. 169; Force, *American Archives*, 4th Series, I, p. 1203.

10. Harrington, *The New York Merchants on the Eve of the Revolution*, p. 51.

11. Champagne, "Sons of Liberty and the Aristocracy in New York Politics," pp. 372-373; Force, *American Archives*, 4th Series, I, p. 144; Evans 14266.

12. McDougall to Josiah Quincy, Jr., April 6, 1775, McDougall Papers, Box 1, New York Historical Society.

13. *South Carolina Gazette*, March 27, 1775.

14. Ibid.

15. Walsh, *Charleston's Sons of Liberty*, p. 67.

16. Ibid., p. 68.

17. Willard, editor, *Letters on the American Revolution*, p. 245.

18. Jonathan Grossman, "Wage and Price Controls During the American Revolution," *Monthly Labor Review* (September 1973): 4; *South Carolina Gazette*, October 31, 1774; *New York Journal*, November 2, 1774; *Newport Mercury*, November 4, 1774.

19. Forbes, *Paul Revere*, p. 225.

20. Goss, *Life of Colonel Paul Revere*, I, pp. 171-176.

21. Foner, *History of Black Americans*, p. 312.

22. Ibid., pp. 312-313.

23. Jones, *New York During the Revolution*, I, pp. 39-40; Force, *American Archives*, 4th Series, II, p. 1364; Morais, "Sons of Liberty in New York," p. 287; Roger J. Champagne, "New York's Radicals and the Coming of Independence," *Journal of American History* 2 (June 1964): 21-23.

24. *New York Journal*, April 29, May 2, June 12, 1775.

25. Francis L. Bronner, "Marinus Willett," *New York History* 17 (July 1936): 272-274.

26. Becker, op. cit., pp. 194-196; Mason, *The Road to Independence*, pp. 82-83, 93-94, 103, 129-133, 141.

27. O'Callaghan, editor, op. cit., VIII, p. 571.

28. Lynd, "The Mechanics in New York Politics, 1774-1788," p. 228.

29. Walsh, *Charleston's Sons of Liberty*, pp. 73-75.

30. Arthur J. Alexander, "Pennsylvania's Revolutionary Militia," *Pennsylvania Magazine of History and Biography* 69 (January 1945): 15-25.

31. Eric Foner, *Thomas Paine and Revolutionary America* (New York, 1976), pp. 54-55, 62-63.

32. Ibid., p. 64.

33. *Pennsylvania Evening Post*, September 14, 19, 1775; David Freeman Hawke, *In the Midst of a Revolution* (Philadelphia, 1961), pp. 106-107, 185-191.

34. Eric Foner, op. cit., p. 64.

35. Ibid., pp. 64-66.

36. David Freeman Hawke, *Paine* (New York, 1974), p. 160.

37. There is still no adequate full-length biography of Paine. The three most recent are Samuel Edwards, *Rebel!* (New York, 1974); Andrew Williamson, *Thomas Paine: His Life, Work and Times* (New York, 1974); and the best of the three, David Freeman Hawke, *Paine*. The account here is based on my introduction to *The Complete Writings of Thomas Paine*, I.

38. Foner, editor, *The Complete Writings of Thomas Paine*, pp. 15-19.

39. Miller, *Origins of the American Revolution*, p. 468.

40. Hawke, *Paine*, p. 163.

41. For the complete text of *Common Sense*, see Foner, editor, *Complete Writings of Paine*, I, pp. 3-46.

42. Ibid., pp. xiv-xv.

43. *New York Packet*, April 11, 1776; Lynd, "Mechanics in New York Politics," p. 230.

44. "Salus Populi" in *Pennsylvania Journal*, March 13, 1776; "Exodus" in

Pennsylvania Packet, April 22, 1776.
45. *Pennsylvania Evening Post,* April 27, 1776.
46. "The Interest of America" in *New York Journal,* June 6, 13, 20, 1776. See also "Independent Whig" and "Essex" in ibid., February 22, 29, March 7, 14, 28, April 4, 1776; "To the Freeborn Sons of America," "On the Different Kinds of Government," "To the Printer of the New York Packet," *New York Packet,* March 21, 28, April 18, 1776; "Cato" and "Cassandra" in *New York Gazette,* April 20, 1776.

Chapter 9

1. "New York Lawyers and the Coming of the American Revolution," *New York History* 55 (October 1974): 303-407.
2. John C. Miller, *Triumph of Freedom, 1775-1783* (Boston, 1948), pp. 348-349.
3. Lamb Papers, Box 1, New York Historical Society.
4. *New York Journal,* June 6, 1776.
5. Force, *American Archives,* 4th Series, VI, p. 725.
6. Mason, *Road to Independence,* p. 164n.
7. Ibid., pp. 160-164; *New York Journal,* June 6, 13, 1776.
8. Mason, op. cit., p. 158.
9. Champagne, "Sons of Liberty and Aristocracy in New York Politics," pp. 505-508.
10. *New York Journal,* June 6, 13, 20, 1776, cited in Champagne, "New York Politics and Independence," pp. 300-301; Klein, "Democracy and Politics in Colonial New York," pp. 231-232; Alfred P. Young, *The Democratic-Republicans of New York, The Origins, 1763-1797* (Chapel Hill, N.C., 1967), pp. 17-22.
11. Theodore Thayer, *Pennsylvania Politics and the Growth of Democracy, 1740-1776* (Harrisburg, Pa., 1953), pp. 173-177; Ryerson, "Leadership in Crisis," pp. 368-371, 467-473, 544-573.
12. A. M. Stackhouse, *Col. Timothy Matlock,* n.p., 1910; Bridenbaugh, *Rebels and Gentlemen,* pp. 120-135.
13. *Pennsylvania Packet,* February 19, 1776; Olton, "Philadelphia Artisans and the American Revolution," pp. 192-197.
14. *Pennsylvania Packet,* November 26, 1776.
15. *The Constitution of Pennsylvania* (Philadelphia, 1776). A full analysis of the Constitution appears in J. Paul Selsam, *The Pennsylvania Constitution of 1776* (Philadelphia, 1936).
16. *Pennsylvania Evening Post,* July 30, 1776. See also John N. Shaeffer, "Public Consideration of the 1776 Pennsylvania Constitution," *Pennsylvania Magazine of History and Biography* 98 (October 1974): 424.
17. John Adams, *Diary,* II, p. 391.
18. *Pennsylvnaia Records,* X, pp. 723-724.
19. Foner, *History of Black Americans,* pp. 313-316.
20. Ibid., pp. 318-320.

Chapter 10

1. Walsh, *Charleston's Sons of Liberty*, pp. 90-96.

2. Jesse Lemisch, "Listening to the 'Inarticulate,' William Widger's Dream and the Loyalties of American Revolutionary Seamen in British Prisons," *Journal of Social History* 3 (1969-1970): 507.

3. Quoted in Herbert Morais, *The Struggle of American Freedom* (New York, 1944), p. 195.

4. Carl Van Doren, *Mutiny in January* (New York, 1943), p. 43; Morris, *Government and Labor in Early America*, pp. 278-280.

5. Morris, op. cit., pp. 281-290; *Pennsylvania Archives*, 1st Series, V, p. 340.

6. Foner, *History of Black Americans*, pp. 324-325, 328.

7. Ibid., pp. 325-327, 329-332.

8. Ibid., pp. 332-333.

9. Ibid., p. 333.

10. Benjamin Quarles, *The Negro in American Revolution* (Chapel Hill, N.C., 1961), pp. 53-57.

11. Foner, *History of Black Americans*, pp. 339-340.

12. Ibid., p. 328.

13. June Sochen, *Her Story: A Woman's View of American History*, I, 1600-1880 (New York, 1974), pp. 84-85.

14. For biographical information on Margaret Corbin and Margaret Hayes (Pitcher), see Elizabeth Ellet, *The Women of the Revolution* (New York, 1850), and Elizabeth Cometti, "Women in the American Revolution," *New England Quarterly* 20 (1947): 329-346. For Deborah Simpson Gannett, see Herman Mann, *The Female Review: Life of Deborah Sampson, The Female Soldier of the American Revolution*, editor, John Adams Vinton, (Boston, 1866), reprinted in 1916 as Extra Number 47 of the *Magazine of History with Notes & Queries*; Julia Ward Stickley, "The Records of Deborah Sampson Gannett, Woman Soldier of the Revolution," *Prologue*, 4 (Winter 1972): 233-241.

Philip Freneau, the "poet of the American Revolution," supported Deborah Gannett's petition to Congress for a pension with a poem: which went:

With the same vigorous soul inspired
As Joan of Arc of old . . .
She marched to face her country's foes
Disguised in male attire . . .
And hostile to the English reign
She hurled the blasting fire . . .
Reflect how many tender ties
A female must undergo
Ere to the martial camp she flies
To meet the invading foe:
How many bars has nature placed,
And custom many more . . . .
All these she nobly overcame,

And scorned a censuring age,
Joined in the ranks, her road to fame,
Despised the Briton's rage;
And men, who had contracted mind,
All arrogant condemn
And make disgrace in womankind
What honor is in them.

15. Anne Benzanson, et al., *Prices and Inflation During the American Revolution*, pp. 12-15.

16. The best study on wage-price regulations during the war is Morris, *Government and Labor in Early America*, pp. 100-135. An excellent brief study is Grossman, "Wage and Price Controls During the American Revolution," pp. 3-10. For the complaints of the soldiers, see Cometti, op. cit., p. 330.

17. Cometti, op. cit., p. 330.

18. *Boston Gazette*, October 4, 1779; *Pennsylvania Colonial Records* (Harrisburg, Pa., 1838-1853), XI, pp. 664-665; *Pennsylvania Packet*, January 16, 1779; Geib, op. cit., pp. 96-97; Rosswurm, op. cit., pp. 120-121.

19. *Boston Gazette*, March 17, April 21, 1777; *Independent Chronicle* (Boston), April 24, 1777; *Familiar Letters of John Adams and His Wife Abigail*, pp. 262, 263, 286-287.

20. Grossman, op. cit., p. 7; *Boston Gazette*, February 3, 1777, August 9, 1779; *Independent Chronicle*, (Boston), April 24, 1777.

21. *Boston Gazette*, September 27, 1779.

22. *Pennsylvania Packet*, January 19, 1779; *Pennsylvania Gazette*, February 10, April 7, 1779.

23. Alexander, "Philadelphia's 'Other Half,'" p. 332.

24. *Pennsylvania Archives*, Selected and Arranged by Samuel Hazard (Philadelphia, 1853), VII, pp. 292-295.

25. Quoted in Frederick B. Stone, "Philadelphia Society One Hundred Years Ago or the Reign of Continental Money," *Pennsylvania Magazine of History and Biography* 3 (1879): 383.

26. Henry D. Biddle, editor, *Extracts from the Journal of Elizabeth Drinker, from 1759-1807, A.D.* (Philadelphia, 1889), entry of May 25, 1779, p. 116.

27. *Pennsylvania Evening Post*, May 29, 1779.

28. Stone, op. cit., p. 384.

29. *Pennsylvania Packet*, May 29, 1779.

30. George H. Ryden, editor, *Letters to and from Caesar Rodney, 1756-1784* (Philadelphia, 1933), p. 303; Elias P. Oberholtzer, *Robert Morris* (New York, 1903), pp. 51-56; Robert L. Brunhaus, *The Counter-Revolution in Pennsylvania* (Philadelphia, 1943), pp. 70-71.

31. *Pennsylvania Evening Post*, June 29, 1779.

32. *Independent Chronicle* (Boston), June 17, 1779; *Boston Gazette*, June 21, 1779.

33. Drinker, op. cit., p. 118.

34. *Pennsylvania Packet*, July 1, 1779.

35. Ibid., September 9, 10, 25, 1779.

36. The best account of the so-called Fort Wilson Riot is by John A. Alexander and appears in three different forms: Appendix E ("Tories, Bread, and Desperation: Philadelphia's Fort Wilson Incident of 1779 Revisited") to his doctoral dissertation, "Philadelphia's 'Other Half': Attitudes Toward Poverty and the Meaning of Poverty in Philadelphia, 1760-1800"; unpublished paper prepared for the 1971 National Meeting of the American Studies Association; and "The Fort Wilson Incident," *William and Mary Quarterly*, 3d Series, 31 (October 1974): 589-612.

For a discussion of the incident which treats the militia as a senseless "mob," see C. Page Smith, "The Attack on Fort Wilson," *Pennsylvania Magazine of History and Biography* 78 (April 1954): 177-188.

37. Letter of Samuel Patterson in Ryden, op. cit., pp. 322-324.

38. *Pennsylvania Archives*, VII, pp. 740, 741, 745, 747-749.

39. *Pennsylvania Evening Post*, October 12, 1779.

40. *To the Merchants and Traders of Philadelphia, and Particularly the Importers and Holders of Salt* (Philadelphia, 1779), pp. 5-6.

41. Morris, *Government and Labor in Early America*, pp. 114-116; Grossman, op. cit., p. 7.

42. Brunhaus, op. cit., p. 58; "Papers Relating to the Whig Club, April 8-17, 1777," in *Maryland Miscellaneous (1771-1838)*, Library of Congress, Manuscripts Division; Eugene P. Link, *Democratic-Republican Societies, 1790-1800* (New York, 1942), p. 26.

43. Van Doren, op. cit., pp. 213-214.

44. *Pennsylvania Evening Post*, October 12, 1779; Evans No. 17658.

45. Foner, editor, *The Complete Writings of Thomas Paine*, I, pp. 66-67.

46. *An Address, Delivered Before the Mechanics and Working Classes Generally, of the City and County of Philadelphia, at the Universalist Church, in Callowhill Street, on Wednesday Evening, November 21, 1827, by the "Unlettered Mechanic." Published by request of the Mechanics' Delegation*, Philadelphia, 1827. The pamphlet was reprinted in *The Butcher Workman*, official organ of the Amalgamated Meat Cutters and Butcher Workmen of North America, AFL-CIO, in four successive issues beginning in September 1975.

47. The literature on these two conflicting interpretations is immense. The following are most useful: J. Franklin Jameson, *The American Revolution Considered as a Social Movement* (Princeton, N.J., 1926); Richard B. Morris, *The American Revolution Reconsidered* (New York, 1967); Herbert Aptheker, *The American Revolution 1763-1783* (New York, 1960); Mary Beard, *Women as Force in History* (New York, 1946); Robert A. East, *Business Enterprise in the American Revolutionary Era* (New York, 1938); Frederick B. Tolles, "The American Revolution Considered as a Social Movement: A Re-Evaluation," *American Historical Review* 60 (October 1954): 1-12.

48. *Independent Journal* (New York), January 21, 1784; William Miller, "The Effects of the American Revolution on Indentured Servitude," *Pennsylvania History* 7 (1940): 134-136.

49. Foner, *History of Black Americans*, pp. 345-377.

50. Cited in Aptheker, op. cit., p. 65.

51. See, for example, advertisements in the *Philadelphia Evening Post*, February 27, 1779.

52. Morris, *Government and Labor in Early America*, p. 200.

53. *National Laborer*, Philadelphia, June 11, 1836.

54. Foner, *History of the Labor Movement in the United States*, I, pp. 116-117.

55. Ibid., pp. 202-209.

56. *The Mechanic* (Fall River), July 13, 1844.

57. *Chicago Tribune*, July 5, 1878.

58. Foner, *History of the Labor Movement in the United States*, I, pp. 241-245.

59. Herbert G. Gutman, "Work, Culture and Society in Industrializing America, 1815-1919," *American Historical Review* 78 (June 1973): 59.

60. *Autobiography of Mother Jones* (New York, 1925), pp. 71-83. The best newspaper account of the March is in the *Philadelphia North American*, July 5-August 18, 1903. The paper sent a correspondent to cover the march from beginning to end.

61. Link, op. cit., p. 151.

62. *New York Journal*, July 4, 1794; *New York Weekly Chronicle*, July 9, 1795; Young, *The Democratic-Republicans of New York*, pp. 405-406, 411-412; Alfred F. Young, "The Mechanics and the Jeffersonians: New York, 1789-1801," *Labor History* 5 (Fall 1964): 258, 271.

63. *New York Journal*, July 2, 5, 1794.

64. *Mechanics' Free Press*, Philadelphia, December 26, 1829.

65. *New York Daily Sentinel*, July 12, 1830.

66. Ibid., p. 124.

Bibliography

Manuscript Collections

Boston Public Library, Boston
  General Thomas Gage Manuscripts.
Historical Society of Pennsylvania, Philadelphia
  William Smith Papers, 1765-1774.
Library of Congress, Washington, D.C.
  "Papers Relating to the Whig Club, April 8-17, 1877," in Maryland Miscel-
  laneous (1771-1838).
New York Historical Society, New York City
  Alexander McDougall Papers.
  John Lamb Papers.
New York Public Library, New York City
  Philip Schuyler Papers.
  Boston Committee of Correspondence Papers.

Unpublished Dissertations and Papers

Alexander, John A., "Philadelphia's Other Half: Attitudes Toward Poverty
  and the Meaning of Poverty in Philadelphia, 1760-1800;" Ph.D. dissertation,
  University of Chicago, 1973.
Beib, George, "A History of Philadelphia, 1776-1780," Ph.D. dissertation, Uni-
  versity of Wisconsin, 1969.
Blacke, Elizabeth May, "Opposition to the Stamp Act in New York City,"
  Ph.D. dissertation, Syracuse University, 1936.
Champagne, Roger J., "The Sons of Liberty and Aristocracy in New York
  Politics," Ph.D. dissertation, University of Wisconsin, 1960.
D'Innocenzo, Michael, "Voting in Colonial New York," M.A. thesis, Columbia
  University, 1950.

Hoerder, Dick, "People and Mobs: Crowd Action in Massachusetts During the American Revolution, 1765-1780," Inaugural Dissertation, Ph.D., Free University, Berlin, 1971.

Lemisch, Jesse, "Jack Tar vs. John Bull: The Role of New York's Seamen in Precipitating the Revolution," Ph.D. dissertation, Yale University, 1962.

Lynd, Staughton, "The Revolution and the Common Man: Farm Tenants and Artisans in New York Politics, 1777-1788," Ph.D. dissertation, Columbia University, 1962.

Olson, Charles S., "Philadelphia Artisans and the American Revolution," Ph.D. dissertation, University of California, Berkeley, 1967.

Rolland, S. B., "Cadwallader Colden: Colonial Politician and Imperial Statesman," Ph.D. dissertation, University of Wisconsin, 1952.

Rosswurm, Steven J., "'That They Were Grown Unruly': The Crowd and Lower-Classes in Philadelphia, 1765-1780," M.A. thesis, Northern Illinois University, 1974.

Ryerson, Richard A., "Leadership in Crisis. The Radical Committees of Philadelphia and the Coming of the Revolution in Pennsylvania, 1765-1776: A Study in the Revolutionary Process," Ph.D. dissertation, Johns Hopkins University, 1972.

Shufro, Joel A., "Impressment and Economic Decline in Boston: Context for Conflict, 1740-1760," paper delivered at the American Studies Association, October 1971.

Towner, Lawrence W., "A Good Master Well Served, A Social History of Servitude in Massachusetts, 1620-1750," Ph.D. dissertation, Northwestern University, 1955.

Young, Alfred, P., "Some Thoughts on Mechanic Participation in the American Revolution," paper delivered at 3rd Annual Conference on Early American History, Newberry Library, Chicago, November 1, 1974.

Broadsides and Pamphlets

Address, An, Delivered Before the Mechanics and Working Classes Generally of the City and County of Philadelphia, at the Universalist Church, in Callowhill Street, on Wednesday Evening, November 21, 1827, by the "Unlettered Mechanic." Published by request of the Mechanics' Delegation, Philadelphia, 1827. Pamphlet.

Brutus, "To the Public," January 18, 1770. New York Historical Society. Broadside.

Chauncey, Charles, A Letter to a Friend, Giving a Concise but Just Representation of the Hardships and Sufferings of the Town of Boston. Boston, 1774.

"For Erecting and Encouraging a New Manufactory," Evans 1555. Pamphlet.

Handbill signed by Timothy Wheelwright and John Chissel, dated September 8, 1734. New York Public Library, Rare Book Room.

"Lover of Liberty and a Mechanics' Friend, A," To the Free and Patriotic Inhabitants of the City of Philadelphia, May 31, 1770, Philadelphia, 1770. Pamphlet.

"New Song—Address'd to the Sons of Liberty on the Continent of America, A,"
    Historical Society of Pennsylvania. Broadside.
Portfolio 37, No. 28. Broadside, Boston, 1770, Library of Congress, Rare Book
    Room.
"Resolutions of the United Sons of Liberty, July 7, 1769," New York Public
    Library, Rare Book Room. Broadside.
Seaver, Henry, An Oration Delivered before the Mechanic Apprentice's Library
    Association, July 4, 1835, Boston, 1835. Pamphlet.
"Song-1734, A," New York Public Library, Rare Book Room. Broadside.
Son of Liberty, A, "To the Betrayed Inhabitants of the City and Colony of New
    York," New York, December 16, 1769, New York Historical Society. Broad-
    side.
"To the Inhabitants of the City," January 22, 1770, New York Historical
    Society. Broadside.
To the Manufactures and Mechanics of Philadelphia, the Northern Liberties,
    and the District of Southwick, Philadelphia, June 8, 1774. Pamphlet.
To the Merchants and Traders of Philadelphia and Particularly the Importers
    and Holders of Salt, Philadelphia, 1779. Pamphlet.
To the Tradesmen, Farmers, and Other Inhabitants of the City and County of
    Philadelphia, Philadelphia, September 24, 1770. Pamphlet.

Newspapers and Journals

American Museum, 1788.
Boston Chronicle, 1769.
Boston Evening-Post, 1765, 1766, 1770, 1771.
Boston Gazette and County Journal, 1765, 1766, 1770, 1772, 1773, 1774, 1777,
    1779.
Butcher Workman, The, 1975.
Chicago Tribune, 1878.
Common Sense, People's Bicentennial Commission, 1976.
Daily Sentinel (New York), 1830.
Independent Chronicle and Universal Advertiser (Boston), 1777, 1779.
Independent Journal or General Advertiser (New York City), 1784.
Magazine of History, The, 1918.
Massachusetts Gazette and Boston Weekly News-Letter, 1773.
Mechanic, The (Fall River), 1844.
Mechanics' Free Press (Philadelphia), 1829.
National Laborer (Philadelphia), 1836.
Newport Mercury or Weekly Advertiser, 1765, 1767, 1772, 1774, 1775.
New York Gazette or Weekly Post-Boy, 1765, 1766.
New York Journal, 1769, 1770, 1773, 1774, 1775, 1776, 1794.
New York Mercury, 1766, 1770.
New York Packet, 1776.
New York Times, 1975.
New York Weekly Chronicle, 1795.

Pennsylvania Chronicle and Universal Advertiser (Philadelphia), 1770.
Pennsylvania Gazette (Philadelphia), 1770, 1773, 1774, 1779.
Pennsylvania Journal and Weekly Advertiser (Philadelphia), 1765, 1770, 1776.
Pennsylvania Packet, or the General Advertiser (Philadelphia), 1776, 1779.
Philadelphia Evening Post, 1775, 1776, 1779.
Philadelphia North American, 1903.
Rivington's New York Gazetteer (New York), 1773, 1774, 1775.
South-Carolina Gazette; and County Journal (Charleston), 1768, 1769, 1770, 1774.

Books

Abbott, W. C., *New York in the American Revolution*, New York, 1929.
Adair, Douglas, and Schutz, John A., editors, *Peter Oliver's Origin and Progress of the American Rebellion: A Tory View*, San Marino, California, 1961.
Adams, Charles Francis, editor, *The Works of John Adams*, Boston, 1850-56.
— —, editor, *Familiar Letters of John Adams and his Wife, Abigail Adams, during the Revolution*, New York, 1876.
Adams, James Truslow, *Revolutionary New England, 1691-1776*, Boston, 1923.
Alvord, Clarence V., *The Mississippi Valley in British Politics*, Cleveland, 1917.
American Revolution: Three Views, New York, 1975.
Aptheker, Herbert, *The American Revolution 1763-1783*, New York, 1960.
Arts and Crafts in New York, 1726-1776, The, New York, 1936.
Autobiography of Mother Jones, New York, 1925.
Bailyn, Bernard, *The Ideological Origins of the American Revolution*, Cambridge, Mass., 1967.
— —, editor, *Pamphlets of the American Revolution*, Cambridge, Mass., 1955.
— —, *The Ordeal of Thomas Hutchinson*, Cambridge, Mass., 1974.
Barck, Oscar, T., *New York City During the War for Independence: With Special Reference to the Period of British Occupation*, New York, 1931.
Beach, Stewart, *Samuel Adams: The Fateful Years, 1764-1770*, New York, 1965.
Beard, Mary, *Women as Force in History*, New York, 1946.
Becker, Carl, *The History of Political Parties in the Province of New York, 1760-1776*, Madison, Wisc., 1909.
Bernstein, Barton J., editor, *Towards a New Past: Dissenting Essays in American History*, New York, 1968.
Bezanson, Anne, et al., *Prices and Inflation during the American Revolution: Pennsylvania 1770-1790*, Philadelphia, 1951.
Biddle, Henry D., editor, *Extracts from the Journal of Elizabeth Drinker, from 1759-1807, A.D.*, Philadelphia, 1889.
Bonomi, Patticia U., *A Factious People: Politics and Society in Colonial New York*, New York and London, 1971.
Boorstein, Daniel J., *The Genius of American Politics*, Chicago, 1953.
Bridenbaugh, Carl, *Cities in Revolt: Urban Life in America, 1743-1776*, New York, 1955.
— —, *The Colonial Craftsman*, New York, 1955.
— —, and Bridenbaugh, Jessica, *Rebels and Gentlemen*, New York, 1942.

Brown, Alice, *Mercy Warren*, New York, 1896.

Brown, Richard D., *Revolutionary Politics in Massachusetts: The Boston Committee of Correspondence and the Towns, 1772-1774*, Cambridge, Mass. 1970.

Brown, Robert E., *Virginia 1705-1786; Democracy or Aristocracy?* Cambridge, Mass., 1964.

——, *Middle-Class Democracy and Revolution in Massachusetts, 1691-1780*, Ithaca, New York, 1955.

Burnett, Edmund Cody, *The Continental Congress*, New York, 1941.

Burnhaus, Robert L., *The Counter-Revolution in Pennsylvania*, Philadelphia, 1943.

Butterfield, L. H., editor, *Letters of Benjamin Rush*, Princeton, N.J., 1951.

Byrdsall, F., *The History of the Loco-Foco or Equal Rights Party*, New York, 1842, reprinted 1967.

Carter, Clarence Edwin, editor, *The Correspondence of General Thomas Gage with the Secretaries of State, 1763-1775*, New Haven, Conn., 1931-1933.

Champagne, Roger J., *Alexander McDougall and the American Revolution in New York*, Schenectady, N.Y., 1975.

Chandler, Allen D., *The Colonial Records of Georgia*, Atlanta, 1908.

Christie, Ian R., *Wilkes, Wyvill and Reform*, London, 1962.

Clark, D. M., *British Opinion and the American Revolution*, New Haven, Conn., 1930.

Clark, Victor S., *History of Manufacturing in the United States, 1607-1860*, Washington, D.C., 1916.

Colden Letter-Books, New York Historical Society *Collections*, New York, 1918-1937.

Commons, John R., and Associates, *History of Labor in the United States*, New York, 1918.

Curti, Merle, *Growth of American Thought*, New York, 1943.

Cushing, Harry A., editor, *The Writings of Samuel Adams*, New York, 1904-08.

Davidson, Philip, *Propaganda and the American Revolution*, Chapel Hill, N.C., 1941.

Dawson, Henry B., *The Sons of Liberty in New York*, Poughkeepsie, N.Y., 1859.

Dickerson, Oliver M., *The Navigation Acts and the American Revolution*, Philadelphia, 1951.

East, Robert A., *Business Enterprise in the American Revolutionary Era*, New York, 1938.

Edwards, Samuel, *Rebel*, New York, 1974.

Ellet, Elizabeth, *The Women of the Revolution*, New York, 1910.

Erlanger, Steven J., "The Colonial Worker in Boston, 1775," U.S. Department of Labor, Bureau of Labor Statistics, New England Regional Office, Regional Report 75-Z, 1975.

Foner, Eric, *Thomas Paine and Revolutionary America*, New York, 1976.

Foner, Philip S., editor, *The Complete Writings of Thomas Paine*, New York, 1945.

——, *History of the Labor Movement in the United States*, New York, 1947.

——, *Organized Labor and the Black Worker: 1619-1973*, New York, 1974.

——, *History of Black Americans: From Africa to the Emergence of the Cotton Kingdom*, Westport, Conn., 1975.

——, *American Labor Songs of the Nineteenth Century*, Urbana, Ill., 1975.

Forbes, Esther, *Paul Revere and the World He Lived In*, Boston, 1942.

Ford, Worthington, et al., editors, *Journals of the Continental Congress*, Washington, D.C., 1904-37.

Frothingham, Richard, *Life and Times of Joseph Warren*, Boston, 1865.

——, *History of the Siege of Boston*, Boston, 1849.

Gibbes, R. W., editor, *Documentary History of the American Revolution*, New York, 1855.

Gordon, William, *The History of the Rise, Progress, and Establishment of the Independence of the United States of America*, London, 1788.

Goss, Elbridge H., *The Life of Colonel Paul Revere*, Boston, 1891.

Hanna, William S., *Benjamin Franklin and Pennsylvania Politics*, Stanford, Calif., 1964.

Harrington, Virginia D., *The New York Merchants on the Eve of the Revolution*, New York, 1935.

Harris, Herbert, *American Labor*, New Haven, Conn., 1938.

Hart, Albert B., editor, *American History Told by Contemporaries*, New York, 1898.

Hawke, David Freeman, *Paine*, New York, 1974.

——, *In the Midst of a Revolution*, Philadelphia, 1961.

Hazard, Samuel, editor, *Pennsylvania Archives*, Philadelphia, 1853.

Henretta, James A., *The Evolution of American Society, 1700-1815*, Lexington, Mass., 1973.

Hobsbawm, Eric, *Primitive Rebels: Studies in Archaic Forms of Social Movement in the 19th and 20th Centuries*, New York, 1959.

Hofstadter, Richard, *The Progressive Historians*, New York, 1968.

——, and Wallace, Michael, *American Violence: A Documentary History*, New York, 1970.

Hurtz, Stephen G., and Hutson, James H., editors, *Essays on the American Revolution*, Chapel Hill, N.C., 1973.

Hutchinson, Thomas, *History of the Province of Massachusetts Bay*, London, 1828.

Hutson, James, *Pennsylvania Politics, 1746-1770; The Movement for Royal Government and Its Consequences*, Princeton, N.J., 1972.

Jameson, J. Franklin, *The American Revolution Considered as a Social Movement*, Princeton, N.J., 1926.

Jensen, Merrill, *The Articles of Confederation*, Madison, Wisc., 1959.

Jernegan, Marcus W., *Laboring and Dependent Classes in Colonial America*, Chicago, 1931.

Kidder, F., *History of the Boston Massacre, March 5, 1770*, Albany, N.Y., 1870.

Labaree, Benjamin W., *The Boston Tea Party*, New York, 1964.

——, *Patriots and Partisans: The Merchants of Newburyport, 1764-1815*, Cambridge, Mass., 1962.

Leake, Isaac Q., *Memoir of the Life and Times of General John Lamb*, Albany, N.Y., 1850.

Letters and Papers of Cadwallader Colden, New York State Historical Society *Collections for 1923*, New York, 1923.

Lincoln, Charles H., *The Revolutionary Movement in Pennsylvania, 1769-1776*, Philadelphia, 1901.

Link, Eugene P., *Democratic-Republican Societies, 1790-1800*, New York, 1942.

Lodge, Henry Cabot, editor, *The Works of Alexander Hamilton*, New York, 1904.

Lossing, Benson J., *Pictorial Field-Book of the Revolution*, New York, 1860.

Lynd, Staughton, *Anti-Federalism in Dutchess County, New York*, Chicago, 1962.

McKee, Samuel J., Jr., *Labor in Colonial New York*, New York, 1935.

McKinley, A. E., *The Suffrage Franchise in the English Colonies*, Philadelphia, 1905.

Maier, Pauline, *From Resistance to Revolution: Colonial Radicals and the Development of American Opposition to Britain, 1765-1775*, New York, 1972.

Main, Jackson Turner, *The Social Structure of Revolutionary America*, Princeton, N.J., 1965.

Mark, Irving, *Agrarian Conflicts in Colonial New York, 1711-1775*, New York, 1940.

Mason, Bernard, *The Road to Independence: The Revolutionary Movement in New York, 1773-1777*, Lexington, Ky., 1966.

Miller, John C., *Triumph of Freedom, 1775-1783*, Boston, 1948.

——, *Sam Adams, Pioneer in Propaganda*, Boston, 1936.

——, *Origins of the American Revolution*, Boston, 1943.

Montressor, James and John, *The Montressor Journals*, New York Historical Society *Collections*, New York, 1882.

Morais, Herbert M., *The Struggle for American Freedom*, New York, 1944.

Morgan, Edmund S., and Helen M., *The Stamp Act Crisis: Prologue to Revolution*, Chapel Hill, N.C., 1953.

Morris, Richard B., *The American Revolution Reconsidered*, New York, 1967.

——, editor, *The Era of the American Revolution*, New York, 1939.

——, *Government and Labor in Early America*, New York, 1946.

——, *The American Revolution, 1763-1783: A Bicentennial Collection*, New York, 1970.

Morton, A. L., editor, *Freedom in Arms, A Selection of Leveller Writings*, New York, 1976.

Nettels, Curtis P., *Roots of American Civilization*, New York, 1938.

Newcomb, Benjamin H., *Franklin and Galloway: A Political Partnership*, New Haven, Conn., 1972.

Oberholtzer, Elias P., *Robert Morris*, New York, 1903.

O'Callaghan, E.B., editor, *Documentary History of the State of New York*, Albany, N.Y., 1850.

——, editor, *Documents Relative to the Colonial History of the State of New York*, Albany, N.Y., 1856.

Olton, Charles S., *Artisans for Independence: Philadelphia Mechanics and the*

American Revolution, Syracuse, N.Y., 1975.

Postgate, R. W., *That Devil Wilkes*, New York, 1929.

Quarles, Benjamin, *The Negro in the American Revolution*, Chapel Hill, N.C., 1961.

Rayback, Joseph G., *A History of American Labor*, New York, 1966.

Reed, William B., editor, *Life and Correspondence of Joseph Reed*, Philadelphia, 1847.

Rudé, George, *The Crowd in History: A Study of Popular Disturbances in France and England, 1730-1848*, New York, 1964.

— —, *Wilkes and Liberty*, London, 1962.

Ryden, George H., editor, *Letters to and from Caesar Rodney, 1756-1784*, Philadelphia, 1933.

Saunders, Frederick, editor, *Our National Jubilee. Orations, Addresses, Poems Delivered on the Fourth of July 1876 in the Several States of the Union*, New York, 1877.

Selsam, J. Paul, *The Pennsylvania Constitution of 1776*, Philadelphia, 1936.

Shy, John W., *Toward Lexington: The Role of the British Army in the Coming of the American Revolution*, Princeton, N.J., 1965.

Smith, Abbott Emerson, *Colonists in Bondage: White Servitude and Convict Labor in America, 1607-1776*, Chapel Hill, N.C., 1947.

Snowden, Yates, *Notes on Labor Organization in South Carolina, 1742-1861*, Columbia, S.C., 1924.

Sparks, Jared, editor, *Diplomatic Correspondence of the American Revolution. . .* , Boston, 1829-30.

Stackhouse, A. M., *Col. Timothy Matlock*, n.p., 1910.

Tea Leaves, etc., with Introductory Notes, and Biographical Notices of the Boston Tea Party, by Francis S. Drake, Boston, 1884.

Thayer, Theodore, *Pennsylvania Politics and the Growth of Democracy, 1740-1776*, Harrisburg, Pa., 1953.

Thompson, E. P., *The Making of the English Working Class*, New York, 1963.

Vance, Clarence H., editor, *Letters of a West Chester Farmer*, White Plains, N.Y., 1930.

Van Doren, Carl, *Mutiny in January*, New York, 1943.

Van Rensselaer, Marianna G., *History of New York in the Seventeenth Century*, New York, 1909.

Vinton, John Adams, editor, *Deborah Sampson, The Female Soldier of the American Revolution*, Boston, 1866.

Walsh, Richard, *Charleston's Sons of Liberty: A Study of the Artisans, 1763-1789*, Columbia, S.C., 1959.

— —, editor, *The Writings of Christopher Gadsden*, Columbia, S.C., 1966.

Warden, G. B., *Boston: 1689-1776*, Boston, 1970.

Ware, Norman J., *Labor in Modern Industrial Society*, New York, 1935.

Warner, Sam Bass, Jr., *The Private City: Philadelphia in Three Periods of Its Growth*, Philadelphia, 1968.

Willard, Margaret Wheeler, editor, *Letters on the American Revolution, 1774-1776*, Boston, 1925.

Williams, Talcott, *Labor a Hundred Years Ago*, New York, 1887.

Williamson, Andrew, *Thomas Paine: His Life, Work, and Times*, New York, 1974.

Williamson, Chilton, *American Suffrage from Property to Democracy, 1760-1860*, Princeton, N.J., 1960.

Winslow, Ola Elizabeth, editor, *American Broadside Verse*, New Haven, Conn., 1943.

Young, Alfred P., *The Democratic Republicans of New York, The Origins, 1763-1797*, Chapel Hill, N.C., 1967.

— —, editor, *Dissent: Explorations in the History of American Radicalism*, De Kalb, Ill., 1968.

Zobel, Hiller B., *The Boston Massacre*, New York, 1970.

Articles

"Account of the Grand Federal Procession in Philadelphia," *American Museum* 4 (1788): 57-75.

Alexander, Arthur, Jr., "Pennsylvania Revolutionary Militia," *Pennsylvania Magazine of History and Biography* 49 (1945): 15-25.

Alexander, John A., "The Fort Wilson Incident," *William and Mary Quarterly*, 3d Series, 3 (1974): 589-612.

Allan, James, and Day, Katherine, "Another Look at the Boston Caucus," *Journal of American Studies* 5 (1971): 19-42.

Anderson, George P., "Ebenezer Mackintosh: Stamp Act Rioter and Patriot," Colonial Society of Massachusetts *Publications* 26 (1924-26): 15-64, 348-361.

— —, "Pascal Paoli: An Inspiration to the Sons of Liberty," Colonial Society of Massachusetts *Publications* 26 (1924-26): 180-210.

Baker, Mary Roys, "Anglo-Massachusetts Trade Union Roots, 1730-1790," *Labor History* 14 (1973): 352-396.

Barker, R. J., "The Daughters of Liberty," *American Historical Register* 1 (1894): 29-36.

Berg, Harry D., "The Organization of Business in Colonial Philadelphia," *Pennsylvania History* 10 (1943): 157-177.

Boyer, Lee R., "Lobster Backs, Liberty Boys, and Laborers in the Streets: New York's Golden Hill and Nassau Street Riots," *New York Historical Society Quarterly* 57 (1973): 281-307.

Boyle, John, "Boyle's Journal of Occurrences in Boston, 1759-1778," *New England Historical and Genealogical Register* 84 (1930): 142-169.

Bronner, Francis L., "Marinus Willett," *New York History* 17 (1936): 273-280.

Brown, Robert E., "Democracy in Colonial Massachusetts," *New England Quarterly* 25 (1952): 291-313.

Cabeen, Francis von, "The Society of the Sons of Saint Tammany in Philadelphia," *Pennsylvania Magazine of History and Biography*, 2 (1901): 433-451.

Calkin, H. L., "Pamphlets and Public Opinion During the American Revolution," *Pennsylvania Magazine of History and Biography*, 44 (1940): 22-42.

Cary, John, "Statistical Method and the Brown Thesis on Colonial Democracy," *William and Mary Quarterly*, 3d Series, 20 (1963): 251-276.

Champagne, Roger J., "The Military Association of the Sons of Liberty," *New*

York Historical Quarterly, 51 (1957), 344-360.

— —, "New York Radicals and the Coming of Independence," *Journal of American History* 2 (1964), 21-42.

— —, "Liberty Boys and Mechanics in New York City, 1764-1774," *Labor History* 8 (1967): 123-135.

— —, "New York and the Intolerable Acts, 1774," *New York Historical Society Proceedings* 45 (1961): 195-207.

— —, "New York Politics and Independence," *New York Historical Society Quarterly* 46 (1962): 3-19.

Cometti, Elizabeth, "Women in the American Revolution," *New England Quarterly* 20 (1947): 329-346.

Countryman, Edward, "The Problem of the Early American Crowd," *Journal of American Studies* 7 (1973): 77-90.

Crane, Verner W., editor, "'The Internal State of America' by Benjamin Franklin," *William and Mary Quarterly,* 3d Series, 15 (1958): 214-227.

Davidson, Philip, "Sons of Liberty and Stamp Men," *North Carolina Historical Review* 9 (1937): 38-56.

Day, Alan and Katherine, "Another Look at the Boston Caucus," *Journal of American Studies* 5 (1971): 19-42.

Dexter, F. B., editor, "The Correspondence and Miscellaneous Papers of Jared Ingersoll," New Haven Colony Historical Society *Papers* 10 (1918): 308-355.

Dickerson, Oliver M., "The Commissioners of Customs and the 'Boston Massacre,'" *New England Quarterly* 27 (1954): 307-325.

Edes, Henry H., "Memoir of Thomas Young," in *Publications of the Colonial Society of Massachusetts, Transactions 1906-1907,* 2-53.

Edwards, George W., "New York Politics Before the American Revolution," *Political Science Quarterly* 35 (1921): 596-602.

Ernst, Joseph A., "An Economic Interpretation of the American Revolution," *William and Mary Quarterly,* 3d Series, 29 (1972), 3-32.

Ford, Worthington C., editor, "John Wilkes and Boston," *Proceedings of the Massachusetts Historical Society* 37 (1913-14): 180-215.

Friedman, Lawrence J., and Shaffer, Arthur H., "Mercy Otis Warren and the Politics of Historical Nationalism," *New England Quarterly* 48 (1975): 194-215.

Greene, Jack P., "'Bridge to Revolution,' The Wilkes Fund Controversy in South Carolina, 1769-1775," *Journal of Southern History* 29 (1963): 19-52.

Grossman, Jonathan, "Wage and Price Control During the American Revolution," *Monthly Labor Review* 85 (1973): 3-9.

Gutman, Herbert G., "Work, Culture and Society in Industrializing America, 1815-1919," *American Historical Review* 88 (1973): 531-588.

Henretta, James A., "Economic Development and Social Structure in Colonial Boston," *William and Mary Quarterly* 3d Series, 22 (1965): 75-92.

Hooper, Richard J., "The American Revolution Seen Through a Wine Glass," *William and Mary Quarterly* 3d Series, 11 (1954): 52-77.

Hoyt, A. H., "Donations to the People of Boston Suffering under the Port Bill," *New England Historical and Genealogical Register* 30 (1876): 368-379.

Jones, Douglas Lamar, "The Strolling Poor: Transiency in Eighteenth Century

Massachusetts," *Journal of Social History* 8 (1975): 28-54.
Klein, Milton M., "Democracy and Politics in Colonial New York," *New York History* 40 (1959): 221-246.
——, "New York Lawyers and the Coming of the American Revolution," *New York History* 55 (1974): 383-407.
Kraus, Michael, "America and the Irish Revolutionary Movement in the Eighteenth Century," in Richard B. Morris, editor, *The Era of the American Revolution*, 332-348.
Kulikoff, Allan, "The Progress of Inequality in Revolutionary Boston," *William and Mary Quarterly*, 3d Series, 28 (1971): 375-412.
Lemisch, Jesse, "Jack Tar in the Streets: Merchant Seamen in the Politics of Revolutionary America," *William and Mary Quarterly*, 3d Series, 25 (1968): 371-407.
——, "New York's Petitions and Resolves of December 1765: Liberals vs. Radicals," *New York Historical Society Quarterly* 49 (1965): 313-323.
——, "The American Revolution Seen from the Bottom Up," in Barton J. Bernstein, editor, *Towards A New Past: Dissenting Essays in American History*, 3-45.
Longley, R. S., "Mob Activities in Revolutionary Massachusetts," *New England Quarterly* 6 (1933): 98-130.
Lynd, Staughton, "The Mechanics in New York Politics, 1774-1788," *Labor History* 5 (1964): 224-246.
Maier, Pauline, "Revolutionary Violence and the Relevance of History," *Journal of Interdisciplinary History* 2 (1971): 119-135.
——, "Coming to Terms with Samuel Adams," *American Historical Review* 81 (1976): 12-37.
——, "The Charleston Mob and the Evolution of Popular Politics in Revolutionary South Carolina, 1765-1784," *Perspective in American History* 4 (1970): 173-198.
Main, Jackson Turner, "Government by the People: The American Revolution and the Democratization of the Legislatures," *William and Mary Quarterly*, 3d Series, 23 (1966): 391-407.
Mark, Irving, and Handlin, Oscar, "Land Cases in Colonial New York, 1765-1767, The King vs. William Prendergast," *New York University Quarterly Review* 9 (1942): 180-208.
Matthews, Albert, "Joyce Junior," *Publications Colonial Society of Massachusetts* 8 (1907): 97-101.
Miller, William, "The Effects of the American Revolution on Indentured Servitude," *Pennsylvania History* 7 (1940): 131-141.
Morais, Herbert M., "The Sons of Liberty in New York," in Richard B. Morris, editor, *The Era of the American Revolution*, 269-289.
——, "Artisan Democracy and the American Revolution," *Science and Society*, 6 (1942): 227-249.
Morgan, Edmund S., "Thomas Hutchinson and the Stamp Act," *New England Quarterly* 21 (1948): 459-463.
Morris, Richard B., "Labor and Mercantalism in the Revolutionary Era," in Richard B. Morris, editor, *The Era of the American Revolution*, 76-139.

Political Science Quarterly 52 (1937): 51-85.

— —, "The American Revolution and the Labouring Classes, Slave and Free: A Reconsideration," *Society for the Study of Labour History Bulletin* 32 (1969): 11-13.

Nash, Gary B., "The Transformation of Urban Politics 1700-1765," *Journal of American History* 60 (1973): 605-632.

— —, "Poverty and Poor Relief in Pre-Revolutionary Philadelphia," *William and Mary Quarterly*, 3d Series, 33 (1976): 3-30.

Nettels, Curtis P., "British Mercantilism and the Economic Development of the Thirteen Colonies," *Journal of Economic History* 12 (1952): 105-114.

— —, "The Menace of Colonial Manufacturing, 1690-1720," *New England Quarterly* 4 (1931): 240-266.

Newcomb, Benjamin H., "Effects of the Stamp Act in Colonial Pennsylvania Politics," *William and Mary Quarterly*, 3d Series, 23 (1966), 257-272.

Oaks, Robert F., "Philadelphia Merchants and the First Continental Congress," *Pennsylvania History* 40 (1973): 149-168.

Olton, Charles S., "Philadelphia's Mechanics in the First Decade of the Revolution, 1765-1775," *Journal of American History* 59 (1972): 311-326.

Parker, Peter J., "Rich and Poor in Philadelphia, 1709," *Pennsylvania Magazine of History and Biography* 99 (1975): 3-17.

Rogers, George C., Jr., "The Charleston Tea Party: The Significance of December 3, 1773," *South Carolina Historical Magazine* 75 (1974): 162-185.

Rudolph, Lloyd, "The Eighteenth-Century Mob in America and Europe," *American Quarterly* 11 (1959): 447-459.

Ryerson, R. A., "Political Mobilization and the American Revolution," The Resistance Movement in Philadelphia, 1765-1776," *William and Mary Quarterly*, 3d Series, 21 (1974): 565-588.

Schlesinger, Arthur M., "A Note on Songs as Patriot Propaganda," *William and Mary Quarterly*, 3d Series, 11 (1954): 78-88.

— —, "Political Mobs and the American Revolution, 1765-1776," *Proceedings*, American Philosophical Society 99 (1955): 243-249.

Seyboldt, Robert J., "Trade Agreements in Colonial Boston," *New England Quarterly* 2 (1929): 307-310.

Shaeffer, John N., "Public Consideration of the 1776 Pennsylvania Constitution," *Pennsylvania Magazine of History and Biography* 98 (1974): 415-437.

Smith, C. Page, "The Attack on Fort Wilson," *Pennsylvania Magazine of History and Biography* 78 (1954): 177-188.

Smith, Glenn C., "An Era of Non-Importation Association," *William and Mary Quarterly* 2d Series, 40 (1932), 52-77.

Stickley, Julia Ward, "The Records of Deborah Sampson Gannett, Woman Soldier of the Revolution," *Prologue* 4 (1972): 233-241.

Stone, Frederick B., "Philadelphia Society One Hundred Years Ago or the Reign of Continental Money," *Pennsylvania Magazine of History and Biography* 3 (1879): 380-398.

Tolles, Frederick B., "The American Revolution Considered as a Social Movement: A Re-Evaluation," *American Historical Review* 60 (1954): 1-12.

Towner, Lawrence W., "The Indentures of Boston's Poor Apprentices, 1734-

1805," *Publications Colonial Society of Massachusetts* 43 (1956-63): 417-434.

Trumbull, J. H., "Sons of Liberty in 1775," *The New Englander* 25 (1892), 308-321.

Walsh, Richard, "The Charleston Mechanics: A Brief Study, 1760-1776," *South Carolina Historical Magazine* 60 (1959): 123-144.

Weer, Robert M., "'The Harmony We Were Famous For': An Interpretation of Pre-Revolutionary South Carolina Politics," *William and Mary Quarterly*, 3d Series, 26 (1969): 473-501.

Williams, William Appelman, "Samuel Adams: Calvinist, Mercantalist, Revolutionary," *Studies on the Left* 1 (1960): 47-57.

Wood, Gordon S., "A Note on Mobs in the American Revolution," *William and Mary Quarterly*, 3d Series, 23 (1966): 635-642.

Woody, Robert H., "Christopher Gadsden and the Stamp Act," *Proceedings of the South Carolina Historical Association 1939*, 3-22.

Young, Alfred F., "The Mechanics and the Jeffersonians: New York, 1789-1801," *Labor History* 5 (1964): 247-276.

— —, and Lynd, Staughton, "After Carl Becker: The Mechanics and New York City Politics, 1774-1801," *Labor History* 5 (1964): 215-224.

Zimmerman, John J., "Charles Thomson: The Sam Adams of Philadelphia," *Mississippi Valley Historical Review* 45 (1958): 464-480.

Index

About the Author

Philip S. Foner, Independence Foundation Professor at Lincoln University, is the author of such works as *Life and Writing of Frederick Douglass* and *History of the Labor Movement in the United States*. The first volume of his *History of Black Americans* was published in 1975 by Greenwood Press.